REMEMBER BUTLER

SIR WILLIAM F. BUTLER
From a photograph in the Public Archives of Canada

REMEMBER BUTLER

The Story of
Sir William Butler

by

EDWARD McCOURT

McClelland and Stewart Limited
Toronto Montreal

The Canadian Publishers
McClelland and Stewart Limited,
25 Hollinger Road, Toronto 16.

Printed in Great Britain

TO

LIEUT.-COL. PATRICK RICHARD BUTLER, D.S.O.

Contents

Illustrations

Preface

THE VICTORIAN AGE, so much of its literature would lead us to believe, was a time when Englishmen roamed through strange places of the earth in search of adventure, fame, pleasure and sometimes the peace of God, pausing from time to time to write books, nearly always in excellent prose, about what they had seen and done. The Victorian world was a world of antimacassars, philistinism, Stags at Bay, insularity, jingoism and Samuel Smiles; but it was also the world of Richard Burton, Charles Gordon, David Livingstone, Lady Hester Stanhope, Charles Doughty and many another gifted and wandering spirit whose like will not be seen again.

In this splendid host General Sir William Butler has been lost sight of, overshadowed by personalities more spectacular than his own, but not always worthier. His claims to notice are many. He was a soldier of great distinction; a traveller in wild and lonely places; and among soldier-travellers the best writer of them all. He was the friend of great men—Victor Hugo, Ruskin, Gordon, Parnell—and like them the champion of lost causes and seeker of impossible goals. Even those of his colleagues whom he tried most sorely acknowledged the nobility of his purposes and the greatness of his spirit.

The unusual charm of his writings derives in part from the fact that they are much more than conventional reminiscences of a professional soldier; they are the revelation of a warm-hearted, many-sided personality and of the eternal seeker-after-truth whose physical wanderings are a true reflection of the wayfaring spirit within.

This book is written in the hope of calling back into memory one who, whatever his faults and foibles, bore throughout his life an honourable and often heroic part in what he himself called 'the ever-recurring fight of day with darkness that gives to man's life on earth its nerving necessity, its ceaseless ideal, its sole nobility'.

I would like to thank the many people to whom I am indebted for assistance in the writing of this book; in particular the librarians of the University of Saskatchewan; Mr. Roger Carter, Q.C., who read part of the manuscript; Mr. Frederick Ormond Butler of Kilshane, Tipperary (a mine of information about the Butlers of Ballycarron); Brigadier John Stephenson and Captain David Askin of the Royal United Service Institution, Whitehall, who placed the Wolseley correspondence at my disposal; and above all Lieutenant-Colonel Patrick Butler and Mrs. Butler, who made available to me the family archives and answered all inquiries with patience and courtesy.

Edward McCourt

University of Saskatchewan

CHAPTER ONE

The Butlers of Ballycarron

A TWELVE-YEAR-OLD BOY crouched on a narrow ledge half-way down the great rockface overhanging Lough Muskry in the heart of the Irish Galtees and with a slender stick fended off the increasingly vicious attacks of an outraged mother eagle whose nest he had come to plunder. The boy had made his descent with the aid of a rope held by a companion, but in scrambling along the ledge towards the eagle's nest he had failed to notice a sudden bulge in the rockface above his head. Now the rope, which he had let go in his haste to snatch an eaglet from the nest, dangled a foot or two beyond his reach. The position was one which might well have caused a twelve-year-old to panic. Without the support of the rope the boy could not make his way back along the ledge, his companion above was unaware of his plight—and if he survived the mother eagle's attacks he had still to face the ignominy of rescue by an organized party of adults and the pain of paternal lashings with tongue and rod.

The boy did not panic. The screaming mother eagle made another pass—her wing touched the rope, flicked it inwards, and the boy caught it. A few minutes later and he stood safe at the top of the rockface.

The capacity for getting into trouble which young William Butler displayed on this occasion was uniquely his own; the courage and resolution with which he faced danger no doubt owed something to the stock from which he sprang.

The Butlers are a great name in Ireland. The founding father, one Theobald, came over in 1177, just seven years after Strongbow, Earl of Pembroke, had landed near Waterford and opened the way for the conquest of the island. Theobald had had the good fortune to be distantly related to the lately murdered Thomas à Becket, and a repentant King Henry II, seeking to placate the ghostly Thomas by providing handsomely for his relatives, bestowed on Theobald the post of King's Butler (hence the family name) and extensive land grants in north Tipperary and Wicklow. In 1328 the Butler of that day was created Earl of Ormond by the English regent, Roger Mortimer; and the exercise of certain grazing and tax-gathering privileges which accompanied the earldom brought the Butlers into direct conflict with another great southern family, the Fitzgeralds, or Geraldines.

The Fitzgeralds—more commonly called Desmonds after the name of the family earldom—had come over with Strongbow himself seven years before Theobald Butler set foot in Ireland and claimed first comer's rights to the rich pastoral lands of Tipperary and to the 'prisage' (tax in kind) of wines unloaded in the ports of Youghal and Kinsale. For nearly three centuries thereafter the Butlers and the Desmonds waged intermittent clan warfare, partly in the hope of settling genuine grievances and partly for the pure pleasure of fighting. They besieged one another's castles, drove off one another's herds and occasionally carried off one another's women. Inevitably Romeo and Juliet situations developed from time to time, for the Butler men were handsome, the Desmond women beautiful. The most unusual variation of the conventional plot-pattern was created by Joan, daughter of the eleventh Earl of Desmond, who must have been very beautiful indeed. Joan married James Butler, later Earl of Ormond, in 1532, thus becoming countess in the house of the hereditary enemies of her own people. So far the conventional romantic pattern is observed. But in 1549, three years after the death of Ormond, to whom she had borne seven sons, Joan married her kinsman Gerald, heir to the house of Desmond and her junior by more than twenty years. Perhaps it was her dream to unite for ever the two great houses, but if so she was disappointed. Between her eldest son, Thomas Butler, 10th Earl of Ormond, and her husband Gerald (stepson and stepfather and both of an age) the ancient feud was soon renewed. It dragged on until 1580, when Thomas Butler was made military governor of Munster with a commission from Queen Elizabeth to 'banish and vanquish those cankered Desmonds'. Butler did the job reluctantly but thoroughly. Gerald, in the end a proscribed outlaw deserted by all except four faithful followers, was hunted to death in 1583, and with him perished the once-great house of Desmond.

The Desmonds were loved by the Irish people, the Butlers

distrusted. The Desmonds intermarried early with the native stock, the Butlers preserved for generations the purity of their Norman blood; the Desmonds were daring men—Gerald a Hotspur among them—ready to revolt against the Crown at the suspicion of injustice or insult; but the Butlers were the King's men, hence even after centuries looked upon as aliens by the native Irish.

Thomas Butler's work in rooting out the Queen's enemies earned him a sonnet from Edmund Spenser—

> In thy person without paragone
> All goodlie bounty and true honour sits—

and an uneasy conscience. He was a sensitive man, brooding, introspective—he has been called an Irish Hamlet—and a good deal less enthusiastic than Spenser about killing Irishmen.

William Francis Butler, the boy who fought the eagle on the mountain ledge, was born in a farmhouse at Ballyslateen, Suirville, County Tipperary, on October 31, 1838, the seventh child of Richard and Ellen Butler. Ballyslateen lay directly across the river—Spenser's 'gentle Shure'—from the estate of Ballycarron which Butlers had held since the seventeenth century. The Butlers of Ballycarron, descended from a younger son of the 9th Earl of Ormond, were Catholics and poor; but they were good fellows all, loyal to the Crown, and they seem to have suffered comparatively little under the ferocious Penal Laws whose object was to break up all Catholic estates in Ireland and reduce the Catholic Irish to the position of 'insignificant slaves, fit for nothing but to hew wood and draw water'. Richard Butler, William's father, was a landholder on a small scale and always hard up. He was a man of ferocious temper, known on occasion to smash a tenant's pipe with his blackthorn stick when the tenant addressed him without first taking the pipe from his mouth. But he was a humane man, too. Much of what little wealth he had he spent during the terrible years of the great potato famine (1845–8) trying with some success to keep his tenants and their families alive. There was not much money left for the education of a large family—nine sons and two daughters—and William's schooling was sketchy and haphazard. He spent two years at Tullabeg, a Jesuit school set in the boglands of King's County, and in later life looked back on those years with horror:

> I was nine years old and thin and delicate; and the cold of the winter, in that elevated marshland which lies to the north of the Slieve Bloom Hills

. . . seemed to strike into the heart and soul of such a frame as mine. All the more did the climatic conditions tell against a small boy because the majority of the other boys were strong. Many of them were rough, and, it is needless to say, were as merciless to their smaller and weaker fry as though the school had been of pilchards.[1]

The winter of 1848–9 he remembered as 'a long night of sorrow'. He was removed from the school he hated, but only because his mother had died and two of his brothers lay ill of a wasting fever.

William later attended a private school in Dublin for a brief period, but most of what he learned from books he snatched at intervals over the years when a fortunate posting gave him access to a good library. Some of his most intensive reading he did during his wanderings in remote places of the earth, for in the conviction that he who runs may read he always found room in his bag for a few books.

But he could never carry enough. 'In the good old days of a soldier's life,' he wrote the year before he died, 'the French knapsack had place kept in it for the Baton. That place is now filled by the Book. Doubtless the change is for the better. But the Book must always be a little one'.[2]

Although the boy's formal education was limited, he was fortunate enough to live in a countryside rich in folklore and legend and history, preserved in an oral tradition which made little distinction between fiction and fact. A few miles north of Ballycarron the Rock of Cashel, crowning-place of ancient Irish kings, rose from the broad central plain of Tipperary; all the land between Cashel and the mighty upthrust of the Galtee Mountains to the south-west was Butler country still, in name if not in fact, and in the tenant cottages of Ballycarron innumerable fine tales of Butler exploits of a former time were to be had for the listening. Only a mile or so downriver from Ballycarron a certain 'Mosh' or Tom Butler, a man 'of desperate fighting tenacity', had fought a duel with the descendant of a Cromwellian settler reputed to wear chain-armour under his clothing. Tom killed his man with a silver coin which his second had slipped into his pistol between powder and wad. On a black day in 1642 a riderless horse galloped over Kilmoyler Hill within easy view of Ballycarron, the empty saddle a mute forewarning of the word that forty rebellious Butlers had died fighting against the loyalist Earl of Ormond in the Battle of Kilrush. Beyond Kilmoyler Hill lay the family burial ground of the Butlers of Ballycarron, and the name of the ground, Killardrigh, was in itself enough to stir the blood, for it meant that a High King of Ireland was buried there.

There were stories, too, to be heard of the world lying just beyond the immediate Butler country, for the Galtee Mountains and the land falling away to the south and west abound in historic names and associations. Edmund Spenser lived fearfully in Kilcolman Castle, whose ruins rise stark and lonely at the foot of the western Galtees. There Sir Walter Raleigh read with passionate enthusiasm the first three books of the *Faerie Queene*; and in his own house at Youghal—not far from Ballycarron as the crow flies—smoked the first pipefuls of tobacco to be burned in Ireland and talked with Spenser about the need to exterminate the Irish. In the lovely wood of Aherlow on the slopes of the Galtees, Gerald, the last of the Desmonds, wandered ragged and starving, an Irish Lear accompanied by a priest, two soldiers and a boy, in the months before his death at Tralee. (Now he sleeps under the waters of Loch Gur and every seventh year rouses himself and rides over the water on a horse shod with silver. When the horse's shoes are worn out he will return and reclaim the lost dominions of the Desmonds.) Anne Boleyn, an English queen with Butler blood in her veins, was born, as every honest Irishman will tell you (though, of course, the English deny it), in a fine manor-house near Cahir, less than ten miles from Ballycarron; and Thomas Meagher, a near-contemporary of William Butler's, who made a name for himself on two continents, grew up in near-by Clonmel. In 1848 Meagher, a leader of the Young Ireland movement, was sentenced to death for treason. The sentence was later commuted to transportation for life. Meagher escaped to the United States in 1852. He served with distinction in the Civil War, rising to the rank of General, and in 1867 was appointed acting Governor of the Territory of Montana. While on an official tour of inspection he fell—or was pushed—off a steamboat into the Missouri River. Today an equestrian statue of Meagher dominates the grounds of the state legislative building in Helena, Montana.

But of all the stories young William Butler listened to those which interested him most were of battles and bivouacs told by men who had been participants in or spectators of mighty events which early in the nineteenth century shook half the world. These excellent story-tellers Butler later epitomized in the characters of the old soldier and the priest who are the childhood companions and mentors of the hero of Butler's admirable juvenile novel, *Red Cloud:*

Sergeant MacMahon was, when I knew him, a man who had passed his sixtieth year. Yet time, despite a score of years of fighting and exposure, had dealt lightly with the old soldier, who still stood straight as the ramrod he had so often driven home upon the bullet of his firelock. . . . He had the battles of the Peninsula by heart, and day after day did he pour forth his descriptions of how Busaco was won, and how Fuentes d'Orono had been decided, and how Lord Wellington had outmatched 'Sowlt' as he used to call him, at Pampaluna, or had outmanoeuvred Marmont at Torres Vedras. His personal adventures were told in another style. He had stories of bivouac . . . of nights on outlying picquet, of escapes when patrolling, and of incidents in action, that he loved to recount to me as we sat by a riverside waiting for a cloud to cross the sun before we tried a cast of flies over some favourite stream. . . .

But I had another schoolmaster at the time. A mile down the glen from our cottage stood the (French) priest's house. . . . Here he lived in the memory of his past life. Nearly half a century had gone by since his eyes had rested on the vine-clad slopes of the Loire, but it was ever an easy task for him to fling back his thoughts across that gulf of time, and to recall the great names that had risen in the sunrise of the century, and flashed such a glory over Europe that the lustre of succeeding time had shone faint and dim in contrast. He had seen the great emperor review his guards in the courtyard of the Tuileries, and had looked upon a group of horsemen that had in it Murat, Ney, Soult, Lannes and Massenna. . . . He never tired of talking of the great campaigns of the consulate and Empire . . . and many a winter's night sped rapidly while the old man, seated before his turf fire, rambled on from battlefield to battlefield, now describing to me the wonderful strategy of some early campaign in Italy, now carrying my mind into the snows of Russia, and again taking me into the plains of France to that last and most brilliant effort of warlike genius, the campaign of 1814. At such times the storm in the mountains would sometimes lend its roar in fitting accompaniment to the old man's story, and then the scene would change to my mind's eye as I listened. The little parlour would fade away, the firelight become a bivouac; and I saw in the grim outside darkness of the glen figures dimly moving; the squadrons charged; the cannon rumbled by; and the pine-tops swaying in the storm were the bearskin caps of the Old Guard, looming above smoke and fire.[3]

The land which William Butler grew up in, apart from the people who occupied it, was in itself a stimulus to the imagination and to the development of that Celtic melancholy, that sense of sadness at the heart of things—the poet's *lacrimae rerum*—which is no mere sentimental fancy but an authentic part of the Irish heritage. It is a melancholy compounded of many elements—among them a mist-shrouded landscape; a long memory; hungry generations; a centuries-old subjugation to a conqueror who has everywhere dotted the land with evidences of his mindless ferocity. 'Wherever the traveller pursues his route in Ireland', Butler said in a speech to the Irish Literary Society of London,

there is one ever-present object in the landscape, whose presence after a time ceases to attract attention through the simple fact of its perpetual recurrence.

It is the ruin.

Ruins of great monastic edifices and abbeys—some set on lonely islands in silvery lakes, some standing amid meadows where winding river-reaches reflect their roofless outlines. Ruins of Plantagenet castles crowning some rock, which itself seems of material scarcely more durable than the remnant of battlement above it. Ruins of hermit's cell, of wayside chapel, of weed-grown cloister, of city rampart, of sea-beaten fortalice, of broken bridge and battered gable—everywhere they rise in view, the silent witnesses to some great historic cataclysm, some vast fact of human destruction, which has wanted no historian to describe it, so largely is it written in characters which even Time is powerless to efface, over the broad page of the entire island.[4]

There are ruined hovels, too, and they were never more numerous than in the mid-nineteenth century. Of all the evidences of human destruction the ruined hovel stirred in young William Butler the greatest sense of outrage, because it was most intimately connected with the suffering of the helpless and oppressed. A scene which haunted him all his life and helped to rouse in him a Swiftian *saeva indignatio* at the spectacle of man's inhumanity to man was that of an eviction—Irish peasants driven from their cottages by a greedy landlord, with no redress possible in law and no place to shelter except a ditch:

At a signal from the sheriff the work began. The miserable inmates of the cabins were dragged out upon the road; the thatched roofs were torn down and the earthen walls battered in by crowbars (practice had made these scoundrels adept at their trade); the screaming women, the half-naked children, the paralysed grandmother, the tottering grandfather, were hauled out. It was a sight I have never forgotten. I was twelve years old at the time; but I think that if a loaded gun had been put into my hands I would have fired into that crowd of villains, as they plied their horrible trade by the ruined church of Tampul-da-voun.[5]

About his choice of profession young Butler seems to have had no doubts whatever. The tales told him by veterans of the Peninsular War had done their work; he would be a soldier, too. But his father was not easily persuaded. For an Irish Catholic lad with few influential friends and no money at all—this at a time when commissions were still obtained mainly by purchase—the Army offered little hope of normal promotion. Richard Butler reminded his son of the fate of their distant kinsman, Theobald O'Doherty, who had taken an active, often heroic part in nearly every great battle of the Peninsular War and retired many years after Waterloo with a most distinguished military record and the rank of captain. True, Theobald's brother Richard had done rather better; he had seen active service only in Guadaloupe and Martinique, but he had changed his religion, dropped the 'O'' from his name and was now General Sir Richard Doherty. Richard Butler looked with disfavour upon a profession which would seem to make his son's advancement dependent, in part at least, on a change of faith and denial of nationality.

None the less, it was Sir Richard Doherty's influence which gained William Butler his commission. He called on Sir Richard in 1857 and was appropriately awed by the appearance and manner of his aged kinsman:

I was under inspection. It was an anxious moment. He was reserved, graciously solemn, and of the type of veteran not uncommon at the time, but now rarely to be seen—the type of Gough, Napier, Harry Smith and a dozen others. He wore a high black silk stock, behind the stiff shelter of which he seemed at times to withdraw a good deal of the lower part of his face in order to regard me to greater advantage from the upper portion.[6]

Young Butler passed the inspection. In 1858, on the recommendation of Sir Richard Doherty, he was nominated to a direct commission without purchase. He passed his qualifying examination at Burlington House and on September 17, 1858, was gazetted ensign in Sir Richard Doherty's old regiment, the 69th Foot.

The regimental training depot was based at Fermoy, some forty miles south-west of Ballycarron, and thither the young ensign went by horsecart. The evening of his arrival at barracks was dark and lowering, but his spirit was high, his mood exalted. He was young and imaginative, of superb physique—the shrinking stripling of Tullabeg school had grown into a strikingly handsome young man of six feet two—and the world was all before him. 'Perhaps no event leaves a more lasting impression on the memory than that which a young officer experiences when he joins the army', he wrote more than thirty years later.

> The entrance to all professions is like passing through the door of life, but the army door strikes the imagination more than any other. The barrack-gate localizes the feeling into a distinct tangible reality; the sentinel without; the armed guard within, the austere buildings, the bugle calls ringing through the squares, the evidence of order and discipline—these things impress the mind with the sense of some great step forward into that vague and vast world which the boy's imagination has been unconsciously endeavouring to pierce and realize.[7]

When William Butler entered the army barracks at Fermoy he carried several books in his knapsack. But he left enough room for the marshal's baton.

CHAPTER TWO

Stations of the East

TO A YOUNG MAN nominated to a commission without purchase 1858 must have seemed a good year to join the Army. The nation was in a state of shock following the disasters of the Crimea and the Indian Mutiny and there was talk on all sides of drastic army reforms. In particular the purchase system, whereby commissions were bought and sold for hard cash, came under heavy fire from the reformers. Defenders of the system pointed out that it had enabled Wellington to reach the rank of colonel at twenty-four and thus exercise his genius for command from an early age; but it was equally true that the purchase system kept many talented officers of small means far below the rank which their ability merited—Sir Henry Havelock, one of Britain's great professional soldiers, remained a lieutenant till the age of forty-three—and permitted such an irresponsible and brutal exhibitionist as the Earl of Cardigan to buy the command of the 11th Light Dragoons for £40,000 and lead them to near annihilation at Balaclava. For the ambitious soldier a military campaign, and particularly one involving heavy casualties, offered the only real hope of advancement. In time of war vacancies caused by death in battle were often filled on the field on the basis of merit. But in peacetime an officer, no matter how able, might languish for years in the same rank and find the vacancies in his own regiment bought over his head by men whose sole claim to promotion was the ability to pay the several thousand pounds which purchase of a commission in a regiment of good reputation usually required.

There was, too, talk of retiring army generals before they reached the last stage of senility. When the Crimean War broke out in 1854 the British Army had on its active list 'thirteen generals with over seventy years' service; thirty-seven between sixty and seventy years'; and one hundred and sixty-three with between fifty and sixty years'.[1] Many of these men held high command during the Crimean War itself—Lord Raglan, the Commander-in-Chief, was nearly seventy—and enough of them survived to dominate the Army and the War Office after the war was over. The general in command at Aldershot when William Butler went there in 1865 'had borne at Inkermann the worst pressure of the Russian attack in the early hours of the fight. When the first reinforcement—Cathcart's Division—came up, that general had ridden forward to ask to what part of the field he should direct his troops. "Anywhere you like, my dear sir; you'll find plenty of fighting all round." '[2]

In 1865 with more than half a century of service behind him this old general was still capable of a passionate interest in the minutiae of military manoeuvres, as Butler gleefully observed:

I can still see this old hero sitting his charger on the top of a knoll over the Basingstoke Canal, across which the engineers had, in manoeuvre language, 'thrown a pontoon bridge' (two pontoons and twenty planks). Over this structure our brigade had to go, and the great point was that they should break step as they crossed, but the poor fellows had been so mercilessly trained to keep step that they couldn't break it to save their lives; and as the canal was only about four feet deep in the centre of its twenty foot width, it didn't matter a pin whether they fell in or not. But from the general's excitement you might have thought that the operation was quite on a par with that of the Russians retreating over their bridge of boats from the south to the north side of Sebastapol. Up we came to the canal in solid serried ranks. The more he swore at us, the more his staff roared at us, shouting 'break step', the more our men stepped as one man as they had been taught and drilled and bullied into doing for years: tramp, tramp, tramp. I can never forget the sight of that fine old soldier; the reins dropped on his charger's neck, his hands uplifted as far as they could go, and a whole torrent of imprecations pouring from under his snow-white moustache. Two ladies who had ridden out with the staff thought it prudent to retire from the scene. The two pontoons withstood it all.[3]

The talk of reform soon died down. In 1858 there was peace everywhere throughout the Empire. Even Ireland was quiet, for following the great potato famine of 1845-8 most of the Irish were dead. True, the Army of the Crimea was dead too, but it could be argued that the War Office and not the generals was to blame. Hadn't the British won every battle they fought against the Russians and didn't the shambles of Balaclava give the Poet Laureate a subject for a poem that made every Englishman's heart swell with pride? Reform was nearly always expensive as well as risky and on the whole it was probably better to bear the ills they had than fly to others they knew not.

Such were the views which prevailed. Prince George, Duke of Cambridge, the newly appointed Commander-in-Chief of the Army—a post he was to fill for nearly forty years—heartily approved promotion by purchase, and held that the right time to make a change 'is when you cannot help it'. Few generals were retired, except of their own free will, and on the Fermoy parade ground Ensign William Butler listened to aged officers bellowing commands unchanged since the days of the Peninsular War:

The colonel, Isaac Moore, had risen from the ranks. He was an old officer with the profile of an eagle, the voice of a Stentor, and a heart of great goodness. . . . He was warned not to use his voice too much on parade, but he persisted in giving the long-drawn-out cautionary commands of the old Peninsular drill days, such as 'The battalion will change front by the wheel and counter-march of subdivisions round the centre' . . . ending by a 'Quick march' that could be heard in the town square at the foot of the barracks hill. One day, after one of these excessive throat exercises, the old man was seen to lean forward upon the neck of his old horse, and they carried him to his quarters to die. He had burst a blood-vessel in the lungs.[4]

But though officers and drill were unchanged—from the beginning of the century it seemed—the rank and file were changed beyond recognition. The Crimean War had destroyed the splendid Army built in the Peninsular tradition, and the sources from which it had mainly been recruited were by 1858 drying up. William Butler idealized the old Army, which he knew through its surviving veterans, and in 1878 wrote a remarkable paper, 'A Plea for the Peasant', a detailed analysis of the make-up of the old and new armies and an attempt to account for what he thought was the overwhelming superiority of the old. Until the mid-nineteenth century the British Army drew its main strength not from England but the peasantry of Ireland and Scotland. Early in the century the Scottish supply was in part cut off. Laws were framed 'to convert the Highland glens into vast wastes untenanted by human beings; to drive forth to distant and inhospitable shores men whose forefathers had held their own among these hills despite Roman legion, Saxon archer, or Norman chivalry—men whose sons died freely for England's honour through those wide dominions their bravery had won for her'.[5]

The evictions swept the Highlands clear of men; the crofters took their talents and their loyalties elsewhere and in the long run the British Army was one of the heaviest losers. None the less, as late as 1853 on the eve of the Crimean War there were 12,000 Scots and 32,000 Irishmen in a total British infantry strength of 100,000. Within a year they were nearly all dead. 'Victorious in every fight,' Butler wrote, 'the army perished miserably from want. With all our boasted wealth, with all our command of sea and steam-power, our men died of the common needs of food and shelter within five miles of the shore and within fifteen days of London.'[6]

The Army was rebuilt, but of different, weaker stuff. The Scottish peasant who might have helped to fill the ranks had emigrated to new lands and the Irish peasant was dead in the great famine. Butler's figures show that as late as 1840 nearly 60 per cent of the rank and file of British infantry were Scots and Irish; in 1853 about 44 per cent, and by 1877 only 30. And the new men, he said, were 'the sweepings of the large crowded towns'. Butler was later guilty of gross unfairness when he blamed the disasters which befell his friend General George Colley in 1881, culminating in Colley's death on Majuba Hill, on the indiscipline and cowardice of the troops under Colley's command; but his charge of a decline in the all-round quality of the British soldier received support from the evidence given by Lord Roberts, an army man for more than half a century, before the South African War Commission in 1903:

> The highest praise I can give the regular soldier of today is to say that he is in no single respect inferior to his predecessor. . . . As a fighting man, however, he was not so expert when he first met the enemy as he might have been. His individuality had been so little cultivated that his natural acuteness was checked, and his want of resourcefulness, especially at the beginning of the campaign, was marked. He was the exact opposite of the Boer, especially in his want of knowledge of ground and how to utilize it; and also in his defective powers of observation. His shooting cannot be described as good.[7]

Other veteran army officers spoke in blunter terms. General Kelly-Kenny referred to 'physical defects due to the modern necessity of recruiting chiefly in the poorest districts of the crowded towns'; and Professor Ogston, a medical man who had served with the forces in South Africa, testified that 'some of the regiments were physically very inferior'. They were, he said, made up of 'boys and sweepings'.[8]

'A Plea For the Peasant' marks the beginning of a campaign which Butler carried on to the end of his life to return the Irishman and the Scot to the land taken from them—for the welfare of the men themselves and the good of the Army. A town-dweller, Butler argued, puts down no roots; he had nothing to love and nothing to fight for. Butler conducted his campaign with no less vigour because he realized its futility. He had much in common with Cyrano de Bergerac; certainly he would have approved Cyrano's philosophy—*one does no fight because there is hope of winning . . . it is much finer to fight when it is no use.*

At the Fermoy training depot Butler was untroubled—for the only time in his life—by the state of the Army. He drilled 'in the balance step without gaining ground', studied manual and platoon excercises, and in his spare time read widely and enjoyed life as only a carefree young man in top physical condition can do. He tramped far and wide through the beautiful country around Fermoy, fished for salmon in the Blackwater, for trout in the Araglin and Bride, won the south of Ireland hurdles championship in the footraces at Limerick and flirted with every pretty woman who crossed his path. He was popular with his fellow juniors, whom he entertained with lively conversation, outrageous puns (to which he suffered lifelong addiction) and scraps of doggerel verse about the food served in the canteen—

> The marmalade is luscious
> Though it's made of turnip peels,
> The sugar is the sweetest,
> Though it only sand reveals—

but the men dear to his heart were the battle-and-bottle-scarred old veterans who formed living links with a romantic past—men who could talk for hours of bivouacs and marches and battles long ago. Men like Captain Robert Weild—'Old Bob Weild, as he was popularly called among us youngsters. He drank a good deal, and smoked pipes of many kinds and colours. He spoke the broadest Lowland Scotch. He took a fancy to me and would often come into my room and sit smoking at the fire and telling me of his early life and service.'

Old Bob had been seriously wounded in the Crimea and owed his life, so he believed, to a pint of brandy which a surgeon had poured down his throat immediately following the injury. Thereafter he lived by the rule that if brandy could save a life it could also preserve it:

Sometimes he would stay late in the little club at the foot of the barracks hill; and as I would be crossing the square to the mess I would encounter my old friend making the best of his way from the gate to his quarters, walking straight to the front but gazing at the ground with a fixed stare and an expression in his eyes that told me it would not be safe to speak a single word to him. He had taken his line from the gate, and he was steering for his door upon a mental compass bearing so fine that the smallest whisper might have deranged it.[9]

While at Fermoy Butler was twice detailed to help preserve order at polling-booths during elections. As late as 1859 many police duties were still assigned to the military, and the execution of these duties contributed greatly to the unpopularity of the Army in peacetime. Butler was shocked by the spectacle of 'free and independent voters' being hustled under escort (and a barrage of stones from the opposition) to register their votes according to the dictates of their landlords; and agreeably entertained by the ladies of the town who spent election day heaping ridicule—occasionally spiced with genuine wit—upon the defenceless soldiers.

Eight months after being commissioned Butler was ordered abroad for service in Burma. He sailed from Queenstown aboard the *Coldstream*—one of more than 200 men crowded into an 800-ton sailing-vessel.

The voyage to India was in no way different from the average run of the time. It took 124 days and during that period those on board saw land twice—Madeira, and St. Paul's Island in the Indian Ocean. The drinking-water rotted in the barrels; it was foul-tasting, foul-smelling stuff, but the men nearly mutinied when they were put on short rations during a heat-ridden three weeks' period of dead calm in the tropics. Catching the trade winds at last, the old tub briskly rounded the Cape of Good Hope, far to the south of land, and 'entered upon a vast ocean of gigantic rollers, a grey limitless waste of waters that came surging after us in stupendous billows as though they would overwhelm the little speck of ship that carried us'.

In spite of a leak that compelled the soldiers to man the pumps round the clock for nearly two weeks, the tough little ship survived the billows and most of the soldiers survived the voyage. Indeed, for a select few the voyage was probably the most agreeable experience of their lives. This handful of adventurous souls penetrated into the ship's hold by sliding down the chain cable, then cut a hole through a bulkhead into a room containing a large cargo of spirits intended for consumption in Anglo-Indian clubs. Here the men, homesick for the familiar pub, created a snug little tap-room furnished with hogshead seats, lighted by butt-ends of candles and stocked with unlimited supplies of liquor; and thither, via the ship's cable, they repaired nightly for several weeks. They were betrayed after inviting a congenial but enormously fat soldier to join the club. The fat soldier slid down the cable with no trouble at all, but was quite unable to climb back up. Abandoned by his companions, he consoled himself in his loneliness first with gin and then with song. The weird sounds reaching the upper deck alarmed the crew, an intensive search for their source was instituted, and the fat soldier at length uncovered. To his undying honour he refused to betray his fellow clubmen and he alone spent the rest of the voyage in chains.

Of such stuff was the old Army made.

Poonamallee, the depot outside Madras where the draft trained for several weeks before going to Burma, could have held few attractions for the average soldier, but Butler was delighted with everything—'the people, the trees, the fireflies in the bamboo hedges, the cicadas in the feathery palm-trees, the bullfrogs in the grassy fields, the endless multiplication of life human and animal everywhere to be seen, heard or felt', to say nothing of the extraordinary sculpture of the near-by Hindu temples 'representing, with an effrontery not to be abashed, the lowest and most direputable lines of the Hindu worship'.

The draft sailed from Madras to Rangoon. The soldiers were roaring drunk for part of the voyage, to the complete mystification of the officers, since no spirits were allowed on board. It was later discovered that many of the oranges which the soldiers bought from the natives at various ports of call had been drained of their natural juice, refilled with arrack, the potent local liquor, and sealed with plugs of rind. No doubt the discovery convinced Butler and his fellow juniors that they were at last coming to grips with the mysterious East.

The draft landed at Rangoon, marched across country to the Sittang River and embarked in a flotilla of native craft bound for the regimental station of the 69th Foot at Tonghoo, twenty-one days and 200 miles upriver. Again the impressionable young ensign was delighted by everything he saw—the forest of reeds flanking the river; the steersman on his lofty seat high above the stern, controlling the boat with a huge spoon-shaped oar; the crewmen who after a day of prodigious toil ate a scanty supper of boiled rice, and played cards the rest of the night; and the innumerable village festivals to celebrate a wedding or a funeral or a religious holiday. He even tackled Burmese food with stout heart and stomach and sagely observed that the native delicacy called Napee—fish pounded to a pulpy mass and left buried in a deep pit until it decomposed—was as civilized a dish as 'a venerable Stilton, a mite-ridden Roquefort, a semi-liquefied Camembert'.

Even to men innured to the damp of an English or Irish winter the Tonghoo environment must have been infinitely depressing. Butler's draft was fortunate enough to arrive in the middle of the dry season, but the disenchanted veterans on the station gave dismal warning of what lay ahead:

In three months the clouds would sweep up over the tree-tops from the sea, and in terrific thunder and lightning the ball of the Monsoon would open. Then for nearly six months it would not be possible to stir beyond the roads of the cantonment. All the forest would be a swamp; the river, which was now thirty feet down in its channel, would be running level with the tops of the banks; the bull-frogs would croak outside every compound; and all creeping things that love heat and damp—scorpions, centipedes, huge spiders, strange lizards, beetles, cobras and pythons—would hold general carnival.[10]

Butler made the most of the few weeks of good weather prevailing before the rains set in. He and a brother officer borrowed three elephants from a Forest Department official and hunted tiger in the jungle. Without success—but no matter. The magnificent teak forests, the abundant and novel wild life, the friendly native villagers—these things were adequate compensation for the failure to make a kill. Butler prided himself on being a good shot and spent many a pleasant day in the field, but he was not a sportsman in the accepted sense of the term. Except when he was hungry he preferred to let birds and animals live.

Even during the rainy season he managed to avoid the appalling boredom which broke many a good man on a station such as Tonghoo. He borrowed books instead of elephants and read omnivorously, mixed as far as possible with the natives of the near-by villages (no Orwellian guilt-complexes to torment him), listened with rapt attention to the talk of the old officers on the station and thanked God there was no likelihood of serving under them in actual combat. One of these 'strange and interesting survivals of an earlier generation' still ordered the troops to 'prime and load' as he had done in the days of the flintlock musket half a century before. 'Recollection of its cumbersome process of combustion,' Butler commented, 'still lingered among our seniors'.

Butler's stay in the jungle was short. The main body of the regiment had languished at Tonghoo for three years now and the men were in bad shape both physically and mentally, beset by the awful depression which was the inevitable consequence of a long stay in a rain-soaked fetid environment with nothing to do beyond routine drill. The sole function of the regiment was to preserve order in a peaceful land. A few of the rankers had been able to bring their wives and families with them and lived miserably in the crowded married quarters of the barracks; the rest found what entertainment they could in native wines and native women.

Conditions were materially better for the officers; but they, too, suffered from the sense of confinement which the jungle environment invariably imposes, and from an awareness that the carrying out of routine duties in a post as remote from the centre of things as Tonghoo added little to their chances of promotion. And there seemed no chance of a military campaign. In the sixties the Burmese were annoyingly peaceful.

Early in 1862 the 69th left Tonghoo, bound for the plains of India, where, it was said, the blistering sun and scorching wind would dry the men out in no time and draw the fetid jungle vapours from their blood. The descent of the Sittang River gave Butler his first staff appointment. The colonel commanding the last of the regimental detachments to move out—an aged veteran with an eye still keen enough to spot the man most likely to do his work for him—appointed the eager young ensign staff officer of the wing, and suddenly Butler found himself 'adjutant, paymaster and quartermaster of some four or five hundred men'. Everything went well; the native boatmen rode out the mighty bore of the Sittang River without losing a single soldier; his own men and the colonel gave

Butler no trouble at all, and he delivered the unit intact and in fair health at the embarkation point in Rangoon.

The troops were carried across the Bay of Bengal in a steamer with a sailing-ship in tow. Butler was aboard the sailing ship—a battered old hulk named the *Tubal Cain*, long since fit only for scrap. She was commanded by a mentally ill captain, undermanned by a crew of Lascars, and overloaded with soldiers, soldiers' families and the strangely assorted throng of camp-followers which even as late as the 1860s formed an unofficial part of every armed force abroad.

Half-way across the Bay of Bengal the transports were hit by a tropical hurricane for which the *Tubal Cain* was totally unprepared. The steamer cut the towline and vanished into darkness; the Lascars were demoralized by the loss of their mate, who was swept overboard by the first big wave to hit the ship; the ailing captain locked himself in his cabin and refused to come out; and the destruction of the *Tubal Cain* seemed certain. But the second mate, a lion-hearted old sailor whose behaviour won Butler's unqualified respect and gratitude, eventually restored order among the crew, infused something of his own courageous spirit into them and made preparation to meet the full onset of the hurricane.

An hour or two later it came. Butler's description of a great storm at sea is worthy of Conrad:

There is no sea running and no sky and no air. They have all become one vast, black, solid, gigantic animal. . . . There is no sea running as in an ordinary storm; beneath this awful wind the sea crouches for a time like a leashed hound. . . . It cannot get up and run before that vast wall of wind. It lies down at first and the wind mows it like grass, shaves it off in swathes of white foam which are caught up into the rushing wind itself, so that no eye can open against it and no face can face its saltness. But the roar is the thing that lives longest in memory; it seems to swallow even the thunder, as though that too, like the sea, had been brayed into it.[11]

The storm subsided before daybreak. By then almost everything movable had been swept away, and the soldiers and camp-followers confined below decks were so ill and battered they cared little whether they lived or died. Even Ensign Butler, suffering agonies of sea-sickness, no longer felt much concern about the future.

The *Tubal Cain*, although a dismantled wreck, remained afloat. A week later the shattered old heroic hulk, still under the command of the second mate, limped into Madras. She had been given up for lost and the names of the soldiers she was carrying struck off the official Army list.

The regiment was marched into quarters at Fort St. George, just outside Madras. Most of the officers went at once on leave—nearly all to Simla, the hill town in the far north which was the nearest approach in all India to 'home'—with the added attraction of lonely dissatisfied Civil Service and Army wives to comfort and eager daughters to woo. Characteristically Butler went off in the opposite direction and he went alone. The most genial of companions in the company of his fellow officers, he was none the less at his best and happiest in some vast lonely world of mountain, plain or desert where his instinctive sympathy for the primitive folk was allowed full play and no mundane official business interrupted his prophetic musings. Already there was formulating in his mind—born of the hideous spectacles of human misery he had witnessed in Ireland and the East—a concept of the causes of man's suffering which was one day to bring him into direct conflict with those in authority over him and make his life as a professional soldier all but intolerable.

But in 1862 the future cast no shadows. Mounted on a tough little Burmese pony which like himself had survived the voyage in the *Tubal Cain*, Butler rode into the Nilgherry Mountains of southern India. He explored the mountains in all directions, rejoicing in the cool pure air and the magnificent scenery. 'If the Garden of Eden was not here,' he wrote, 'it might well have been. There are points of the eastern ramparts of this paradise from which in gardens hung with roses and jessamine, one can sit and look down from a clear, bracing atmosphere upon a hundred miles of the fevered, quivering plains of Southern India seven thousand feet below."[12]

The trouble with life in the Garden of Eden is that it must always be temporary. After two months Butler's leave was up, and he rode down from his mountain paradise into the dusty hell of the Indian plains.

CHAPTER THREE

The Burning Plains

FOR A SENSITIVE MAN life in India in 1862 was an experience to be endured rather than enjoyed. The great Mutiny was only four years past; and the British were still shaken, as never before in their history, by the moral implications of a war fought with limitless brutality and no quarter given on either side, and by the knowledge—which previously not even the history of Ireland had been able to teach them—that the conquered do not always love their conquerors. Henceforward there could be no trust and no fellowship between Englishman and Indian; and from 1857 onwards the rift between the two peoples widened rapidly to the point where permanent separation became an inevitability.

Nor did the India of 1862 offer many opportunities of advancement to the ambitious professional soldier. Except in the far north, where the hill tribes maintained a state of more or less continuous petty border warfare, the peace of death lay over the land. Butler and his fellow officers spoke enviously of their American cousins who were winning renown in the bloodiest civil war in history. Their sympathies lay entirely with the South, except on the single occasion when the Civil War touched in a practical way their own lives. The American ship which regularly carried ice from Boston to Madras failed to arrive on schedule; and in messes and clubs throughout India men drank lukewarm whiskies-and-sodas and cursed the *Alabama*, the Confederate raider suspected of having sunk the ice-ship. But the ice-ship turned up at last with its precious cargo and immediately, so Butler reported, 'the Federal cause went down again to zero, like the temperature in our glasses'.

Butler rode down from the Nilgherry Mountains to find Fort St. George a huge pest-house. Cholera and the savage midsummer heat were killing the men of the 69th like flies—the colonel of the regiment and his young son died the same day—and those still on their feet were debilitated and apathetic. Living conditions at Fort St. George were far worse than anything the men had known in the jungles of Burma. Every night they lay down in their crowded quarters, worn out by boredom and heat and senseless out-of-date drill in heavy woollen uniform; and every night at midnight the outlet of a huge sewage drain leading from Madras into the sea a few hundred yards from Fort St. George was opened. The current piled the revolting mass of sewage up on the shingle directly opposite the Fort, and the stench made further sleep impossible for the exhausted soldiers.

There was no thought among the authorities of moving the men. After all, the Fort had been built long before the sewage drain.

Butler was fortunate enough to be moved to a musketry training range in the country a few miles from Fort St. George, and here he was able to observe at first hand the life of the native peasant. What he saw shocked him—it was worse than anything he had known in Ireland—and the full strength of his sympathies went out to the sad work-worn tillers of earth—

> people who bend and toil in the paddy-fields; who dwell in mud huts without the commonest articles of household furniture; who have scarcely any clothes; who are lean of leg and shrunken of body and hollow of stomach . . . who are patient beyond any limit of patience known to white men; who live and die scratching the hot soil and pouring water upon it; the poor, starved race, the feeble foundation of all the wealth, splendour and magnificence, the very name of which has made the hungry mouth of the rapacious host water for the last four hundred years.[1]

Butler believed that British rule in India could not long endure, because the work which the British were engaged upon 'lacked the greatest element of stability—sympathy with the people of India'. There were some exceptions, but the average Britisher in India, whether of Army or Civil Service, was an alien working not for the welfare of the native Indian but for the profit of his employers. Imperialism, Butler conceded, was sometimes beneficial to the conquered, but hardly ever by deliberate intention. And in his notebook for 1862 the young officer, then aged twenty-four, wrote with prophetic insight:

> For my part I am inclined to think that the edifice we are uprearing in India has its foundation resting upon sand. . . . The Indian knows that by violence and bribery, often times by treachery and fraud, we obtained

possession of his land. He knows that by force of arms and strength of discipline we hold our possessions; nevertheless he hates and fears us, and while he adopts and uses the discoveries of our civilization, he still holds that civilization in contempt. . . . I can see signs that this great structure we are building will be a ruin before it is completed.[2]

In 1863 Butler obtained a two months' leave and set out to explore the southern peninsula of India, dragging two lethargic fellow officers, one an elderly colonel, with him. The little party crossed by rail from Madras to Calicut on the romantic spice-scented Malabar coast, in Vasco da Gama's time a city of wealth and splendour, but in 1863 'a straggling town hidden in cocoa-nut palms, its old harbour silted up, a big sea breaking ceaselessly upon its straight sandy shore'.

From Calicut the party moved slowly south towards Cape Cormorin, Butler chivvying, cajoling, exhorting like an enthusiastic scoutmaster almost every step of the way. His geniality and conversational talents no doubt made him an admirable after-dinner companion over a pipe and glass; but his two fellow officers, weaker than he in both flesh and spirit and by now wistfully recalling the coolness of the Madras clubs and the peace of the fishing-streams near the city, must have found him an exhausting daytime-tour conductor.

Cochin, once one of the great commercial centres of the East, now 'a museum of almost extinct European races', fascinated Butler, but he felt it unsafe to linger there, for his companions were talking more and more earnestly of a retreat to Madras. At Quillon they were entertained in the local regimental mess; and there the elderly colonel, corrupted by renewed contact with the fleshpots, abandoned the party and turned back to Madras, leaving Butler and his fellow junior, Lieutenant Mansfield, to enjoy by themselves the pleasure of exploring southern India by bullock-cart and on foot.

In Travancore, the most southerly province of India, they turned away from the coast to hunt in the great forests running down the spine of the lower peninsula. Butler's bag included a python (found in the mountain bungalow he and Mansfield shared for several days) and a splendid forest bison; but the wild life of the region interested him less than did the people. Here in Travancore the natives were happier and better fed than the poor starved wretches of the interior plains; and the man and the poet in Butler were stirred by sight of 'those graceful Nair and Tier women with their rich golden skins and black, silky tresses, wading in the warm inland waters or working in their island gardens amid all the spice plants of the earth'. Women who were, he believed, 'the descendants of the people whom Camoens saw on this coast, and sighed after and wrote about in the dread days of misfortune and captivity'.

Near a desolate crumbling old fort called Oodagherry, Butler found the graves, now almost completely obliterated by fallen debris and tangled foliage, of British soldiers, many of them belonging to his own regiment, who had died in the conquest of Travancore more than half a century earlier. To Butler the forgotten men in the forgotten graves, humble soldiers of the rank and file, were, like the peasants from whose homes the best of them came, the exploited of earth. They were the men who won India for Britain and their only reward was oblivion. In his notebook he wrote: 'Here, close to Cape Cormorin, and one thousand five hundred miles northward and east and west from Orissa to the Arabian Sea they lie in countless graves, those old, forgotten, heroic soldiers, unthanked and unthought of by the millions to whom their deaths gave untold riches and unequalled Empire.'

The two officers pushed on by bullock-cart to where Cape Cormorin, the southermost tip of India, 'slanted gently into the sea', then turned north along the east coast towards Madras. They covered part of the way by bullock-cart, but when Butler fell ill hired a 'dhoney', a native boat of some 20 tons manned by an Indian family, and made the last 200 miles by sea. Altogether they had travelled over 1,200 miles by rail, horseback, bullock-cart, dhoney and on foot.

It is probably true to say that the average army officer learned less about India in ten years than Butler did in two months.

The neglected graves of the men of his own regiment at Oodagherry haunted him; and it was at this time that he conceived the idea of writing a history of the 69th Foot, to be based on the sketchy regimental records preserved in the orderly room, the reminiscences of old soldiers, and such books of military history as he might have the good fortune to lay hands on in a country where libraries, both public and private, consisted mainly of sentimental Victorian novels. In the interests of the proposed history and to satisfy his almost insatiable curiosity about people and places, Butler visited the great inland fortress of Vellore, built by the early Mohammedan conquerors of the Carnatic, and the scene in 1806 of a mutiny of native troops in garrison with the 69th Foot. The rising took place at night; the mutineers thrust their muskets through the windows of the barracks and shot the British soldiers as they slept. A few survivors escaped to the ramparts and held off the mob of mutineers until help, summoned by a daring native houseboy who had managed to slip out of the fort, arrived from Arcot twenty miles away, and the mutineers were in turn massacred.

Butler rode to Vellore, about eighty miles inland from Madras, in the height of the scorching summer season. Inside the fort, built in one of the hottest regions of the Carnatic—'red rocky hills surround it, the radiation from which makes the night almost as fevered as the day'—he found the graves of the men of the 69th killed in the 1806 uprising. To his amazement he also found a huddle of miserable huts housing aged pensioners of the Indian Army. There were no survivors of the Vellore mutiny among the pensioners, but Butler came upon one old man who had fought with Nelson's fleet at the Battle of the Nile more than sixty years before. His description of the great naval engagement was unsatisfactory. 'What was the battle like?' Butler roared in his ear (the old man was very deaf). 'Like the sound of the water-wheel of a big mill,' the old man said, and refused to talk about the battle any more.

On his return to Madras, Butler at once circulated a subscription list to raise funds for a memorial to the men of the 69th who had died at Vellore. The required amount was quickly realized and Butler had the satisfaction of personally supervising the erection of 'a fitting monument in the graveyard at Vellore to the memory of the gallant men who lay there'.

Early in 1864 the remnant of the 69th Foot was ordered home. The death-rate from typhoid, cholera, sunstroke and alcohol among men already debilitated by three fever-ridden years in the jungles of Burma was appallingly high; and so many of those who had thus far survived were so seriously ill that the *Lord Warden*, the transport ship in which Butler sailed with the left wing of the regiment, was virtually a floating hospital.

The homeward voyage via the Cape of Good Hope took only three months compared with more than four for the outward run; and for Butler the tedium of the voyage was compensated for by a stay of two days at St. Helena—days 'so steeped in thoughts of glory and of grief that if I lived for a thousand years they would live with me'. In Butler's view Napoleon was, quite simply, the greatest and noblest human being who ever trod the earth; and it was here, on the island where his hero died, that the grand design first took shape in his mind of writing a definitive account of Napoleon's last days. The study of Napoleon was thenceforth to occupy him off and on for the rest of his life.

During his two days on the island Butler hardly slept at all. He talked with everyone who might conceivably have had first- or second-hand knowledge of Napoleon, and was overjoyed to meet a grizzled ancient who had been one of Napoleon's guards in the days of the captivity half a century before. As so often happened in Butler's experience, the conversation following the meeting was not entirely satisfactory. Very old people (like the soldier who remembered the Battle of the Nile as a sound and not a spectacle) tended to fix their minds on what the eager collector of reminiscences regarded as irrelevancies. The old man gave Butler a disconnected account of the 'drawing-in' of the sentries at night so that they stood almost elbow to elbow around Longwood, the bleak prison-house where the great Emperor had spun out the last threads of life, but his interest and only clear memories reached much farther back to the time of his Irish boyhood. 'Did you ever hear tell of Sligo?' were the words constantly on his lips.

When he could find no more old men to talk with Butler studied the topography of St. Helena with a passionate regard for detail that fixed the lineaments of the island for ever in his memory, so that when at length he came to write of Napoleon's last days he wrote of the island itself, and in particular the immediate environs of Longwood, more vividly and precisely than anyone before or since:

(On the sea side) the plateau of Longwood ends in a rock, called Horse Point, beneath which the cliff drops in a tremendous precipice, 1,400 feet, straight into the sea. A grey gloom hangs over this portion of the island. The scanty grass of the plateau is grey. The roads are grey. The ocean is grey. The clouds drifting in from the ocean and clinging to the central mountain cast over the lower ridges their grey sombre shadows. The few stunted trees growing upon the plateau lean before the pressure of the never-ceasing south-east trade wind; they, too, are grey. They stretch out gaunt arms and ragged branches from which wisps of old grey moss hang and wave in the wind. All down the sides of the enormous ravines which flank the plateau strips of lava and ashen-grey cinder-strat, wrinkled and furrowed by the rain of ages, stretch and wind like gigantic serpents crawling seawards. Beyond these gorges the line of the sea-cliff wall rises—all grey too—its skyline cut into huge teeth-like protuberances, or piled up in masses of rock from whose outlines it needs no imagination to shape distorted features and goblin figures along a visual horizon of some eighteen miles circumference. Everything within that dreary circle looks exactly what it is—the grey ruin of some extinct volcanic world. Of this gloomy circumference Longwood farmhouse is the centre.[3]

And yet St. Helena was perfect in its way—a unique memorial, lonely and defiant and enduring, to a giant among men:

Now, when all are gone—gaolers and guards, majesty and meanness, persecuted and persecutors—the lonely island takes its true place, a mightier monument of the strength of a single mortal than is to be found elsewhere in our world. Ocean-girt, vast, lonely—always seen above the centuries, this colossal death-bed, held high between heaven and earth, will remain ever visible to man[4]

In the days before the Suez Canal, St. Helena was a port of call for ships from many parts of the world. Among the ships in the roadstead when Butler visited the island were several American whalers from the Antarctic hiding from the *Alabama*, the Confederate raider which in the spring of 1864 was still at large and a terror to Federal merchant shipping. Always on the look-out for new experiences, Butler went on board one of the whalers and breakfasted with the captain on a plate of hardtack and a bottle of raw spirits. He declined the captain's invitation to stay to lunch.

The officers and doctor of the *Lord Warden* had foretold that a number of sick soldiers aboard would die as soon as the ship came in sight of the English coast. So it fell out. Perhaps the prophecy and its fulfilment reflected something more than superstition borne out by coincidence; within sight of journey's end there might indeed be a tendency on the part of the very ill to relax the tenuous hold on life. There were burials at sea almost within sight of the Lizard Head, and a day later the *Lord Warden* cast anchor in Portsmouth Harbour.

Lieutenant Butler rejoiced in the greenness of the English countryside and with high heart looked forward to the adventures brave and new which he was sure lay just ahead. Could he have foreseen what the next five years would bring, he would almost certainly have resigned his commission on the spot.

CHAPTER FOUR

Years of the Locust

ALDERSHOT, where the 69th went into camp early in 1865, following an eight months' stationing in Gosport, was little more than a dismal expanse of sand dotted with wretched huts in which men and officers were quartered. (The pleasantly landscaped Aldershot of a later time is the creation of Colonel Laffan, a green-thumbed officer of the Royal Engineers). 'Twenty years all round the worruld and a dommed cowshed at the end of it,' Butler heard one disillusioned veteran mutter as the weary men of the 69th marched into camp.

But in spite of the irritations, at both Gosport and Aldershot, of almost daily sandstorms, antiquated drill routines, bad food and lack of money, Butler found in the individuality of crusty old officers and tough veterans of the line who had soldiered over half the world and survived the hazards of warfare, typhus, cholera, syphillis, coconut toddy and methylated spirits enough of interest to make life tolerable. And there was by way of supplement the occasional unexpected and novel experience. Once when on leave from Gosport he saw, sitting in a Dover hotel lunch-room, four men in American Federal uniform—officers from the man-of-war *Kearsarge* then anchored in Dover harbour waiting for the Confederate raider *Alabama* to come out from Calais, where she was enjoying brief sanctuary under international law. As Butler studied the Americans with interest the door opened and several men dressed in oddly assorted civilian clothes came into the room. They stared hard at the Federal officers for a few seconds, then abruptly turned heel and went outside. They were Confederate officers from the *Alabama* who that morning had crossed over by mail-boat from Calais to have a close look at the *Kearsarge*.

A few days later the *Alabama* made a run for open sea and was quickly hunted to death by the bigger and faster Federal cruiser.

Besides the old soldiers not yet quite faded away, Aldershot held another attraction for Butler—an excellent library which was the gift of the late Prince Consort. As might be expected of a library donated by Albert, only books likely to improve the minds of serious young officers were admitted to its shelves. It was particularly rich in military history. Butler usually had the library to himself, and here he spent many agreeable hours gathering material for his two literary projects—a history of the 69th Foot (the work of most immediate concern) and the definitive account of Napoleon's last years.

But to read of manoeuvres and marches and countermarches and the clash of great armies was not enough. Butler scraped together £20, packed a few essentials in a knapsack and spent a glorious two weeks' holiday tramping alone over the battlefields of Belgium and northern France. The names he read on the signposts—Ligny, Quatre Bras, Namur, Waterloo—stirred his blood like a trumpet call and yet, because the places named had existed for so long in his imagination, he found it hard to accept their physical reality:

I had been reading of these places, great hinges of history, graveyards of human glory, for years in all sorts of places, trying so hard to transfer their printed names into brain pictures, that now when I came upon them, not in the flesh but in corn ridge and pasture slope and cottage plot, it seemed impossible they could be what the milestones and fingerposts said they were—themselves.[1]

For Butler the memory of his days among the battlefields was one of the most cherished of his later years, when he recalled even more vividly than the battlefields themselves the people with whom he talked and lived during his rambles; the charming peasant girls riding home from the cornfields in a wagon, 'laughing and talking under large lace or fringe-bordered caps', who invited him to share their ride; Monsieur and Madame Dubois who kept the inn in the little old Flemish town of Antoing and prepared for the famished young hiker a meal fit for the great Emperor himself—'a fillet, a partridge, a salad, an omelette, a bottle of Bordeaux, grapes, coffee, and a *petit verre*'; and the old Flemish peasant, head of the village commune, who dined with Butler in a cottage in Frasnes and charmed him with his dignity and spontaneous good manners.

There was a dessert of grapes and two or three peaches, one of the latter being redder and riper than the others. My companion had the plate of fruit in front of him; he turned it carefully around until the big peach was facing where I sat, and then courteously offered the plate to me. It was a simple thing, but I have never forgotten it. . . . Civility goes a long way. . . . In the case of my peasant friend at Frasnes it has gone more than forty years.[2]

In 1866 the 69th moved from Aldershot to the Channel Islands and the six months which followed were among the happiest of Butler's life, even though he knew that his negligible military duties were not of a kind likely to earn him promotion. He was stationed on the island of Guernsey, where he found the scenery a delight to the eye, the people hospitable, the social order Utopian: 'No very rich and no very poor in it; moderate comfort everywhere; fruits and flowers everywhere; the land and the sea giving a two-handed harvest to the inhabitants.' But even more attractive to Butler than scenery or native hospitality was the presence on the island of a great man. Here on Guernsey, Victor Hugo lived in self-imposed exile. Butler, who had recently read *Les Misérables* and considered Hugo's description of Waterloo the best account of the battle ever written, longed for a chance to talk with the old revolutionary. Partly with this end in view, he took lessons in French conversation from an odd and charming old Frenchman, M. Hannett de Kesler, who had edited a republican newspaper in Paris, fought at the barricades in the rising of 1851 and gone into exile with his idol Victor Hugo. Kesler was sadly broken by disease and semi-starvation, but he was still man—and Frenchman—enough to be enchanted by the coquetry of a flirtatious sixteen-year-old living across the street from him. He wrote verses to the girl—*Elle a le charme, elle a la grâce*—but had wit enough not to send them to her. He read them to Butler instead.

In due time Hugo invited Butler, whom he had heard of through Kesler, to his home. Victor Hugo enjoyed hero-worship, but he was quick to see in Butler not only a worshipper but a kindred spirit. 'Take care of him,' he roared to the assembled company one evening, pointing at Butler. 'He is an *enfant terrible.*' On another evening he announced in characteristically expansive mood that he, too, was an Irishman. 'I love Ireland,' he said, 'because she is to me a Poland and a Hungary, because she suffers.'

Although Hugo loved Ireland he had never seen her, and he invited Butler to be his guide on an Irish pilgrimage which he said he was planning for the following year.

Hugo wrote in a sleeping-room which he had built on the roof of his Guernsey house between two blocks of chimneys. In design he seems to have anticipated the modern picture window, for Butler tells us that half the room was walled with glass and the view it commanded magnificent. Hugo slept on a simple camp cot with writing materials within easy reach. Every morning he made *café-au-lait* for himself on a small wood-burning stove, then set to work at a desk enclosed in a glass alcove. (He wrote *Les Misérables* and *Toilers of the Sea* while living on Guernsey.) As he wrote he numbered the sheets of paper and dropped them to the floor together with discarded odds and ends of verse and prose, the numbered sheets to be gathered later and arranged in proper order. He called the desk his carpenter's bench, the papers littering the floor shavings. Butler held his head high among his peers, but humbled himself before those whom he regarded as truly great; and among his few surviving private papers are some scraps of 'shavings', including a line or two from *Toilers of the Sea*, which he saved from Hugo's workshop floor and cherished to the end of his life.

Butler passed the winter of 1866-7 in this idyllic spot. He bathed in the sea every day, listened nearly every evening to Victor Hugo's compulsive talk and after a few months was able to follow with fair comprehension what the great man said. But Guernsey was a dead end; and though Butler left the island in the spring of 1867 with many regrets he looked forward eagerly to finding a more active service elsewhere.

The 69th spent the early summer in Ireland at the Curragh. In August the regiment was ordered to Canada; and for the first time in his nine years' service Butler had reason to hope that he might see military action. The Fenians, a nuisance for nearly two years now, had assembled in alarming numbers along the Canada-U.S. border and were threatening yet another invasion of the newly created dominion.

The Fenian Brotherhood, organized in New York City in 1859, was the American branch of the Irish Revolutionary Brotherhood founded in Dublin a year earlier. The Fenian brotherhood was largely made up of Irishmen who had immigrated to the United States during or shortly after the great famine in 1845-8. To the natural antagonism of Irishman towards Englishman was added a sense of bitter injustice stemming from the sufferings of the people during the famine. Many Irishmen honestly believed that England had deliberately allowed a fearful catastrophe to run its full course in the hope of achieving by 'natural' means that extermination of a whole people which more than one politician considered the only permanent solution to the Irish problem.

The Fenians elected a government-in-exile to govern a non-existent Irish republic, created a militia of sorts and talked grandly of driving the English out of Ireland and from Ireland striking directly at the heart of the Empire and burning London to the ground. At first no one except the Fenians themselves took the movement seriously; but after the Civil War the ranks of the Brotherhood were swelled by thousands of discharged soldiers—tough fighting men who liked war better than peace, many of them more interested in winning plunder for themselves than freedom for Ireland.

When an uprising of the Revolutionary Brotherhood in Ireland proved abortive the Fenians settled for the conquest of Canada as a first step towards the overthrow of the British Empire. The Canadian Government awoke suddenly to the fact that several thousand maniacal Irishmen armed with Civil War rifles and hundreds of gallons of whisky were swarming towards Canada's straggling and all but undefended frontier eager to kill. The Government appealed to England for immediate military aid and called for local volunteers to assist the militia in policing the border. Fourteen thousand men, not all of whom could shoot, answered the call to arms, and Colonel Garnet Wolseley, a rising young officer destined to become the most successful British general of the Victorian age, came out from England to direct cadet training and organize the local militia and volunteer units against the threat of invasion.

Had the Fenians been able to achieve any sort of discipline in their ranks, they might have caused a good deal of trouble along the border. They were well armed, many were trained fighters and the Government of the United States at first did little to check their activities, perhaps on the grounds that no government could be expected to recognize the army of a non-existent republic. But the leaders squabbled incessantly among themselves, and most martial exercises carried out by the Brotherhood ended in drunken brawls. True, a two-pronged attack in the early summer of 1866 achieved some slight success. Eight hundred Fenians under the command of 'general' John O'Neill crossed into Canada near Fort Erie, wrecked a few farm homes and inflicted some casualties on the Canadian volunteers who hurried out to oppose them; and farther east 1,800 Fenians crossed from Vermont into the Eastern Townships below Montreal and plundered two small towns before withdrawing back over the border. A state of alarm was maintained along the border until well into the following year; but by the time the 69th Foot reached Canada the Fenian hosts had been dissolved in their own alcohol, Colonel Wolseley was on his way back to England and Canada was lapped in profoundest peace.

The posting to Canada contributed nothing to Butler's advancement in his profession, but it gave him a chance to satisfy the most fondly cherished ambition of his childhood and youth—an ambition born of the books he had read in the long winter nights at Ballyslateen.

Nineteenth-century writers of juvenile fiction and travel books exercised an incomparably greater influence over the minds and lives of their youthful readers than do their present-day counterparts. Contemporary writers of juveniles speak with less authority than the Victorians because their audience is more difficult to reach. Today's youth are less circumscribed and more sophisticated than the young Victorians; less innocent and more easily bored. The immensely wide range of entertainment media at their disposal diffuses their interest; and a single writer rarely captures their attention long enough or strongly enough to affect in any way the pattern of their lives. By contrast the average Victorian youngster grew up with his favourite authors—writers who could be counted on to produce year after year solidly constructed juveniles of adult length combining instruction, adventure and high moral tone in proportions which made them welcome reading to all members of the Victorian household. Of the Victorian writers of juveniles George Alfred Henty was the most prolific and popular (his bibliography lists nearly two hundred titles) with Rider Haggard and R. M. Ballantyne not far behind. Henty wrote from two to six juveniles a year for more than a quarter of a century; and if one accepts the premise on which most of his stories are founded, that England can do no wrong, what follows is a most entertaining mixture of exciting adventure and surprisingly accurate history. Writers like Henty and Ballantyne occupied the role usurped in our own time by the guidance counsellor and aptitude test—they frequently determined a youngster's choice of career for him. Many an English boy was drawn into the Army in the hope of sharing there the adventure and high romance and rapid promotion which the heroes of the Henty books never failed to find; and R. M. Ballantyne's admirable semi-autobiographical stories of life in the Canadian far north probably made it easier for the Hudson's Bay Company to recruit young men for its lonely trading-posts.

James Fenimore Cooper had been young William Butler's favourite author. 'In boyhood,' he tells us,

> I read the novels of Fenimore Cooper with an intensity of interest never to be known again in reading. Leatherstocking, Lucas, Chingaghook, the Mohicans, the Hurons, the scenery of the Thousand Islands—all these had been things quite as real to me in imagination as the actual scenes through which we were now passing. Only the Indians and the wild animals were wanting. Where were they? Gone from the west of Canada, but still to be found west of the Mississippi and Missouri.[3]

West of the Mississippi and Missouri therefore he would go. He obtained three months' leave of absence, bought a railway ticket to Omaha, Nebraska, and accompanied by his good friend Lieutenant Mansfield set out to realize a childhood dream.

It is pleasant to know that he realized it. In the course of an adventurous life Butler was to see much of the world, but no other part of it, not even his native Tipperary, was ever as close to his heart as the vast prairie and parklands region of the North American west—the great lone land of his most popular book. To that region he returned time and time again, in body and in spirit, drawn by an extraordinary sense of comradeship with the native red man whom he idealized, by the glorious freedom of a life lived far from the vexations and restraints of what the world was pleased to call civilization, and by the melancholy grandeur of those vast lonely places where more than anywhere else on earth Butler felt at peace with himself and in harmony with the universe.

Everything about the journey west delighted him, and especially the friendliness of the Americans whom he and Mansfield met *en route*:

> We knew nobody, nobody knew us, and yet it was simple truth to say that everybody befriended us. You met a man on board the train going to Chicago; he couldn't do enough for you; he passed you on to some other good fellow who knew somebody else five hundred or a thousand miles nearer the setting sun; and when you alighted at the longitude of that particular location you found that man as friendly as though he had been expecting you for years.

In Omaha, where the two Britishers made a short stop-over, Butler saw for the first time a typical western frontier town with the usual quota of gambling saloons, honky-tonks and brothels, where every man carried a gun and, in Butler's inspired phrase, 'policed himself with a kind of murderous solemnity'. From Omaha, Butler and Mansfield took a train to Kearney Station in western Nebraska and from the station rode in an army mule-wagon across six miles of billiard-table prairie to Fort Kearney. An American Army Officer whom they had met in Chicago had recommended them to the Fort commandant, whose hospitality they were now to enjoy.

At Fort Kearney, an army outpost in Indian territory, Butler spent two weeks living in the flesh the life he had lived vicariously in boyhood through the novels of Fenimore Cooper. He saw his first buffalo herd—'A rifle bullet might have reached the nearest of the herd; two hours' hard riding would not have carried you to the farthest'—shot his first buffalo in true plainsman fashion, from horseback after a long and hazardous pursuit across the plain, ate buffalo steaks with insatiable appetite and drank whisky in bed before breakfast. (This last at the insistence of the Fort doctor, a genial old sot who visited Butler and Mansfield every morning at six, a demijohn over his shoulder from which he poured liberal shots of bourbon for the Commandant's guests. 'Whisky's as good outside as in,' he would say when he slopped some of the liquor over the bedclothes.)

Butler's appraisal of the American frontiersman reflects the enthusiasm he felt for a way of life in many respects at opposite poles from the one he had so far known in the Army. Here on the prairies every day was the first day, all men started from scratch and the strongest and wisest rose to the top by the use of their strength and their wits. Family connections carried no weight, money could not buy rank, for there was no rank to buy. The west which Butler found was a young man's country where the race was to the swift and the battle to the strong; where the spirit of enterprise was not broken by mindless routine and where each man was an individual and not a unit of the mass.

Nobody dreamt, except when he slept, everybody acted when he was awake. They drank a good deal, but you seldom saw a man drunk, and never dead drunk. They sometimes shot each other, they never abused each other; they were generous, open-hearted, full of a dry humour, as manly as men could be; rough but not rude; civil, but never servile; proud of their country and boastful of it and themselves.[4]

With his love of fine phrases and vivid imagery Butler found the language of the American frontiersman a source of endless fascination and delight:

One day, in company with an American officer, we were following, as usual, a herd of buffalo, when we came upon a town standing silent and deserted in the middle of the prairie. 'That,' said the American, 'is Kearney City; it did a good trade in the old wagon times, but it busted up when the railroad went on farther west; the people moved on to North Platte and Julesburg—guess there's only one man left in it now, and he's got snakes in his boots. . . .' Marvelling what manner of man this might be who dwelt alone in the silent city, we rode on. One house showed some traces of occupation, and in this house dwelt the man. We had passed through the deserted grass-grown street, and were again on the prairie, when a shot rang out behind us, the bullet cutting up the dust away to the left. 'By G— he's on the shoot,' cried our friend; 'ride, boys!' and so we rode. Much has been written and said of cities old and new, of Aztec and Peruvian monuments, but I venture to offer to the attention of the future historian of America this sample of the busted-up city of Kearney and its solitary indweller, who had snakes in his boots and was on the shoot.[5]

To add to his pleasure in America Butler for the first time since joining the Army enjoyed the prestige of senior rank. Throughout the American west he was at no time addressed as less than colonel, and most frequently as general.

Back once more with his regiment, now stationed at Brantford, Ontario, Butler was again a humble lieutenant committed to the carrying out of mechanical routine duties. But the tedium of the daily round was relieved when he discovered close at hand an immensely valuable source of first-hand information for his history of the 69th Foot. An aged army officer, Colonel Cotter, then living out his last years on the shores of Lake Erie some forty miles from Brantford, had joined the 69th in 1804, sixty-five years earlier, and fought with the regiment at Waterloo.

Butler found the old man living a lonely and unhappy life in a world that had proved too much for him. He was one of the many British Army half-pay officers who following the Napoleonic wars had taken up large grants of land in the Ontario bush in the expectation of creating substantial country estates, and had found themselves physically and temperamentally unsuited to the rigours of pioneer life. Part of their story is told in Mrs. Susannah Moodie's *Roughing It in the Bush*, a classic of nineteenth-century life in the backwoods of Ontario.

Colonel Cotter had some good stories to tell of early days in the regiment, and particularly of Waterloo, where the 69th had borne the heat and labour of the day with the best of them. Six months later the old man paid a last visit to the regiment, then stationed at London, Ontario. When the regiment was paraded he took his place, at Butler's suggestion, 'between the colours in the front rank, exactly fifty-three years after he had stood in square with them at Waterloo'.

Early in 1868 Butler succeeded Lieutenant Redvers Buller of the 60th Rifles—a promising young soldier with whom he later saw much action and shared many dangers—as patrol officer charged with the monthly inspection of a series of army look-out posts centring on London. Butler found the work, which involved up to 1,500 miles of riding every month, immensely congenial. Most of the time he was on his own; the southern Ontario landscape was beautiful in summer; and the men he talked with at the outposts were the old soldiers whose stories, no matter how outrageous or oft-repeated he never tired of.

It was at this time that Butler was invited by a Yankee bearing the unlikely name of Horatio Nelson Case to invest money in an oil-well.

Oil had been found in Ontario as early as 1862 near the village of Enniskillen, a few miles from the present refinery city of Sarnia. The name of the village was changed to Petrolia in honour of the strike, more wells were drilled and production boomed. (In 1895 it reached a peak of 800,000 barrels per annum.) In 1869 prospecting techniques were relatively primitive and although several oil-wells in the immediate vicinity of Petrolia were in profitable production the extent of the field was as yet undetermined. Horatio Nelson Case, a shrewd Yankee horsetrader 'of restless eye, straight upper lip and firm-set lower jaw', whom Butler met at a village inn while on patrol, had selected a 200-acre plot of heavy forestland as being in the line of a subterranean oil-stream already profitably tapped closer to the town. He would, he said, supply the brains and the know-how if Butler, either by himself or in partnership with a fellow officer, would supply the £800 needed to buy the land.

Horatio Nelson Case caught his man at the right time. A few weeks after the meeting between the two men Butler was removed from his congenial patrol duties and sent with his regiment to Montreal. He went with such reluctance that he knew he had reached a cross-roads in his life. He had served the Army faithfully and well for more than ten years and was still a lieutenant. Worse still, there seemed no chance of promotion in the foreseeable future, for he had saved little money from his meagre pay; and it infuriated him to find vacancies in his own regiment being filled over his head by men younger than he whose only claim to promotion was the money to pay for it. No wars were threatening anywhere in the British Empire and Butler's future in the Army looked bleak. All that he could see ahead were a succession of routine postings, a life lived not for the profession of arms but the leaves it permitted, and at the end an inadequate pension, humble lodgings and swift oblivion.

There was an additional cause of dissatisfaction. America had been an unsettling experience. It stirred dormant ambitions, promised rewards commensurate with the merit of the man, not the length of his purse, welcomed that individuality which the Army so rigidly circumscribed:

This America was a great mind-stretcher. All these lakes, these immense prairies, these deep forests, these rivers of which the single lengths are greater than the width of ocean between Canada and Europe; all the throbbing of life that one saw everywhere, on road and river, in the cities, on the plains; this great march that was going on—all seemed to call with irresistible voice to throw one's little lot with the movement. It all seemed the exact opposite of the profession to which at this time I had given ten years of my life. There one seemed to be going around in a circle; here the line of march was straight to the west. I had seen a sunset over the prairies of Nebraska, and the dream of it was ever in my mind—a great golden mist, a big river flowing from it, a dark herd of buffaloes slowly moving across the prairie distance to drink at the river. And the sun itself seemed to linger above the horizon as though he wanted to have a longer look at the glory he had made below.[5]

But few men, no matter what their disappointments, give up easily a career begun with fair hope and followed conscientiously for ten years or more. In the end Butler temporized. Before making an irrevocable commitment he would return to Ireland and try to raise £400 to invest in Horatio Nelson Case's oil scheme. If oil was found he would be able to buy the captaincy long since morally due him; if not, he would resign his commission and go west.

Butler returned to Ireland on leave, and for the first time in several years visited the family home at Ballyslateen. The visit was tinged with sadness, for Richard Butler, an old man now, was failing sadly. He died in the spring of 1870 and was buried in Killardrigh churchyard at the foot of the Galtee Mountains, where William Butler himself was some day to lie.

Butler inherited nothing from his father, who died almost penniless, but through the full exercise of his very considerable powers of persuasion he was able to borrow from various relatives the £400 he needed for his oil investment. The relatives were understandably reluctant to part with money sure to be lost on a madcap gamble, and it was then, perhaps, that they first raised a cry to be many times repeated, not only by relatives, but—in forms more vehement and often blasphemous—by agitated statesmen and confused generals—'What is William up to now?'

Before rejoining his regiment in Canada, Butler paid a hurried visit to London, where his last tenuous hope of promotion by seniority was blasted by a military secretary at the Horse Guards who told him that all existing vacancies in the 69th were to be filled, as before, by purchase. It was at this point, when his fortunes seemed to have touched rock bottom, that he learned through a newspaper item of the proposed dispatch of a military force from Canada to the North-West Territories to restore order in the newly created crown colony of Assiniboia where a malcontent half-breed named Louis Riel had seized the civil power. The expedition was to be led by Colonel Garnet Wolseley, whom Butler had met briefly in Montreal. The newspaper report added that arrangements for the dispatch of the force were nearly complete.

Butler did not hesitate. He went at once to the nearest telegraph office and in complete violation of military etiquette sent to Colonel Wolseley the telegram which was to prove the most momentous communication of his life:

'Please remember me. Butler, 69th Foot.'

Then he hurried to the office of the Cunard Steamship Company and booked passage in the next ship to Canada.

CHAPTER FIVE

A Roving Commission

UNTIL WELL PAST the middle of the nineteenth century the only area of concentrated settlement in Canada west of Ontario was the Red River Valley, where the descendants of the white settlers brought out by the Earl of Selkirk in 1812, and the Métis, a people of mixed French and Indian blood, constituted the largest ethnic groups. The Métis lived along the Red and Assiniboine Rivers on farms laid out in the old seigniorial fashion, each farm a long narrow strip of land fronting on water. They grew some cereals and vegetables and raised livestock, but they were not by nature farmers; their true home was the great western plains country where all summer long they led a nomadic life. The buffalo rather than the land supplied their needs. It gave them food, clothing, and surplus hides to trade at the Hudson's Bay Company posts for blue capotes with brass buttons, tasselled caps, guns, blankets, and such luxuries as tea and tobacco. Their way of life had its inevitable hardships, but the Métis appear through the haze of time and distance as an Arcadian folk living in a kind of golden age, for a fleeting moment enjoying the best of two worlds—that of the Indian and that of the white man. The civil authority over the huge area of Canada lying west of Ontario was the Hudson's Bay Company, which ruled its subjects with paternal authority and benevolence and protected them against the free trader's whisky. And since it was in the Company's interest to keep the west a wilderness it offered no encouragement to future settlement.

But Arcadias, like Edens, do not last. In 1868 the Dominion and British Governments entered into negotiations with the Hudson's Bay Company for the purchase of the Company's territorial rights to the huge area of land reaching west and north from the border of Ontario to the Pacific and Arctic oceans. The opening of new areas to settlement could no longer be delayed. The American mid-west was being settled with astonishing rapidity and there was a real danger that the westward-moving tide of immigration might lap over the border into Canada. Sir John A. Macdonald, the Canadian Prime Minister, reported to the Imperial Government that 'the United States Government are resolved to do all they can, short of war, to get possession of the western territory and we must take immediate and vigorous steps to counteract them'. So long as the north-west was the preserve of the Hudson's Bay Company it was vulnerable.

Unfortunately the fifteen thousand inhabitants of Assiniboia, as the well-settled Red River Valley country was called, were not consulted about the transfer. Long before negotiations were complete surveyors sent by the Dominion Government moved into the Valley and began dividing the land into square section-blocks without regard for the seigniorial pattern of the Métis holdings. The Métis chased the surveyors out of the Valley, but by this time profound disquiet had spread throughout the territory of Assiniboia. The Métis in particular were seriously disturbed. They knew that once Company rule ended settlers from the east would pour into the Valley and overflow far out on the plains. Settlement meant the destruction of their traditional system of landholding and the annihilation of the buffalo; it meant the end of a way of life the Métis loved.

It was at this point, when negotiations for the transfer were proceeding amicably between the two governments and the great Company, that the most controversial figure in Canadian history makes his appearance.

Louis Riel, a Métis born in the Red River Valley and educated in Montreal, was an ideal leader of revolt; for he added to the natural eloquence which was perhaps a part of his Indian heritage a passionate belief in the nationhood of the Métis and in himself as his people's Messiah. He was shrewd enough to recognize the inevitability of Dominion expansion westward, but he was determined to force the Canadian Government to negotiate with the inhabitants of Assiniboia as well as with the Company and to guarantee them clear titles to the land they lived on. Taking advantage of an interim period when no civil authority was functioning in the Valley—the Company having already surrendered its rights, the Dominion Government not yet having assumed its responsibilities—he created a provisional government with himself at its head, seized Fort Garry (a Hudson's Bay Company post and the administrative centre of Assiniboia), and imprisoned within the Fort a few citizens who refused to acknowledge his authority.

Many of the white settlers of Assiniboia were at first sympathetic to the provisional government, for their interests were in most respects identical with those of the Métis; but they were soon alienated by Riel's dictatorial behaviour—which they might have tolerated in a fellow white man but never in a half-breed. Things came to a head when the more aggressive among the white settlers made a raid on Fort Garry to release Riel's prisoners. The raid proved a fiasco; the raiders were quickly surrounded and captured, and themselves locked up inside the Fort with those whom they had come to rescue.

So far Riel had acted with at least a show of discretion. He was convinced that the creation of a provisional government was legally justifiable, and therefore so was the maintenance of its authority against armed aggression. But now, prompted by motives which are still obscure, for he was never a bloodthirsty man, Riel was guilty of a crime which made the destruction of the Métis cause inevitable. He ordered the execution of one of the raiders, Thomas Scott, whose only offence seems to have been insolence to his captors. The sentence was carried out at midnight on March 4, 1870, by a Métis firing-squad, and Scott's body hastily interred in the stone wall of Fort Garry. Scott was an Orangeman from Ontario, and on word of his death every Protestant in the land howled for Riel's blood. The Government was naturally sensitive to the demands of the voting majority, and since it was not feasible to send a gunboat up the Red River to shell the natives in approved Empire fashion it was agreed in Ottawa and Westminster to send a military expedition overland to bring the rebellious Métis to heel.

Lieutenant Butler had no doubt at all about the cause of hostilities in Assiniboia:

> Any ordinary, matter-of-fact sensible man would have managed the whole affair in a few hours; but so many high and potent powers had to consult together, to pen despatches, to speechify, and to lay down the law about it, that the whole affair became hopelessly muddled. Of course ignorance and carelessness were, as they always are, at the bottom of it all. Nothing could have been easier than to have sent a commissioner from England to Red River, while the negotiations for the transfer were pending, who would have ascertained the feelings and wishes of the

people of the country relative to the transfer, and would have guaranteed them the exercise of their rights and liberties under any and every new arrangement that might be entered into.[1]

But the politicians hadn't sent a commissioner, they were sending a military expedition instead, at a cost of hundreds of thousands of pounds, to subdue the people whom Sir John A. Macdonald had contemptuously dismissed from consideration as mere 'eaters of pemmican'. And whatever the rights and wrongs of the issue Butler was determined to be in at the death. He caught up with the Red River Expedition at Toronto and hurried to see the commander, Colonel Garnet Wolseley.

Yes, Colonel Wolseley remembered Butler of the 69th. No, he could do nothing for him. Nothing at all. Every berth on the Expedition was already filled.

'I think, sir,' Butler said, 'there is one berth still vacant.'

'What is it?'

'You will want to know what they are doing in Minnesota and along the flank of your march and you have no one to tell you.'

Wolseley agreed that he needed an intelligence officer to keep an eye on the Americans, and more particularly the Fenians, on the southern flank of the Expedition. Indeed, according to Wolseley's version of the meeting between the two men he himself had earlier recognized the importance of nominating a highly intelligent and resourceful officer to a roving commission and had already marked Butler as the man for the job:

Before leaving Montreal for Lake Superior I received this telegram from home, 'Remember Butler, 69th Regiment.' I had made that officer's acquaintance when his battalion was quartered at Montreal in the following way. Every summer some half-dozen regimental officers were employed on a military survey of the frontier between Canada and the United States. Among the applicants in 1868 was Lieutenant Butler. When he came to see me on this business I was much struck by the bright clearness of his intelligence and with his all round intellectual superiority to the general run of our officers. I inquired about him from those who knew him well, and ascertained that he was not only by far the cleverest man in his battalion, but was well known generally for his energy and varied talents. Unable to employ him on this survey, I made a note of his name in case I should ever require the services of an officer who was evidently a good, active, talented and trustworthy man. . . . Lieutenant Butler was just the man that I wanted to go round through the United

States to the Red River for the purpose of finding out how matters really stood there, and then to come and meet me when I had made about half the distance to Fort Garry. . . . I explained that I wanted an able soldier, whom I could trust implicitly, to go via the United States to the Red River Settlement, to judge for himself as to the conditions of affairs there. . . . This roving commission that required so many rare qualities was one after his own heart, and he was just the man to carry it out admirably.[2]

Who suggested the commission does not matter. What matters is that Butler was at last given an opportunity, by the man who in 1870 was the rising star of the British Army, to exercise his initiative and imagination.

Colonel Garnet Wolseley, later Field-Marshal Lord Wolseley, is a hard man to come to grips with. He was brave to the point of being suicidal; he planned his campaigns with the precision of a scientist; he was passionately dedicated to army reform; he was well read, and a score of associates including Edmund Gosse—it is true to say he had no friends—have testified to his sense of fun and the charm of his talk. Unfortunately there was no Boswell in any group around him and his social and conversational gifts must be taken on faith. He was an immensely prolific letter-writer even in a letter-writing age, but what he wrote is oddly trivial. The more than two thousand letters to his wife Louisa harp constantly on two related themes—the extent to which the worth of his achievements exceeds their rewards, and the need for his dear little Snipe (Periwinkle, Runtyfoozle, etc.) to cultivate the right people—those who might materially assist his career. (Louisa, who dearly loved the right people, was delighted to oblige.)

But Wolseley himself was not trivial. Far from it. He was the most successful and efficient British soldier of the Victorian Age. But efficiency is a chilly virtue, and though Wolseley was admired by the public and respected by his soldiers he was never loved. Even the Commander-in-chief, the Duke of Cambridge, a bumbling anachronism born half a century after his time who fought tooth and nail to block Wolseley's proposed army reforms—all of them admirably designed to improve the soldier's lot—commanded the affection of the rank and file as Wolseley himself was never able to do.

In 1870 Wolseley still had his way to make. Burma, the Crimea and the Indian Mutiny had given him a flying start. Now he held his first independent command, the Red River Expedition of twelve hundred regulars and militia; and he at once took steps to gather round him that brilliant group of staff officers which was later known as the Wolseley Ring, a group into which nothing but ability—preferably supported by influential family connections—could gain a man admission. A large measure of Wolseley's success—indeed his genius for command—lay in his ability to choose able subordinates. His immediate recognition of remarkable qualities in Butler is evidence of that ability.

While waiting for confirmation of his appointment as special intelligence officer to the Red River Expedition, Butler, for the first time in his twelve years of active service in the Army, came under enemy fire. Reports of renewed Fenian concentrations along the border of the Eastern Townships led to the dispatch of the 69th Foot to the trouble spot, and Butler accompanied his regiment. While on patrol near the village of Hinchinbrook he nearly rode head on into a force of three hundred Fenians. He escaped with bullets rattling the bushes on either side of the trail along which he galloped. Later he took part in the charge of the 69th on a hop field bordering the Trout River where the Fenians were said to have gone to ground. Butler's old company, now under the command of his friend Mansfield, who had purchased the captaincy over Butler's head, led the way. The troops fired volley after volley into the hop field, then charged with fixed bayonets, but were unable to find any Fenians. Contemporary local accounts of the engagement speak of severe casualties being inflicted on the invaders; according to Butler the 69th could legitimately claim only a single 'possible'. But the troops made enough noise and fired off enough ammunition to convince the enemy that if they stayed in the vicinity any longer someone might get hurt. After the Battle of Trout River the Fenians disbanded and went home.

It is easy to understand and share Butler's emotions when his appointment as Wolseley's intelligence officer was confirmed. He was once more going west to the great plains that drew him more strongly than any other part of the earth he had so far known; and for the first time since joining the Army he was being given a chance to exercise independent judgement and initiative. The instructions given him were vague, but he knew that Wolseley was anxious to learn by first-hand report something of the real state of mind of the people of Assiniboia, both whites and Métis, and of the likelihood of raids into Assiniboia from Dakota and Minnesota, where the Fenians were said to be assembling large quantities of firearms and whisky. It was typical of Wolseley that he should make every effort to find out what kind of campaign he might have to wage under any one of a dozen possible sets of conditions. From a distance the 'revolt' in Assiniboia seemed little more than a childish gesture of defiance, but if a united Métis people supported by a strong force of rabid Fenians chose to fight, Wolseley, with only five hundred regulars and seven hundred militia-men under his command, might be in for real trouble.

Butler crossed the border into the United States from Toronto and rode a train west as far as St. Cloud, Minnesota. From St. Cloud he travelled north-west by stage-coach to Fort Abercrombie and there, on July 15, 1870, saw for the first time the muddy rolling waters of the Red River flowing north towards Fort Garry and Lake Winnipeg. In the frontier hotel at the Fort he heard news of the Expedition which was then fighting its way through dense forest and swamp towards Fort Frances and the Lake of the Woods, roughly along the route taken by the fur-traders of the North-West Company nearly a century earlier. Forty soldiers were said to have drowned shooting a single rapids (in actual fact not one man was lost during the entire campaign), and American frontier opinion held that the Expedition would never get out of the bush. Butler, having learned that the troops were actually on their way from Fort William to Fort Frances, at once laid plans for crossing into Canada by Red River steamboat. He was determined to visit Fort Garry and if possible talk with Riel himself. Wolseley had not suggested that Butler go to Fort Garry, but he probably suspected that his impetuous and enthusiastic subordinate would do so on his own initiative unless expressly forbidden.

Butler caught the Red River steamer *International* at a place called Frog Point a short distance below the border. He had ridden the last forty miles to Frog Point on horseback and on the way met the full fury of that one-time scourge of the plains—the mosquito:

There rose around us vast numbers of mosquitos—choking masses of biting insects, no mere cloud thicker and denser in one place than another, but one huge wall of never-ending insects filling nostrils, ears and eyes. . . . I had seen many vast accumulations of insect life in lands old and new, but never anything that approached to this mountain of mosquitoes on the prairies of Dakota. To say that they covered the coat of the horse

I rode would be to give but a faint idea of their numbers; they were literally six or eight deep upon his skin, and with a single sweep of the hand one could crush myriads from his neck. Their hum seemed to be in all things round. To ride for it was the sole resource. Darkness came quickly down, but the track knew no turn, and for seven miles I kept the pony at a gallop, my face, neck and hands cut and bleeding.

Even the *International* offered no sanctuary from the pests:

They came after us in millions . . . until in a very short space of time the interior of the boat became perfectly black with insects. Attracted by the light they flooded into the saloon, covering walls and ceilings in one dark mass. We attempted supper but had to give it up. They got into the coffee, they stuck fast in the soft, melting butter until at length—feverish, bitten, bleeding and hungry—I sought refuge beneath the gauze curtains in my cabin and fell asleep from sheer exhaustion.[3]

Once the *International* got under way downriver the mosquitoes were less troublesome and Butler was able to enjoy the novelty of steamboating through a prairie landscape, even though he felt some doubts about the capacity of the battered old craft to reach her destination. By 1870 the handwriting was on the wall for the steamboats of the Red River, and their owners were making little effort to keep them in repair. The *International*'s paint was peeling, her boards warped, her engines held together by rope and wire, her decks constantly catching fire from sparks that showered from her rust-pocked smoke-stack. Butler was the only man aboard who showed concern at the sight of a flame-burst rising from the deck: 'I shouted vigorously for assistance, and will long remember the look of surprise and pity with which the native regarded me as he leisurely approached with the water-bucket and cast its contents along the smoking deck.'

Butler passed the border post of Pembina into Assiniboia without incident, but shortly after the *International* started downriver on the last lap of the journey to Fort Garry he saw two horsemen riding hard across the plain towards the Fort and knew that his coming would be provided for. Sight of the horsemen, who had obviously been posted along the river to spy on his movements, impressed on Butler the dangers of his undertaking. It was possible that Riel might treat a British officer in civilian clothes as a spy, or at least detain him long enough to defeat the object of his mission. Butler therefore decided to bypass the Fort and the adjoining village of Winnipeg and make his way downriver another twenty miles to Lower Fort Garry, the centre of a predominantly loyal Anglo-Saxon community, and from there assess the situation and make up his mind whether or not to communicate with the Métis leader.

The plan was easy to evolve, difficult to execute. The land on either side of the river was flat and open, and it seemed unlikely that a man could go far without being seen. In the end Butler accepted an offer of assistance from a fellow passenger named William Dreever, a resident of Winnipeg hostile to Riel. Dreever explained that when the steamer reached the junction of the Red and Assiniboine Rivers and turned into the Assiniboine to draw alongside the Fort Garry landing-stage her bow grazed the north bank of the river. At the moment of contact he and Butler would leap ashore under cover of darkness, slip past Fort Garry and be in Winnipeg almost as soon as the boat reached the landing. Dreever would then set Butler on the road to the Lower Fort, and if possible provide him with a horse.

Toward midnight Butler and Dreever took their places in the bow of the steamer. Butler was encumbered with a six-shooter, a rifle, and a large dog on a lead. Where he picked up the dog he never explains. Or why. He liked dogs—perhaps that was reason enough. (Three years later a dog was to be his constant companion on a 6,000-mile journey from Fort Garry to Boston via northern British Columbia and San Francisco.) The *International* shut off steam and began to swing its cumbersome length from the Red River into the Assiniboine. Ahead, the light of flickering lanterns cast into clear relief the dozen or more figures congregated on the landing-stage. The bow of the *International* touched the north bank of the Assiniboine and Butler, Dreever and the dog leapt ashore. They scrambled up the steep bank to the level plain less than 200 yards from Fort Garry and with Dreever showing the way slipped past the Fort to the huddle of shacks which in 1870 formed the village of Winnipeg. Here Dreever left Butler at a bridge on the road to the Lower Fort and went off for the horse he had promised him. When Dreever failed to return Butler turned loose his dog and struck out on foot for Lower Fort Garry.

At daybreak he found food and shelter in the rectory of St. Andrew's Church about four miles above the Fort. Dreever's sister Mary was a visitor at the Rectory. Fascinated by the appearance and talk of the handsome officer who had appeared mysteriously out of the night, she at once offered to carry a letter for him to Fort Garry and deliver it to the *International*. She tucked the letter (a report to Ottawa that Butler considered urgent) into her blouse and set off by buckboard for Fort Garry. She was intercepted by Métis scouts, who questioned her closely and searched the buckboard. They were, however, too modest and gentlemanly to find the letter.

Six years later Mary Dreever married Colonel James Macleod, a distinguished commissioner of the North-West Mounted Police.

Information which Mary Dreever and others brought back from Fort Garry made it clear that Butler had indeed been in danger of arrest. The reception party waiting for him on the landing-stage had included Riel himself, Adjutant-General Lepine, and Riel's Fenian secretary, a man named O'Donoghue. Furious because their quarry had escaped them, the Métis leaders confiscated Butler's luggage, then arrested the captain of the *International* and William Dreever and threw both into gaol. When he learned what had happened Butler at once abandoned all hope of meeting Riel and moved from the Lower Fort to St. Peter's Indian Settlement near the mouth of the Red River. Here through an interpreter he harangued the Indians with an eloquence worthy of one of their own chiefs, assured them—unfortunately without warrant—that when the redcoats came they would be rewarded for their loyalty to the great white queen over the water, and made preparation for a long journey by canoe and on foot up the Winnipeg River to the Lake of the Woods, where he hoped to meet the Red River Expedition.

Shortly before the time he had set for departure Butler received a conciliatory message from Fort Garry assuring him of the loyalty of the Métis to the Crown and inviting him to visit the Fort. He accepted the invitation on condition that his baggage be returned to him, that William Dreever be at once released from prison (the captain of the *International* had been freed several days earlier), and that the Métis flag—a fleur-de-lis and a shamrock on a white background symbolizing Métis and Fenian unity against a common foe—be lowered from the Fort flagstaff. By thus casting himself in the role of representative of Dominion and Empire condescending to meet with petty violators of the law, but only after they had acknowledged the error of their ways, Butler won a significant psychological advantage over the Métis leaders.

He carried off his meeting with Riel with equally high hand. As soon as his baggage was restored to him and Dreever released he drove at once to Fort Garry, accompanied by the messenger Riel had sent to act as escort. The Métis flag still flew over the Fort, but side by side with the Union Jack, and Butler accepted the compromise. The messenger led Butler to a substantial private house inside the Fort. In the living-room a young Métis was practising billiard-shots. Would Lieutenant Butler call on M. Riel? the messenger asked. 'Call on him? Certainly not,' Butler said with a fine assumption of outraged dignity, and picking up a cue he invited the billiards-player to a game. 'But if he calls on you?' That was different. 'Then I'll see him,' Butler said.

The messenger disappeared. Presently the door opened and into the room came 'a short stout man with a large head, a sallow puffy face, a sharp, restless, intelligent eye, a square-cut massive forehead overhung by a mass of long and thickly clustering hair and marked with well-cut eyebrows—altogether a remarkable-looking face'.[4]

The moment was an awkward one. Butler, very much the representative of Empire, inquired if M. Riel played billiards. M. Riel didn't. 'Capital game', Butler said, and made what he admitted was an absurd stroke. With a muttered, 'I see I am intruding here', Riel left the room. The messenger hurried after him and persuaded him to come back. This time Butler laid down his cue. His billiards opponent and the messenger skipped quickly out of the room and Butler and the leader of the Métis were left face to face and alone.

The conversation which followed was stilted and unsatisfactory. At a later time Butler would undoubtedly have felt greater sympathy for Riel, whose cause he admitted was in many ways just; but at their meeting he seems to have been struck more by Riel's patent vanity and the absurdity of his presumptions than by the arguments he advanced to justify the setting-up of a provisional government. 'I only want to retain power until I can resign it to a proper government,' Riel said. 'I have done everything for the sake of peace, and to prevent bloodshed among the people of this land.' And he added, speaking with a sudden heat that revealed the intensity of his feelings towards the white settlers of Assiniboia, 'But they will find if they try, these people here—to put me out—they will find they cannot do it. I will keep what is mine until the proper government arrives!'[5]

Butler listened unmoved. He was impressed only by the fact that Riel, in talking about the Expedition which he knew was on its way, made no mention of a possible amnesty for himself. But he failed utterly to see in the pale-faced man in the frock-coat and moccasins the passionately dedicated leader whose devotion to a lost cause was to bring him, fifteen years later, to the gallows and create a breach between French and English-speaking Canada which the passage of nearly a century of time has done little to close.

Butler left Fort Garry feeling like a second Daniel. He had dared the lion in his den and found him toothless. It was with an exalted sense of mission almost accomplished that he took his place in his canoe at St. Peter's Settlement and gave the 'All right—away!' to his crew of Indian and half-breed paddlers. He was on the last lap of the long journey that would lead him to Colonel Wolseley and the Red River Expedition.

His way lay down the Red and through the marshy reed-grown estuary into Lake Winnipeg, along the southern shore of the lake to the mouth of the Winnipeg River, and thence up the Winnipeg 160 miles to Rat Portage and Lake of the Woods. The first night out he and his men camped on the shore of a deep bay backed with evergreen and rocks, and the memory of that evening—his first in the wilds in the company of the native red man—was to return to him many times with the grace of a benediction:

When I lay down to rest that night on the dry sandy shore, I long watched the stars above me. As children sleep after a day of toil and play so slept the dusky men around me. It was my first night with these poor sons of the lone spaces; many a night afterwards I lay down to sleep beside these men and their brethren . . . but custom stales even Nature's infinite variety, and through many wild bivouacs my memory still wanders back to that first night out by the shore of Lake Winnipeg.[6]

The Winnipeg is a mad river. From its source in Lake of the Woods to its end in Lake Winnipeg, a distance of 160 miles, it falls 360 feet; and to the voyager, whether going up or coming down, seemed nothing but an endless succession of falls, rapids, eddies, whirlpools and interminable portages. The river cuts its way through the rugged rock and forest and muskeg country of the Laurentian Shield, and even today it is little known, for it lies off the beaten paths of men and is useless for navigation.

During the days of toil up the river in the face of raging waters and formidable portages Butler found his childhood idealization of the noble savage justified. Here in the wilderness, paddling the canoe he had made himself from materials he found around him, living off the land and not the white trader, the Indian led a life in which every element, every aspect of the natural world had value and meaning, a life which comprised a perfect harmony between man and nature. Inevitably that harmony was destroyed by the alien white man who slaughtered the Indian's food supply, drove him from his land, and if he let him live made him a pariah in a world he hated and could never understand. For the Indian of the west Butler felt not only admiration but an immense sympathy knowing that his doom was certain; and in the middle of what was until now the most exciting adventure of his life he brooded long and darkly over the fate of the race.

For mixed blood Butler felt pity, but no admiration. The only member of the crew who failed to carry his share of the work and ate more than his share of pemmican was a half-breed named Thomas Hope, a former mission-school teacher whose boastful talk served as inadequate cover for a cowardly spirit. Butler's finest crewman was a full-blooded Indian named William Prince, whom he was to meet again many years later 10,000 miles from the roaring Winnipeg.

Seven days and innumerable portages out from St. Peter's Settlement, Butler reached Rat Portage—then a Hudson's Bay post, now the flourishing resort town of Kenora—on the north shore of Lake of the Woods. No one at the Portage could tell him anything about the Expedition, but he was warned that strange men and canoes had been seen in and around the islands of the lake for several days past. It was generally believed that the strangers were Métis scouts sent by Riel to observe the size and progress of the Expedition. Butler, filled to the bursting-point with information and rumour and wildly impatient to communicate all he had learned to Wolseley, engaged a Hudson's Bay Company York boat at the Portage and set sail across the lake to the mouth of Rainy River seventy miles away on the southern shore. He landed at the Hudson's Bay post near the mouth of the river and eagerly questioned some half-starved Indians he found hanging around the post about the Expedition. To his unbounded relief and delight he learned that a great army of white braves had indeed been sighted 'where the road slants down to the lake'.

'What were they like?' Butler asked.

'They were like locusts,' an old Indian said, unwittingly using the perfect simile.

No one seemed able to identify the lake where the soldiers had been seen, but Butler did not care. The troops were on the march, they could not be far off, and he now hoped to effect a rendezvous at Fort Frances, some eighty miles from the mouth of Rainy River. He was in a fever to be on his way, but the Indians at the post were reluctant to let him go until he had made a speech. Butler obliged. 'Tell your chief that I am sorry he is poor and hungry,' he said. 'But let him look around; the land on which he sits is rich and fertile. Why does he not cut down the trees that cover it, and plant in their places potatoes and corn? Then he will have food in the winter when the moose is scarce and the sturgeon cannot be caught.' His audience listened without enthusiasm. Butler was a true Victorian in his belief in the spiritual and material benefits of hard work and sobriety, and to the end of his life was faintly baffled by the refusal of people to act on the sound advice he was always ready to give them. For the most part this eagerness to advise did Butler no great harm, but when in later years he took to lecturing commissioners and generals as if they were improvident and rather stupid Indians the consequences were occasionally serious.

With a spanking breeze astern, the York boat sailed in fine style up the wide reaches of Rainy River. Twenty-odd miles from Fort Frances the wind died and the boat drifted to a standstill. Butler had anticipated the contingency by bringing along a birch-bark canoe. He now left Thomas Hope, the half-breed mission teacher, in charge of the York boat and with three splendid Indian paddlers to assist him set off on the last stretch to the Fort.

The canoe sprang a leak. Butler requisitioned another from a band of Indians whom he found camped on the river bank, and he and his men paddled upstream all night. They reached Fort Frances at daybreak and Butler found time to marvel at the beauty of the Chaudière Falls in the eerie light of dawn before hurrying to the Hudson's Bay post and rousing the factor from his bed. No, the Expedition had not yet arrived—but the factor had been warned to expect Colonel Wolseley for breakfast.

In twelve days Butler had covered well over 400 miles through some of the roughest and wildest country in Canada; he was already 200 miles beyond the point at which he had originally planned to meet the Expedition, he had paddled all night to cover the last lap to Fort Frances—and he was still unsatisfied with his performance. He could not endure the thought of being found 'within the stockades of an Indian trading-post as though one had quietly taken one's ease at an inn'. He allowed his men an hour's rest, then roused them and said, 'The Colonel is close at hand. It will be well for us to go and meet him.'

One feels that Butler could have played to perfection the role of the French messenger boy who, having brought word to Napoleon of the storming of Ratisbon, answered Napoleon's query, 'You are wounded, boy?' with a firm, 'No, Sire—killed!'—and smiling fell dead.

Two miles above the Fort, at the rapids formed by the waters of Rainy Lake spilling into Rainy River, Butler and his men went ashore and climbed a rock from which they had an uninterrupted view across the lake. It was Butler who first caught the glint of the morning sun on metal and announced that the Expedition was in sight. A short time later a large canoe propelled by eight Iroquois paddlers and carrying a British army officer pulled in close to shore.

'Where on earth have *you* dropped from?' the officer shouted.

Butler saluted. 'Fort Garry, sir,' he said. 'Twelve days out.'

The officer was the commander of the Expedition—Colonel Wolseley himself. For Butler the meeting on the shore of Rainy Lake was one of the proudest moments of his life. What he had done was—as events proved—of no great importance in the sum of things, but he had carried out a difficult assignment with efficiency and dash and a complete disregard of personal danger. He had every reason to be pleased with himself.

The men of the Red River Expedition had performed great deeds, too. They had hacked and clawed their way from Fort William to Rainy Lake through a fearful forest tangle, they had built forty miles of road over rock and muskeg and carried enormous loads of supplies over countless portages. They were bitten raw by mosquitoes and blackflies, scorched by the sun and bleached by the rain, but they had licked the wilderness and opened the way to Fort Garry and God help Riel when they got there. Wolseley's meticulous planning had paid off.

Butler accompanied the 60th Foot (the vanguard of the Expedition) across Lake of the Woods and down the Winnipeg, travelling in his own canoe with his own Indian paddlers. Twelve days after leaving Rat Portage the troops entered the mouth of the Red River and started upstream towards Fort Garry. Butler borrowed a horse named Tacitus—appropriately Roman-nosed—from a settler at the Lower Fort, and rode as scout along the right bank of the river through deserted rain-soaked country. A few miles above Fort Garry the troops went ashore, climbed into Red River carts requisitioned by Wolseley and creaked over the dismal muddy prairie towards the Fort they had crossed half a continent to capture. Presently skirmishers were thrown out, cannon unlimbered, and the soldiers left the carts and advanced on the Fort in fighting formation. But the gate was wide open, the Fort deserted except for a Hudson's Bay Company factor who stood on the steps of the Government House and 'alternately welcomed with uplifted hands the new arrivals and denounced in no stinted terms one or two miserable-looking men who seemed to cower beneath his reproaches'.[7] Riel and his councillors had fled only a few minutes before.

The expedition had travelled dry all the way from Toronto to Fort Garry—Wolseley was known among his men as the 'teapot general'—and now the soldiers, and more particularly the voyageurs, hastened to make up for the long weeks of abstinence and thirst. The Winnipeg saloons, whose number and variety astonished Butler, sold anything that would intoxicate, and casualties were heavy. So many bodies lay stretched out on the prairie as sodden as the earth beneath them that anyone unfamiliar with what had happened might reasonably have assumed that he was looking at a battlefield littered with the as yet unburied dead.

The liquor ran out, everyone sobered up more or less, the militia arrived to police the settlement; and on September 6, 1870, the Honourable Mr. Adams Archibald was installed as Lieutenant-Governor of the newly created province of Manitoba and the North-West Territories. A member of the Canadian militia named Sam Steele, later a North-West Mounted Police commissioner and folk-hero, attended the installation and was notably impressed by the appearance of Lieutenant Butler. Steele was himself a giant of a man, and it was Butler's physique which caught his eye: 'Lieutenant Butler and Dr. Schultz arrived together, both remarkable for their magnificent physique and almost gigantic stature as well as for the contrast they afforded, Butler being dark-haired and bearded, Schultz golden-haired like a Viking of old.'[8] (As events were to prove, the contrast between the two men extended to character as well as complexion, for Dr. Schultz, the newly appointed Medical Health Officer of the North-West Territories, was later notorious for supplying whisky to the Indians.)

Four days after the installation of the Lieutenant-Governor the regular troops left for the east. Butler stayed behind in Fort Garry. He could have accompanied the troops, but he said he preferred to go back the way he had come.

The truth is that the west was in his blood and he did not want to leave it.

CHAPTER SIX

The Great Lone Land

IN WINNIPEG Butler lived for some time as the guest of Mr. Donald Smith (later Lord Strathcona and Mount Royal), a governor of the Hudson's Bay Company who had carried on the civil government of Assiniboia during the brief period between the arrival of the troops and the installation of Mr. Archibald. Butler talked a great deal with his well-informed host, hunted in desultory fashion in the marshlands of the Red River delta, and brooded about his future, which in spite of the good work he had done for Wolseley seemed as dark as ever. A few days after the departure of the regulars for the east he learned of the overwhelming defeat of the French Army by the Prussians at Sedan and the surrender of Napoleon III. Butler loved France and the French, feared and hated Germany and the Germans, and at once a fantastic plan took root in his mind. He would do as thousands of Irishmen had done since the days of Cromwell—become one of the Wild Geese (as Irish continental mercenaries were called) and take service in a foreign army. Almost certainly he would have made the quixotic gesture, entirely in keeping with his character, of 'offering to France in the moment of adversity the sword and service of at least one sympathizing friend'—what, after all, is more romantic in prospect than fighting and dying for a lost cause?—had he not told his host what he planned to do. Donald Smith was in his way an empire-builder, one of the great pioneers of western Canadian settlement, and he had Wolseley's eye for bright young men. He was quick to see in Butler not only frustrated ambition but a physical energy and restlessness which could be satisfied only by decisive and exciting action; and confident that Butler's resolution to throw in his lot with the French Army was born as much of boredom and depression as devotion to the cause of France he resolved not to let him go.

A few days later Lieutenant-Governor Archibald, acting on Donald Smith's advice, asked Butler to come and see him at Government House.

'I am going to ask you if you will accept a mission to the Saskatchewan Valley and through the Indian countries of the West,' the Lieutenant-Governor said. 'Take a couple of days to think it over and let me know your decision.'

Butler's answer echoed those of a score of heroes of the juvenile fiction he had read in his youth. 'There is no necessity to consider the matter, sir. I have already made up my mind and, if necessary, will start in half an hour.'

His resolve to join the French Army was forgotten on the instant. Butler shared with Emerson the view that with consistency a great soul has nothing to do. 'I know nothing so fixed as the mole, so obstinate as the mule, or so steady as a stone wall,' he wrote, 'but I don't particularly care about making their general characteristics the rule in my life.'

His instructions were set forth at some length in a document handed to him shortly before his departure. These instructions made it clear that the Government of Canada was preparing, however reluctantly, to assume full responsibility for the administration of an enormous empire hitherto the preserve of the Hudson's Bay Company and, as late as 1870, populated by only a few scattered Indian tribes and occasional small settlements of Scotch and Indian half-breeds.

The Governor's bill of instructions said in part:

Representations have been made from various quarters that within the last two years much disorder has prevailed in the settlements along the line of the Saskatchewan, and that the local authorities are utterly powerless for the protection of life and property within that region. . . . It is the desire of the Lieutenant Governor that you should examine the matter entirely from an independent point of view, giving his Honour for the benefit of the Government of Canada your views of the state of matters on the Saskatchewan in reference to the necessity of troops being sent there, basing your report on what you shall find by actual examination. . . .

Secondly you are to ascertain, as far as you can, in what places and among what tribes of Indians, and what settlements of whites, the small-pox is now prevailing. You are to take with you such small supplies of medicines as shall be considered by the Board of Health here suitable and proper for the treatment of small-pox, and you will obtain written instructions for the proper treatment of the disease, and you will leave a copy thereof with the chief officer of each fort you pass, and with any clergyman or other intelligent person belonging to settlements outside the forts.

You will also be expected to ascertain, as far as possible, the nature of the trade in furs conducted upon the Saskatchewan . . . and generally make such enquiries as to the source of trade in that region as may enable the Lieutenant-Governor to form an accurate idea of the commerce of the Saskatchewan.[1]

In brief, Butler was to explore the conditions under which the Indians, half-breeds and few whites were living in the country between Fort Garry and the Rockies—more particularly along the line of the North Saskatchewan River—and recommend to the Government of Canada the best way, compatible with small expense to the taxpayer, to ensure the establishment of the rule of law in the North-West Territories well in advance of settlement.

The execution of the commission so casually offered and eagerly accepted posed extraordinary difficulties. Not only was Butler expected to cover an enormous expanse of primitive wilderness but he would have to do much of his travelling in the dead of winter. On the western prairies temperatures of forty degrees below zero are not uncommon, and blizzards strike with a ferocity which even today in a well-settled country of normally excellent communications can isolate and kill. In 1870 there was no settlement to speak of west of Winnipeg. Here and there at strategic points stood the trading-posts of the Hudson's Bay Company, with occasionally a mission house near by, and that was all. The half-breeds and Indians—Crees, Blackfeet, Bloods, Piegans, Salteaux, Lurcees and Assiniboine—were nomads; a few had pitched their tepees more or less permanently near the Hudson's Bay posts, but the majority were forever on the move, the line of movement dictated by the course of the buffalo and the whereabouts of fur-bearing animals. The land which only a few decades later was to be known as the bread-basket of the world stretched from the Red River to the Rockies, unchanged in appearance and character from the day of creation; and its loneliness, its immensity, roused Butler's brooding Celtic spirit to an instantaneous sympathetic response:

The great ocean itself does not present more infinite variety than does this prairie-ocean of which we speak. In winter, a dazzling surface of purest snow; in early summer a vast expanse of grass and pale pink roses; in autumn too often a wild sea of raging fire. No ocean of water in the world can vie with its gorgeous sunsets; no solitude can equal the loneliness of a night-shadowed prairie; one feels the stillness, and hears the silence, the wail of the prowling wolf makes the voice of solitude audible, the stars look down through infinite silence upon a silence almost as intense. This ocean has no past—time has been naught to it; and men have come and gone, leaving behind them no trace, no vestige of their presence. Some French writer, speaking of the prairies, has said that this sense of the utter negation of life, this complete absence of history, has struck him with a loneliness oppressive and sometimes terrible in its intensity. Perhaps so; but for my part, the prairies had nothing terrible in their aspect, nothing oppressive in their loneliness. One saw here the world as it had taken shape and form from the Creator. Nor did the scene look less beautiful because nature alone tilled the earth, and the unaided sun brought forth the flowers.[2]

Over this vast ocean of land Butler now prepared to journey. His proposed route, the Carlton Trail, was one long familiar to the fur-traders and missionaries, and more recently to the advance guard of the Métis of Red River, many of whom—dreaming vain dreams of escaping the white settlers—were preparing to leave Manitoba and seek new homes along the South Saskatchewan. The Trail ran straight west of Winnipeg through the settlement of Portage la Prairie (founded by La Verendrye in 1738) to Fort Ellice at the junction of the Qu'Appelle and Assiniboine Rivers, thence north-west to the Hudson's Bay posts strung along the North Saskatchewan River at Carlton, Battleford, Fort Pitt, Victoria and Edmonton. From Edmonton, Butler proposed to strike south and west through heavy bush country to Rocky Mountain House, the last Hudson's Bay post east of the Rockies, and, if he could hire a reliable guide, continue straight south from Rocky Mountain House through the dangerous Blackfeet country across the international border into Montana. In Montana he hoped to learn something of the activities of the free traders who were crossing the border into what is now southern Alberta with the utmost impunity and corrupting the Indians with rotgut whisky.

On October 24, 1870, just one week before his thirty-second birthday, Butler left Fort Garry and turned his face towards the Rocky Mountains nearly twelve hundred miles west. With him went a Hudson's Bay factor returning to his post on the Saskatchewan and an energetic half-breed named Pierre Dionne who was to act as Butler's teamster as far as Carlton. Butler rode a splendid little western pony named Blackie to whom he quickly became much attached. Pierre Dionne drove the horse-drawn Red River cart that carried Butler's personal kit, the party's food supplies and two chests of medicines for distribution in the smallpox-ridden districts through which Butler expected to pass. In army rank Butler was still only an insignificant lieutenant, but before leaving Fort Garry he had been appointed Justice of the Peace for Rupert's Land and the North-West, a title that gave him jurisdiction over an area so vast, that, as he himself observed, 'the only parallel to be found in the world exists under the title "Czar of all the Russians"'.

A few hours out of Portage la Prairie, the last settlement of consequence in Manitoba and jumping-off place for the North-West Territories, the little party came upon the grave of a man who had died of smallpox beside the trail only a day or two before. That night they camped near by, on what Butler named the Prairie of the Lonely Grave. It was then that the magnitude of his undertaking seems to have at last struck home. Haunted by recollection of the lonely grave beside the trail, conscious for the first time of the awesome impersonality of the prairie ocean on which he was now launched, he allowed a melancholy awareness of 'the vastness, the inscrutability and the ultimate sadness of nature' to possess his imagination:

> When the fire flickered low and the wind wailed and sighed amongst the dry white grass, it was impossible to resist a feeling of utter loneliness. A long journey lay before me, nearly 3000 miles would have to be traversed before I could hope to reach the neighbourhood of even this lonely spot itself; this last verge of civilization; the terrific cold of a winter of which I had only heard, a cold so intense that travel ceases—a cold which freezes mercury, and of which the spirit registers 80 degrees of frost—this was to be the thought of many nights, the ever-present companion of many days. Between this little campfire and the giant mountains to which my steps were turned, there stood in that long 1200 miles but six houses, and in these houses a terrible malady had swept nearly half the inhabitants out of life. So, lying down that night for the first time with all this before me, I felt as one who had to face not a few of those things from which is evolved that strange mystery called death, and looking out into that vague dark immensity around me, saw in it the gloomy shapes and shadowy outlines of the bygone which memory hides but to produce at such times.[3]

The melancholy fit did not last long. October is often the finest time of year on the prairies. The air is bracing, the sun not yet

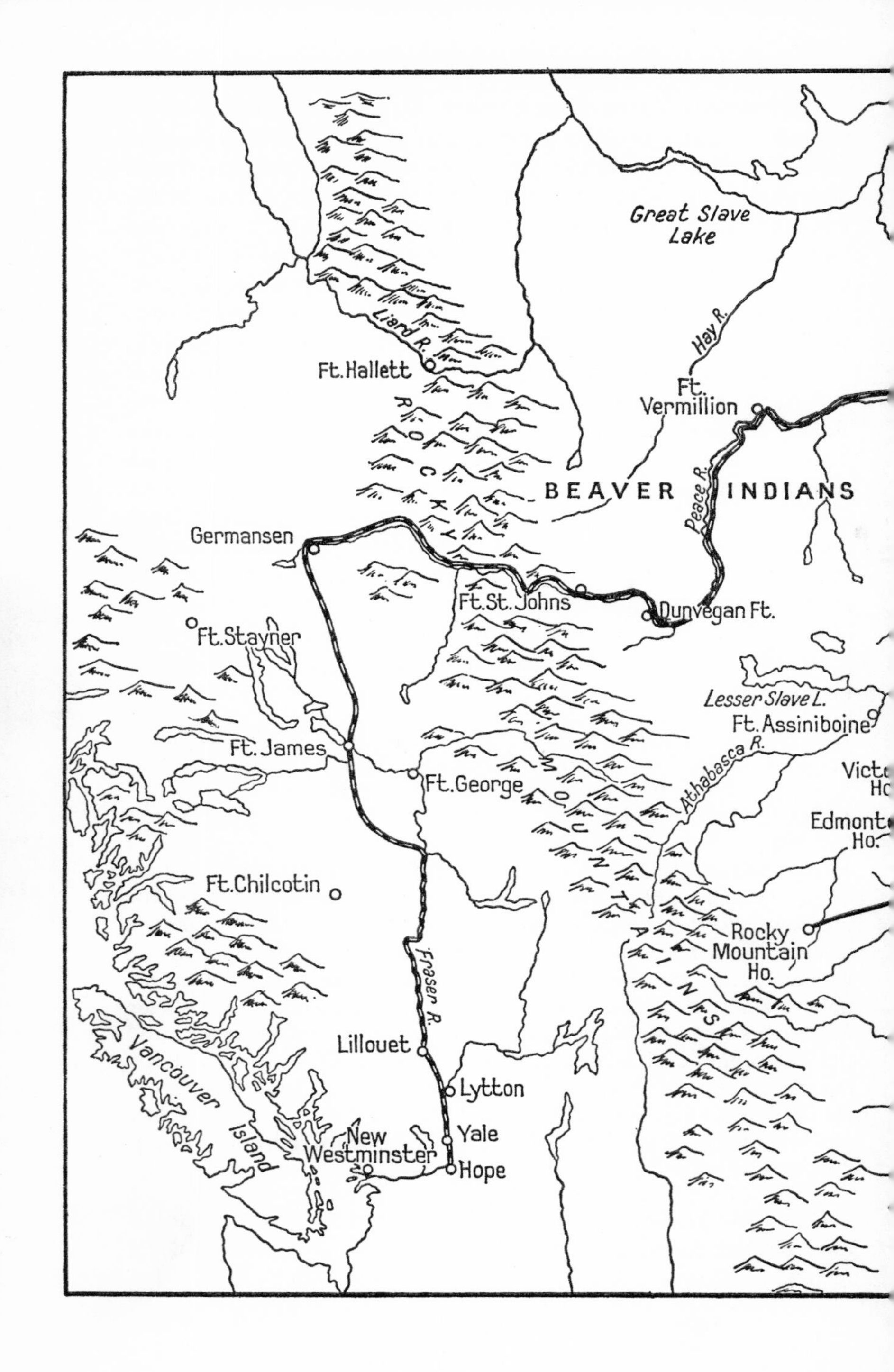

Great Slave Lake
Hay R.
Liard R.
Ft. Hallett
Ft. Vermillion
R O C K Y
BEAVER INDIANS
Peace R.
Germansen
Ft. St. Johns
Dunvegan Ft.
Ft. Stayner
Lesser Slave L.
Ft. Assiniboine
Ft. James
Athabasca R.
Ft. George
M O U N T A I N S
Edmont
Ho.
Ft. Chilcotin
Rocky Mountain Ho.
Fraser R.
Lillouet
Lytton
Vancouver Island
New Westminster
Yale
Hope

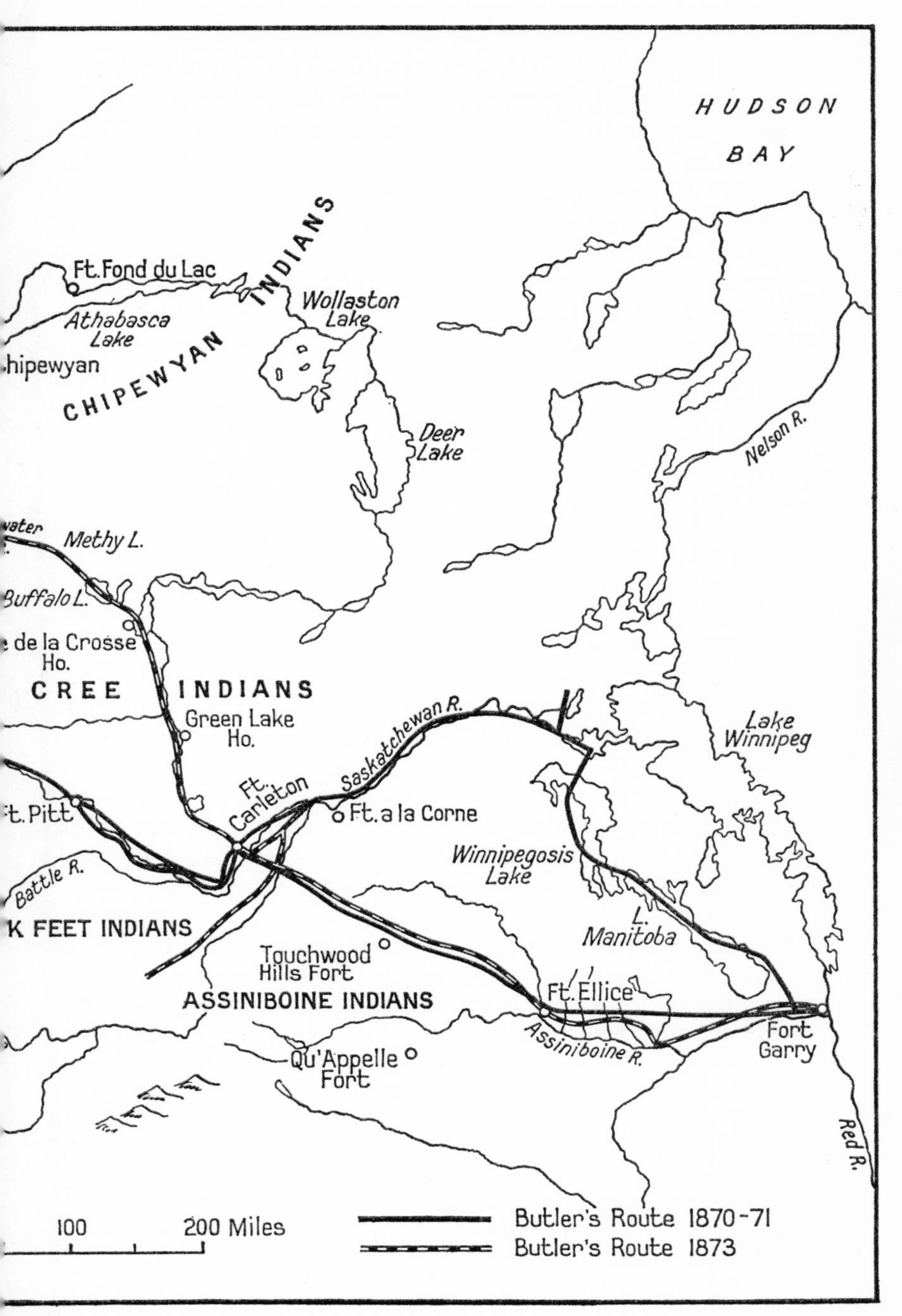

Drawn from the map illustrating Butler: 'The Wild North Land' (1873)

wholly vanquished, and one sees all things with an awareness and intensity impossible in the warm summer-time, when the oncoming winter sends no premonitory chills before. Butler revelled in the sights and sounds of the brief sunlit days; and fell asleep at night under a shimmering many-coloured canopy of northern lights in the sense of utter content induced by a long day's ride in the open, a meal of fried pemmican fit to subdue the most ravenous appetite (by sheer weight if nothing else), and the knowledge of work well done. In truth Butler had reason to feel gratified with his progress. His party covered fifty miles or more a day, forded ice-choked streams, rode for hours soaked to the skin with no thought of stopping to light a fire, and gloried in the sheer unthinking joy of being alive. Never again was Butler to know quite the exhilaration of those late fall and early winter days when, senses alert to every new impression, body responsive to every demand made upon it, he rode into the great lone land on the kind of mission precisely suited to his temperament—a mission to help the red man, and bring law and justice into a lawless unjust world. Or so he dreamed. And perhaps his dream did not go wholly unfulfilled.

Half-way between Fort Ellice and Carlton, Butler entered upon the region then known as the Touchwood Hills (the name is almost forgotten now)—a land of high ridges, poplar thickets (call 'bluffs' in the Canadian west), and abundant grass rooted in a rich dark soil. From a high point of the Hills, Butler was able to look over an enormous expanse of fire-blackened plain dotted with bleaching buffalo bones, once the dominion of the red man, now utterly empty of life. 'There is something unspeakably melancholy in the aspect of this portion of the north-west,' he wrote.

From one of the westward jutting spurs of the Touchwood Hills the eye sees far away over an immense plain; the sun goes down, and as he sinks upon the earth the straight line of the horizon becomes visible for a moment across his blood-red disc, but so distant, so far away, that it seems dreamlike in its immensity. There is not a sound in the air or on earth; on every side lie spread the relics of the great fight waged by man against the brute creation; all is silent and deserted, the Indian and the buffalo gone, the settler not yet come. You turn quickly to the right or left; over a hilltop close by a solitary wolf steals away. Quickly the vast prairie begins to grow dim, and darkness forsakes the skies because they light their stars, coming down to seek in the utter solitude of the blackened plains a kindred spirit for the night.[4]

West of the Touchwood Hills in the first week of November a wild blizzard roared out of the north and Butler awoke in the morning to find himself at last exposed to the unique terrors of snow driven in long slanting lines before a savage wind, all landmarks obliterated in a hard-driving whiteness. The horses had strayed from camp and the three men went to look for them, Butler refusing to plead a tenderfoot's privilege and stay behind. The Hudson's Bay factor, a veteran of prairie winters, lost his way, and it was Butler who found him floundering in the wrong direction and guided him back to safety.

On his way out from camp Butler had kept the wind on his left shoulder, on the way back his right, and thus avoided the danger of travelling in a circle. He was immensely proud of this bit of plainscraft, which he had learned from the novels of Fenimore Cooper.

On November 7 the party reached the south branch of the Saskatchewan River at a point where the two branches run parallel in a northerly direction before swinging east to their junction forty miles beyond Prince Albert. The temperature had fallen far below freezing for many nights now, and Butler was amazed and indignant to find that down the middle of the great river the water still ran black and fast between solid ice-masses extending to either shore. A delay of several days would not have seriously upset the party's time-table, but Butler was determined to reach Carlton, some twenty miles west, on the day he himself had named when he drafted his itinerary. Besides, the pemmican had run out and for hungry men a mixture of fried flour and grease made a poor substitute.

At Butler's insistence the three men spent a cold, miserable day trying to convert the factor's wagon-box into a boat, using a sheet of oilcloth for waterproofing. Butler and Pierre Dionne actually ventured into the water aboard the ridiculous craft and were fortunate to suffer no more than a soaking in ice-cold water. They even managed after prodigious exertions to save the wagon-box. That night the cold was intense; when morning came the ice stretched unbroken from shore to shore. In the centre it easily sustained the weight of a man—but what about the horses? There was, perhaps, some excuse for Butler's misjudging the strength of the ice, but none at all for Pierre's or the factor's. Perhaps they had caught something of Butler's impatience—or perhaps they could not endure the prospect of another day in the shipyards. They believed, they said, that the horses could cross in safety.

The first horse made the perilous journey unharmed, although a sudden bend in the ice at the centre of the river should have warned the men that luck alone had brought him across. It was little Blackie's turn next. Pierre led the pony, Butler following close behind lest he balk at a crucial point.

Unfortunately Blackie showed complete confidence in Pierre and his master and unhesitatingly walked to the centre of the river. With appalling suddenness the ice gave way. Butler leapt back just in time to save himself, but Blackie was plunged into the cold, fast-running water. The ice was thick all round him, he could not break it with his knees, and to drag him from the water was far beyond the strength of the three men.

'Is there no hope at all?' Butler shouted to his companions. He did not wait for their answer, for he knew what it would be. He ran back to camp and snatched up his rifle. When he returned Blackie was still swimming, but his strength was almost gone. Butler shot the pony between the eyes and then, so he tells us, went back to camp and cried like a child.

It would be pleasant to record that the sad little episode taught Butler caution. The truth is that to the end of his life he showed a marked inclination to walk where the ice was thinnest.

Everywhere in the Carlton country, it seemed, the taint of death was in the air. Carlton House, which Butler reached the day following the loss of Blackie, stood on low ground adjoining the North Saskatchewan River about sixty miles south-west of Prince Albert. It consisted of a huddle of houses surrounded by twenty-foot palisades. Just outside the palisades were the snow-covered mounds marking the graves of the victims of the smallpox epidemic which had raged the summer before throughout the plains country, and nowhere more virulently than at Carlton House. Of sixty inhabitants of the House thirty-six had contracted the disease. Thirty-two, including the Hudson's Bay factor, were dead.

Butler stayed four days at Carlton House. He found to his disgust that the medical supplies he had dragged in the Red River cart across hundreds of miles of prairie were largely useless. They had been carelessly packed in uninsulated wooden crates; jars were broken, liquids frozen. Butler could do little more as a precaution against future epidemics than leave his pamphlets of printed instructions with the persons least likely to burn them.

He was assiduous in gathering material for his report to Lieutenant-Governor Archibald. He made copious notes on conditions among the Indians (they were a hungry lot around Carlton, for the buffalo had moved far beyond reach of their hunting parties), on the flora and fauna of the district, the nature of the soil, the kinds of cereals and vegetables grown with success in the Carlton country, and the possibility of extensive land cultivation taking the place of the vanishing buffalo in the prairie economy. He was, as one who knew him well said later, 'at once doctor, lawyer, diplomat, historian, geographer, census enumerator, agriculturalist',[5] and he took himself seriously in each of the roles he had assumed.

The pattern of inquiry he established at Carlton was the one he adhered to for the rest of his journey west to Rocky Mountain House. At every post along the way—Battleford, Fort Pitt, Victoria, Edmonton—he talked with Hudson's Bay men, missionaries, Indians, half-breeds—and everywhere the story he pieced together was the same, the sordid drama of the destruction of a race. 'The American and Canadian are only names that hide beneath them the greed of united Europe', he wrote in a fit of savage anger.

> Terrible deeds have been wrought out in that western land; terrible, heart-sickening deeds of cruelty and rapacious infamy. . . . If on the long line of the American frontier from the gulf of Mexico to the British boundary, a single life is taken by an Indian . . . the fact is chronicled in scores of journals throughout the United States, but the reverse of the story we never know. . . . My God, what a terrible tale could I not tell of these dark deeds done by the white savage against the far nobler red man! From southernmost Texas to most northern Montana there is but one universal remedy for Indian difficulty—kill him.[6]

Butler's admiration for the Indian was curiously founded. It is quite literally true that to the end of his life when he thought of the Indian his imagination conjured up a picture not of the red men whom he had actually met, talked and worked with on the western plains, but of Fenimore Cooper's idealized braves. None the less, however poor and degraded the Indian of real life might have been, he must have commended himself to Butler because of his unselfishness. He lacked the white man's greed—greed which Butler, haunted all his life by memory of the evictions he had witnessed as a child, was coming to believe was the greatest evil in the world—greater even than the love of power and more corrupting. 'This wild man . . . is the only perfect socialist or communist in the world', he wrote.

He holds all things in common with his tribe—the land, the bison, the river, the moose. He is starving and the rest of the tribe want food. Well, he kills a moose, and to the last bit the coveted food is shared by all. . . . There is but a scrap of beaver, a thin rabbit or a bit of sturgeon in the lodge; a stranger comes, and he is hungry; give him his share and let him be first served and best attended to. If one child starves in an Indian camp you may know that in every lodge scarcity is universal and that every stomach is hungry. . . . The most curious anomaly among the race of man, the red man of America is passing away beneath our eyes into the infinite solitude. The possession of the same noble qualities which we affect to reverence among our nations makes us want to kill him. If he would be our slave he might live; but as he won't be that, won't toil and delve and hew for us, and will persist in hunting, fishing, and roaming over the beautiful prairie which the Great Spirit gave him; in a word, since he will be free—we kill him.[7]

In his less passionate moments Butler freely admitted that the Indian way of life was wasteful in the extreme; that the vast plains over which the tribes roamed could sustain many times the number of tribesmen. He had no intention of playing a Canute-like role and trying to hold back the tide of western Canadian settlement which he knew must come. But it was with a sense of absolute dedication that he studied ways and means whereby the remnants of the Indian race in western Canada might be saved from the fate of their brothers in the United States. The law must come before the settler, its chief function in the Canadian west to protect the Indian from the white man rather than the other way about.

Around Butler's visit to Fort Pitt, an isolated Hudson's Bay post on the North Saskatchewan roughly between Carlton and Edmonton, there lingers a pleasing aura of romance. The last day's ride to Fort Pitt over gully-seamed, heavily wooded and snow-logged country was an unusually long and strenuous one, and to compound the party's difficulties the half-breed guide whom Butler had engaged at Battleford lost his way. The Hudson's Bay Company factor who had been Butler's companion all the way from Fort Garry favoured camping out for the night, but Butler, whose sense of direction was uncanny, took charge of the party and led the way through trackless country and in darkness to the Fort. The factor, a Scot named John Sinclair, welcomed the cold and famished travellers with true frontier hospitality, and soon they were devouring an immense meal of buffalo steak and potatoes served by the factor's daughter Mary, according to Butler 'the

WORKING UP THE WINNIPEG
An illustration from 'The Great Lone Land' published in 1872

THE ROCKY MOUNTAINS AT THE SOURCES OF THE SASKATCHEWAN

brightest-eyed little lassie, half Cree, half Scotch, in the North-West'. Those who knew her say that Mary Sinclair was indeed beautiful, and about her meeting with Butler a romantic legend has taken form, with how much basis in truth no one can say. Mrs. Albina Hamilton, the wife of a Saskatchewan pioneer newspaper man, thus records the story as she says she heard it from Mary Sinclair herself:

William MacKay's wife (Mary Sinclair), when she was young, had the reputation of being the most beautiful girl in all the Saskatchewan country. Years afterwards, when her daughter Mary had become the wife of William Peterson of Regina, an old friend of my husband's family, Mrs. MacKay was visiting her. Four of us—Mrs. MacKay, Mrs. Peterson, my husband and I—were sitting around the fireplace one winter's evening talking about old days on the prairie. Mrs. MacKay said, 'It is a pleasure for me to be here in my daughter's house, where she is happy with her children and has one of the finest husbands in the world. You know,' she continued, 'it is the best thing in the world to have a good husband and a happy home.' Then she added reminiscently, her voice taking on that softness characteristic of women who have some of the native blood in their veins: 'I have had a long and happy life with my William, but once long ago, when I was a young girl, there was an officer who came to Fort Pitt. He was tall and very good looking, and he could talk so well. I thought I could have loved him. He came out of the snow and storm one night like someone from a different world. He went on to Fort Edmonton and when he was away I thought of him often. Afterwards he came back and I was glad. He spoke to me about his home in Ireland and asked me to marry him and go with him to the Old Country. I did like him very much but I was a child of the North-West and what would I do in other lands? Perhaps I cried a little, but I sent him away without me. . . .'

After Sir William Butler's death his autobiography . . . was published and there was a name in it that gave us the clue. When calling on Mrs. MacKay my husband said: 'Did you know a Captain Butler long ago?'

Her eyes, still bright and clear, softened with a mist of tears at the well-remembered name, and the memory of the fine old woman, surrounded by her grandchildren and still beautiful in spite of encroaching age, must have leapt across the years and she replied, 'Oh yes, Mr. Hamilton, that was the officer of whom I told you'.[8]

The marriage proposal need not be dismissed out of hand as a conventional embellishment added by Mrs. Hamilton or Mary Sinclair herself to round out a romantic tale. Butler was no doubt strongly attracted by the young girl's beauty and innocence; he was enamoured of the land she belonged to and of the way of life her people led. It is unlikely though that he would have suggested taking her to Ireland—unless prompted by a perverse inclination to shock his relatives. If he offered marriage to Mary Sinclair he almost certainly did so with the intention of resigning his commission and settling permanently in the North-West.

The inmates of Fort Pitt itself had escaped the smallpox, but the Cree Indians of the surrounding district suffered terribly. Driven by a forlorn hope that the white man might be able to help them, they had fled back to the Fort from their hunting-grounds far to the south as soon as the epidemic struck; but long before they reached the vicinity of the Fort their line of march was marked by the bodies of the unburied dead who had almost literally died in their tracks. In order to safeguard as far as possible the men and women within the Fort, the factor had imposed a strict quarantine while the disease ran its frightful course. The ghastliest time of all came when the Indians, knowing at last that they could expect no help from the white man, sought to rid their tortured bodies of the smallpox by transference; and day after day the inmates of the Fort were witnesses to the hideous spectacle of the stricken and desperate Indians rubbing their pustule-disfigured bodies against the palisades and doors and window-frames of the Fort before they lay down and died. Only a few weeks before Butler's arrival had the remnants of the band given up their macabre picketing of the Fort and scattered into the heavy bush country lying to the north.

After a stop of two days at Fort Pitt, Butler engaged fresh horses and set off once more along the line of the Saskatchewan towards Fort Edmonton. The country between Fort Pitt and Edmonton along the great valley of the North Saskatchewan River is richly loamed, rolling, heavily wooded with poplar, willow and evergreen. It is today one of the best mixed-farming areas in the Canadian west, as Butler predicted it would be, and although much of the land is now cleared its general appearance is almost the same as it was when he first saw it, for the hills and the valleys and the river itself are unchanged, and from ground-level the observer gets an impression of a land heavily wooded and not altogether subdued to the purposes of man.

Edmonton, today a booming oil town of more than 400,000 people, was in 1870 a palisaded fort set high on the banks of the

North Saskatchewan in the middle of one of the most lawless regions of the North-West. William Christie, a chief factor of the Hudson's Bay Company in charge of the Fort, admitted to Butler that it was not possible for the Company to preserve law in the North-West as it was understood in the rest of Canada. Four known murderers were among his Indian customers; and here in the vicinity of Fort Edmonton the Crees and their implacable enemies the Blackfeet—whose traditional hunting-grounds extended far to the south and west—came into frequent and bloody contact.

Before continuing his journey to the mountains Butler took time to visit the French Mission at St. Albert a few miles north-west of Edmonton. His meeting with the Oblate Fathers in charge of the Mission excited in him the sympathy he always felt, not for missionaries as such, but for the men of a nation he idealized whom he found living in self-imposed exile far from all those things uniquely French which they had once known and still loved and would never see again:

> He who has travelled through the vast colonial empire of Britain . . . must often have met with men dwelling in the midst of wild, savage peoples whom they tended with a strange and mother-like devotion. If you asked who was this stranger who dwelt thus among wild men in these lone places, you were told he was the French missionary; and if you sought him in his lonely hut, you found ever the same surroundings, the same simple evidences of a faith which seemed more than human. . . . And it has ever been the same, East and West, far in advance of trader or merchant, of sailor or soldier, has gone this dark-haired fragile man, whose earliest memories are thick with sunny scenes by bank of Loire or vine-clad slope of Rhone or Garonne, and whose vision in this life, at least, is never destined to rest again upon these oft-remembered places.[9]

Of the 900 French half-breeds who originally made up the mission congregation of St. Albert 300 had died of smallpox. The news which Butler brought from the outside world to the good French fathers was not such as to lighten their gloom, for it was he who told them of the disaster of Sedan and 'the closing of the high-schooled hordes of Teuton savages around Paris'.

On December 1, 1870, Butler said good-bye to William Christie, the chief factor at Fort Edmonton, and set out for Rocky Mountain House nearly two hundred miles south-west of Edmonton and the last post of the Hudson's Bay Company east of the Rockies. Two new men, half-breeds, accompanied him—Rowland Sinclair, brother of 'the bright-eyed little beauty at Fort Pitt', and Paul Foyale, who had lost his wife and only child in the smallpox epidemic. They formed a companionable trio. Butler, as always, loved the long daily rides—through beautiful pastoral parkland now—and the meal of fried pemmican and hot tea eaten and drunk in enormous quantities around the nightly campfire, and afterwards the wonderfully deep and relaxing sleep within the shelter of a sleeping-bag so soundly insulated from the cold as to make tent or brushwood shelter a superfluity.

Three days out from Fort Edmonton, Butler looked west from the summit of a high hill and saw for the first time the stupendous jagged peaks of the Rocky Mountains serrating the far-off skyline:

> The snow had cleared the atmosphere, the sky was coldly bright. An immense plain stretched from my feet to the mountains—a plain so vast that every object of hill and wood and lake lay dwarfed into one continuous level, and at the back of this level, beyond the pines and the lakes and the river courses, rose the great range solid, impassable, silent—a mighty barrier standing sentinel over the plains and prairies of America, over the measureless solitudes of the Great Lone Land.[10]

On December 5, a day when the early-morning thermometer registered twenty-two degrees below zero, Butler reached Rocky Mountain House. He had been on the trail from Fort Garry for forty-two days, and in twenty-seven days of actual travel had ridden and walked just under twelve hundred miles. At Rocky Mountain House he remained for eight days, enjoying the companionship and advice of the factor and of the 'black-robed voyageur', Father Lacombe, an almost legendary figure in the history of western missions. From the factor and the good father, Butler gathered much valuable information about conditions of life in the farthest reaches of the Saskatchewan country. The Indians in the immediate vicinity of Rocky Mountain House were the remnants of the once-powerful Assiniboine tribe whom war and smallpox had all but wiped out. Here, too, came Bloods and Blackfeet from the southern plains region. They were the most warlike of the western tribes, and Rocky Mountain House was elaborately safeguarded against the possibility of surprise attack during the times when the Indians came in large numbers to trade furs for Company goods. Deeds of violence were common in the vicinity of the post. Sometimes they originated in clashes between naturally hostile tribesmen which the Company could do nothing to quell, and sometimes in family quarrels. Butler was greatly moved by the tale he heard of two proud brothers of the Blood Indian tribe between whom a sudden fierce dispute flared up over some trivial matter. One of the brothers whipped out a knife and stabbed the other, inflicting a ghastly wound, and immediately stalked to his own tent, where he sat 'silent and impassive'. The wounded man contrived to load his rifle, and, holding his terrible wound closed with one hand, staggered to his brother's tent, placed the muzzle of the rifle against his brother's chest and shot him through the heart. Then he took his hand away from his wound, letting the blood gush out, and died almost instantly beside his brother. From the moment the knife flashed until both brothers lay dead neither had spoken a word or uttered a sound. No doubt the tale, as Butler heard it, lost nothing in the telling, but for him it had the ring of authenticity, for the brothers had behaved in obedience to the heroic Indian tradition he had read about in Fenimore Cooper; and before leaving Rocky Mountain House he found time to visit their graves in the near-by woods and salute their departed shades.

But the chief cause of violence in the Saskatchewan country was the free trader. Butler had learned enough of the methods of the old East India Company to feel a profound distrust of company monopolies—later experiences in South Africa were to strengthen this distrust—but for the Hudson's Bay Company he was disposed to make an exception. The Company treated the Indians and half-breeds with as much fairness as the need to declare substantial dividends permitted; it advocated, in its own interest as a continuing organization, a long-term conservationist policy for buffalo and fur-bearing animals; and it refused to sell whisky to the Indians. The free trader by contrast adopted a short-term hunting policy; he encouraged the Indians to kill indiscriminately, because the reckless slaughter of buffalo and beaver meant big profits today—and who cared anything about tomorrow? Worse still, the free trader took pride in being a sharp dealer. 'Wherever I have gone, among wild or semi-wild men,' Butler wrote years after his Canadian mission, when he had journeyed over half the world, 'I have found one idea prevalant in the minds of white men trading with natives. That idea was that it was perfectly fair and legitimate to cheat the wild man in every possible way.'[11] The easiest way to cheat and rob the Indian of the western plains was first to make him drunk. From the factor and Father Lacombe, Butler learned something of the scenes enacted at Rocky Mountain House in the days —only ten years past—when the Company itself had used alcohol as a stimulus to trade:

In former times, when rum was used in the trade, the most frightful scenes were in the habit of occurring in the Indian room. The fire-water, although freely diluted with water, soon reduced the assemblage to a state of wild hilarity, quickly followed by stupidity and sleep. The fire-water for the Crees was composed of three parts of water to one of spirit, that of the Blackfeet, seven of water to one of spirit, but so potent is the power which alcohol exercises over the red man that the Blackfeet, even upon his well-diluted liquor, was wont to become helplessly intoxicated. The trade usually began with a present of fire-water all round —then the business went on apace. Horses, robes, provisions, tents, all would be proffered for one more drink of the beloved poison. Nothing could exceed the excitement inside the tent, except the excitement outside. There the anxious crowd could only learn by hearsay what was going on within. Now and then a brave, with an amount of self-abnegation worthy of a better cause, would issue from the tent with his cheeks distended and his mouth full of the fire-water, and going along the ranks of his friends he would squirt a little of the liquor into the open mouths of his less fortunate brethren.[12]

In his capacity of Justice of the Peace, Butler was the bearer of an order-in-council from Lieutenant Governor Archibald 'prohibiting the sale, distribution or possession of alcohol in the North-West Territories'. He was, however, absolutely without means to enforce the prohibition. On one occasion he told the chief of a band of Crees that henceforth, when a trader brought whisky into the Cree camp, he could order his braves to take it from the trader by force. But he was uneasily aware that the chief's joy in the news stemmed from what he thought was a chance, not to destroy the whisky trade, but to acquire a supply of free fire-water.

Butler could find no one at Rocky Mountain House willing to guide him through the dangerous Blackfeet country, and on December 12, 1870, he turned his face towards the east and Fort Garry. At Fort Edmonton he was able to exchange his horses for three teams of mongrel sleigh-dogs. After several days' experience on the trail he reached the conclusion that sleigh-dogs shared most of the vices common to mankind (they were cunning, cowardly, sometimes brutal)—but on balance they were long-suffering, overburdened and underfed servants who deserved a better life than the one man compelled them to lead.

The cold was now of an intensity which Butler had never before known. Even his deerskin sleeping-bag, made with the hair inside and covered with canvas, failed him when the temperature dropped to forty degrees below zero, and it was then that he began to appreciate more fully the worth of the sleigh-dog. He made an excellent foot-and-body warmer, and Butler enthusiastically welcomed any or all of the dogs who chose to sleep beside or on top of him.

He spent Christmas Day in the Methodist Mission House at Victoria, sixty miles east of Edmonton, as guest of the Rev. George McDougall, who next to Father Lacombe was the best-known missionary in the North-West. It was the most melancholy Christmas of Butler's life. His host made some attempt to provide a festive meal, and in the evening the girls played the little organ in the Mission parlour and sang duets; but two members of the family had died of smallpox a few weeks earlier and not even the faith of dedicated Christians could triumph at Christmas-time over the bitter reality of death.

The cold deepened, more than once reaching fifty degrees below zero. But every reader of *The Great Lone Land* must be impressed by the superb assurance—pleasure even—with which Butler endured the cold and labour of the day. Blow wind come snow he took the lead on the trail, worked the hardest gathering firewood when the short day was ended and darkness fell, ate his fried pemmican and drank his hot tea with heroic appetite; made his notes—enormously detailed, recording all things seen and done and surmised during the day—in the uncertain light of the campfire, often with fingers numbed to the point where they could hardly hold a pencil; and afterwards crawled into his sleeping-bag, pulled the flap over his head, and with a dog or two stretched across the bag for communal warmth slept soundly until the pale northern winter daylight crept over the vast white sea of land.

Only once on the return journey to Fort Garry were Butler's assurance and equanimity seriously shaken—this when he acted as escort, between Carlton and Prince Albert, to the wife of a Hudson's Bay Company factor and her eight-months-old baby. The night they spent in the open half-way to Prince Albert was for Butler a long night of horror. He had relinquished his beloved sleeping-bag to his charges and spent the interminable hours of darkness huddled under a few inadequate blankets listening to the howls of the baby which hardly subsided all night long. At daybreak he rose, bleary-eyed and wretched, and 'gathered the fire together in speechless agony'. The temperature stood at forty degrees below zero, the baby's nose was frost-bitten, the water-resistant qualities of the sleeping- bag tested from the inside out. 'A baby at any period of a man's life is a very serious affair,' Butler afterwards commented. 'But a baby below zero is something appalling.'

From Carlton House, Butler chose to follow a return route to Fort Garry running farther north than the one he had followed when outward bound. It traced its way through the heavily-wooded country of the North Saskatchewan River valley north-west from Prince Albert to Cumberland House, thence swinging sharply south-east to Lake Winnipegosis and continuing south over Lake Manitoba to Fort Garry. The region beyond the junction of the north and south branches of the Saskatchewan, some forty miles east of Prince Albert, forms a part of the great subarctic forest where, so Butler reported, 'the earth dwelt in the perpetual gloom of the pine-trees'. And here his prophetic vision for once failed him, for looking down at the junction of the rivers from a favourable vantage-point he foresaw a time not far distant when the junction would be an important centre of commerce and civilization.

> It is impossible [he predicted] that the wave of life which rolls so unceasingly into America can leave unoccupied this great fertile tract; as the river valleys farther east have all been peopled long before settlers found their way into the countries lying at the back, so must this great valley of the Saskatchewan, when once brought within the reach of the emigrant, become the scene of numerous settlements. As I stood in the twilight looking down on the silent rivers merging into the great single stream which here enters the forest region, the mind had little difficulty in seeing another picture, when the river forks would be a busy scene of commerce, and man's labour would waken echoes now answering to the wild things of plain and forest.[13]

Today the river forks are as silent as they were in Butler's time, and echoes still answer only to the wild things of plain and forest.

At Fort-a-la-Corne, twenty miles below the forks of the river, Butler hoped to intercept the northern packet of mail, the 'winter express' which under the direction of the Hudson's Bay Company left Fort Garry in mid-December to distribute mail, either directly or through subsidiary carriers, to posts as far away as the Mackenzie River delta nearly two thousand miles from Fort Garry. Sometimes a week-long blizzard, accident or sudden death might play havoc with the mail-packet time-table, yet nothing in the story of the fur-trade is more impressive or dramatic than that of the winter express which ran with a punctuality hardly surpassed by any of the mail-carriers in operation today. Butler had been told when he left Fort Garry in October that the packet was due at Fort-a-la-Corne, 500 miles from Fort Garry, about January 21. It arrived on January 22, the carrier having been delayed twenty-four hours by a blizzard of unusual severity.

Here at Fort-a-la-Corne, hundreds of miles from the nearest white settlement, Butler learned from a months-old newspaper brought in by the mail-carrier that Paris was still holding out against the Germans. There was still time, perhaps, to offer his sword to France, and his burning desire now was to reach Fort Garry as quickly as possible, write his report for Lieutenant-Governor Archibald and take ship to Europe. The journey along the northern line was adding little to what he had already learned; here in the forest and swamp lands the Indians were few, lawlessness the exception (the free trader preferred the plains country), administrative problems trifling compared with those met with farther west. So on and on Butler journeyed, hour after hour, day after day, on snowshoe and dog-sled through the bitter burning cold that now in the most savage time of year called upon the totality of man's physical resources to fight it. Movement, food, fire, sleep—these were the essentials of survival in the Great Lone Land where a man stood alone with nothing except his own courage, his own strength to depend on.

Near Cumberland House Butler came upon an Indian wigwam in which the inmates—an aged Indian, two women and several children— were mourning the death of the old Indian's son-in-law, a Métis named Joe Miller, who had died of exhaustion after running down a silver fox in the deep snow. 'He hunted for us, he fed us,' the old man said. 'I am too old to hunt. I can scarce see the light. I would like to die, too.' It was characteristic of Butler that he delayed his journey long enough to assist in the burial of Joe Miller, even to the point of helping to dig the grave in the frozen earth. His account of the interment reads in part like an echo of a poem once familiar to every schoolboy—*The Burial of Sir John Moore:*

We buried Joe Miller in the pine-shadowed graveyard near the Fort. Hard work it was with pick and crowbar to prise up the ice-locked earth and to get poor Joe that depth which the frozen clay seemed to grudge him. It was long after dark when his bed was ready, and by the light of a couple of lanterns we laid him down in the great rest. The graveyard and the funeral had few of those accessories of the modern mortuary which are supposed to be the characteristics of civilized sorrow. There was no mute, no crape, no parade, nothing of that imposing array of hatbands and horses by which man, even in the face of the mighty mystery, seeks still to glorify the miserable conceits of life; but the silent snow-laden pine-trees, the few words of prayer read in the light of the lantern, the hush of nature and of night, made accessions full as fitting as all the muffled music and craped sorrow of church and city.[14]

At Cumberland House, Butler saw for the first time a dog-team made up of true sleigh-dogs—two magnificent Esquimaux and two cross-breeds (Esquimau predominating)—and by this time thoroughly fed up with the recalcitrant and ill-mannered Hudson's Bay Company mongrels he had put up with all the way from Fort Edmonton, promptly spent most of the little money he had with him to buy the Esquimaux team. 'Cerf Volant, Tigre, Muskymote, Cariboo—they were splendid dogs all, aristocrats of the trail who pulled by instinct and loved their work. But among them Cerf Volant, the Speedy Deer who carried his fine curled tail like a panache, was from the first Butler's especial favourite and quickly claimed the right, never once abandoned, to sleep at night on top of his master.

At a place called Cedar Lake, Butler broke away at last from the dismal frozen swamps and marshlands of the Saskatchewan and swung south to Lake Winnipegosis and thence to Lake Manitoba, covering thirty to forty miles a day on the ice and hard-packed snow of the far-reaching lake surfaces. On February 20, 1871, he came at last to Fort Garry after having travelled 3,700 miles in four months. His feelings, when he passed beneath the familiar gate of the Fort were a mingling of exultation for a tremendous task well done and regret for an experience that could not be sustained indefinitely.

He who has once tasted the unworded freedom of the western wilds [he explained] must ever feel a sense of constraint within the boundaries of civilized life. The Russian is not the only man who has the Tartar close underneath his skin. That Indian idea of the earth being free to all men catches quick and lasting hold of the imagination—the mind widens to grasp the reality of the lone space and cannot shrink again to suit the requirements of fenced divisions. There is a strange fascination in the idea 'Wheresoever my horse wanders there is my home'; stronger, perhaps, is that thought than any allurement of wealth, or power or possession given us by life. Nor can aftertime ever wholly remove it; midst the smoke and hum of cities, midst the prayer of churches, in street or salon, it needs but little cause to recall again the wanderer to the image of the immense meadows where, far away at the portals of the setting sun, lies the Great Lone Land.

The report which Butler submitted to the Honourable Adams G. Archibald, Lieutenant-Governor of Manitoba, for transmission to the Dominion Government is remarkable in the accuracy of its information about the population of the North-West Territories, the number and distribution of the Indian tribal bands, the extent of the smallpox ravages and the value of prairie soil for agriculture. It is valuable for its suggestions about the best way of opening the Canadian west to settlement without unduly disturbing the Indians and, above all, the most appropriate means of establishing law and order throughout a vast area where so far no law existed. Butler emphasized that the Hudson's Bay Company could hardly be expected to do more than preserve order within and around the Company posts; and missionary enterprise was not, in his view, a significant civilizing influence:

Many of them (the missionaries) have toiled with untiring energy and undaunted perseverance in the work to which they have devoted themselves [he wrote], but it is unfortunately true that the jarring interests of different religious denominations have sometimes induced them to introduce into the field of Indian theology that polemical rancour which so unhappily distinguishes more civilized communities.

Specifically, Butler recommended the appointment of 'a Civil Magistrate or Commissioner, after the model of similar appointments in Ireland and India', who would be required 'to make semi-annual tours through the Saskatchewan for the purpose of holding courts'. The Commissioner would be assisted by the civil magistrates of the Hudson's Bay Company, and other such magistrates 'to be appointed from amongst the most influential and respected persons of the French and English half-breed population'.

More far-reaching in its consequences was Butler's recommendation calling for the creation of 'a well-equipped force of from 100 to 150 men, one-third to be mounted', for the purpose of maintaining law and order within the North-West Territories and bringing violators of the law to justice. Significantly Butler, who had visited American Army posts on the western frontier some three years earlier, rejected the plan advocated by some influential Canadian politicians and specifically referred to in Lieutenant-Governor Archibald's directive, that soldiers be employed to police the prairies. The men of the police force, Butler insisted, should be 'specially recruited and engaged for service in the Saskatchewan; enlisting for two or three years' service, and at the expiration of that period to become military settlers, receiving grants of land, but still remaining as a reserve force should their services be required'.

Butler's recommendation led to the formation, two years later, of what has since become the best-known body of law-enforcement officers in the world—the North-West Mounted Police.

What strikes a reader of the Report today is not so much the shrewdness of its recommendations or the accuracy of its predictions as its immense readability. In this sense it intimates things to come, for few of Butler's actions in later life gave greater offence to his colleagues and superiors than the introduction into reports and communiqués of a highly individual style utterly at odds with the colourless formality characteristic of the orthodox and approved official document. The Report to Lieutenant-Governor Archibald abounds in alliterative phrases, antitheses, extravagant imagery, genial asides and purple passages—all the devices and affectations in which Butler took unaffected delight; and it concludes with a peroration which is at once an impassioned prophecy and an appropriately unorthodox conclusion to one of the great documents in the history of Western Canada:

Such, Sir, are the views which I have formed upon the whole question of the existing state of affairs in the Saskatchewan. They result from the thought and experience of many long days of travel through a large portion of that region to which they have reference. If I were asked from what point of view I have looked upon this question I would answer—From that point which sees a vast country lying, as it were, silently awaiting the approach of the immense wave of human life which rolls unceasingly from Europe to America. Far off as lie the regions of the

Saskatchewan from the Atlantic sea-board on which that wave is thrown, remote as are the fertile glades which fringe the eastern slopes of the Rocky Mountains, still that wave of human life is destined to reach those beautiful solitudes, and to convert the wild luxuriance of their now useless vegetation into all the requirements of civilized existence. And if it be matter for desire that across the immense continent, resting upon the two greatest oceans of the world, a powerful nation should arise with the strength and the manhood which race and climate and tradition would assign to it—a nation which would look with no evil eye upon the old mother land from whence it sprung, a nation which, having no bitter memories to recall, would have no idle prejudices to perpetuate—then surely it is worthy of all toil of hand and brain, on the part of those who today rule, that this great link in the chain of such a future nationality should no longer remain undeveloped, a prey to the conflicts of savage races, at once the garden and the wilderness of the Central Continent.[15]

CHAPTER SEVEN

The Wild North Land

LIEUTENANT-GOVERNOR ARCHIBALD was delighted with Butler's report. He expressed the hope that Butler would remain in the North-West in an official capacity—perhaps as Commandant of the Territories—to supervise the implementing of the main recommendations of the report and in particular the establishment of a police force. Nothing could have suited Butler better, and it must be a matter of regret to Canadians that the eminent politicians whom he waited on in Ottawa—Sir John A. Macdonald, Sir George Cartier, Sir Francis Hincks and Joseph Howe—congratulated him on his excellent work, assured him of their lasting interest in his welfare and dismissed him from their doors and minds. In London, where Butler went after being summarily cold-shouldered in Ottawa, his reception was even more frustrating. The Colonial Office strongly recommended him to the attention of the Secretary of War, Mr. Edward Cardwell, but Cardwell flatly rejected Butler's petition for a half-pay company. After twelve years of conscientious and at times brilliant service for the Empire, Butler was still a lieutenant, and an angry and embittered man. Once again he had come, so it seemed, to a dead end. He could no longer make even the quixotic gesture of offering his sword to France, for Paris had long since fallen and now the city was torn by ferocious civil war between Government and Commune.

But he could still go to France, for his leave had not yet expired. In May 1871 he crossed the Channel, and by the exercise of cunning, diplomacy, personal charm and dogged perseverance, won his way to the heart of the capital. The stories he heard, the scenes he witnessed, were to haunt him thereafter for many years—in particular one story and one scene. The story, which he heard from an English surgeon doing volunteer ambulance work, reads like a condensation of de Maupassant: 'An old woman was found crouching under an upturned cart behind a barricade; the troops advanced thinking the barricade had been abandoned by everybody; the old woman shot with a revolver the first soldier who approached her. "I have had three sons killed in the fighting," she said, "and I swore that I would kill one enemy. You may shoot me now." They did so.'

The scene he remembered above all others, and which provided material for one of the finest passages of his *Autobiography*, was that of a woman riding in a cart past the Palace of Versailles to her death—the eternal revolutionary whom the bullets of the firing-squad might silence for a decade or a generation or a century, but never wholly destroy:

Presently we could see movement and commotion going on far down the broad avenue towards Paris. Troops were advancing up the roadway between the elm-trees; a wave of shouting and gesticulation accompanied them. The head of the column was soon abreast of where we stood—cavalry horses and men lean and hungry-looking, faces grimed and greasy, uniforms dust-covered and worn. Behind these came a great straggling band of Communist prisoners, men, women and children, ragged, fierce, powder-marked, streaming with perspiration; such people as I had never seen before, and have never seen since; faces at the last gasp of exhaustion; faces that looked scornfully at the howling mob of bourgeois, that shouting, racing crowd which ran under the elms on either side and out of the cafes, throwing vile epithets over the heads of the soldiers. At the end of this dismal column came the carts of the wounded. In one of these there sat, bolt upright, a woman in the prime of life; her black hair hung loose upon her shoulders, her olive face had a great gash across one cheek from which the blood was still flowing, her hands were tied behind her back; two or three wounded men lay at her feet helplessly stricken, but had there been a thousand dead or dying around her it would not have mattered. It was her face that held the eye. I have never forgotten the face and figure of that proud, defiant, handsome woman. The cart passed with the rest, but I followed it with my eyes while it was in sight, and ere it passed into the distance I saw the figure against the background of the great chateau as the terrible cortege filed away into the open space before the palace. There it all was, grouped, set, framed, and told as never pen could write it, nor picture paint it. Two hundred years of French history were there; the great King, the shameless Court, the wreck of France. And so, until after sunset the stream flowed on; the dirty, ill-horsed dragoons, the cowardly crowd along the sidewalks, the struggling, shambling masses marching in the roadway. Every phase of human age and misery was there; white-haired men of seventy, desperado boys of sixteen, old battered women, young girls clinging on the arms of wild-looking youths—all tired, hungry, blood-stained—this time the defeated ones in the everlasting strife between rich and poor, marching into the twilight. . . .[1]

When his leave was up Butler rejoined the 69th Foot in its new regimental depot at Chatham. Here his chief pleasure was not in soldiering but in writing the story of his experiences in the Canadian North-West which was later published under the title of *The Great Lone Land*. His *History of the 69th Regiment*, on which he had worked intermittently for six years, had been published while he was in Canada—a curiously stiff and stilted little work in which the author's personality rarely asserts itself. But *The Great Lone Land* is above all an intensely personal document—the work of an enthusiastic idealist proud of his strength, confident of his abilities, still young enough to feel himself immortal, overflowing with sympathy for his less-fortunate fellow men and resolute to break a lance with any and all of their oppressors. Butler was to write many books; but none other with quite the same freshness, zest for living and curiosity about all things under the sun which help to make *The Great Lone Land* a classic in the literature of travel.

In the spring of 1872 Butler's fortunes took a mild upswing. He was gazetted to an unattached infantry company—on half-pay it is true—the manuscript of *The Great Lone Land* was enthusiastically accepted by the first publisher he sent it to, and—miracle of miracles—oil was found in paying quantities on the land owned by the Horatio Nelson Case syndicate. From the sale of the land, negotiated by Case, Butler cleared one thousand pounds. There was no doubt in his mind about what to do with the money; he would apply for extended leave, return to the Canadian North-West and wander wherever inclination led him in the land which now claimed his affection as did no other part of earth.

It is difficult to escape the conviction that the underlying motive of his return was the need of reassurance, of testing himself anew against the indifferent forces of nature. It is hardly possible to explain in any other terms why Butler eventually chose to journey in the coldest months of the year far to the north of the region he had travelled through two years earlier, battling blizzards and temperatures of fifty degrees below zero, living on moosemeat and pemmican and sugarless tea for weeks on end, sleeping night after night in the great northern forest wilderness with no com-

SUNSET SCENE, WITH BUFFALO

An illustration from 'The Wild North Land' published in 1873

AFTER THE BATTLE OF TEL-EL-KEBIR. *From the painting by Lady Butler*

panionship except that of the half-breeds and Indians he engaged as assistants along the way. Butler was in his mid-thirties now, but the adolescent in him died hard; and he needed desperately to feel pride in physical achievement as compensation for his failure to win military distinction. His army career had so far earned him little reputation; but among the men of the Canadian North-West, whom he admired as he did few others, he held an honourable place. And in the back of his mind a plan was shaping—to take up land in the new country he had helped to open, and become one of the first white settlers in the valley of the Saskatchewan.

He followed the familiar route by rail across the United States as far as St. Cloud, Minnesota, thence north by stage-coach and Red River steamer to Fort Garry. At a small Hudson's Bay post in Dakota territory he went ashore with an acquaintance who wished to exercise two mighty deer-hounds he had brought with him from England. The deer-hounds were immediately set upon by a trio of bushy-haired Esquimau sleigh-dogs and ignominously overthrown. To his astonishment and delight Butler recognized the leader of the sleigh-dogs—the magnificent plume-tailed Cerf Volant, his companion and sleeping-bag warmer of two years before. On the spot he bought Cerf Volant and his fellow huskies, took them to Fort Garry by steamer and from Fort Garry ran them across 600 miles of prairie to the Forks of the Saskatchewan. Thither he had been preceded by his old friend, Captain Mansfield of the 69th, who had retired from the Army and was considering going into partnership with Butler in a ranching venture in the Saskatchewan River country. The partnership never materialized. It is possible that Mansfield did not share Butler's enthusiasm for pemmican and temperatures of forty degrees below zero and a degree of isolation from his fellow men which nothing in his previous experience could have prepared him for. In November the two men rode far to the west of the Forks and in the company of a party of Métis hunters stalked and killed enough buffalo to provide them with a winter's supply of meat and pemmican. On the return journey to the Forks, which occupied sixteen days, they did not meet a single human being.

Towards the end of January 1873, Butler set out on his perilous journey to the north and west. There was a sound enough reason for travelling in the northern forest country in winter-time. Then the rivers, in summer treacherous fast-moving streams flowing east from the mountains against boat or canoe, formed splendid frozen highways through swamp and muskeg and tangled deadfalls which at any other time of year were all but impassable. The route which Butler proposed to follow ran almost straight west from the Forks of the Saskatchewan to Carlton, thence north and west over Green Lake to Isle à la Crosse, through the valleys of the Clearwater and Athabasca Rivers to Lake Athabasca, west again along the frozen Peace River to Dunvegan (founded and named by a MacLeod of Skye) and Fort St. John's, fifteen hundred miles from the Forks. At Fort St. John's, which he expected to reach about the time of the spring break-up, Butler planned to abandon his dog-sleighs and snowshoes and continue west through the Rockies by canoe, horse and foot.

The story of his extraordinary journey by dog-sled to Fort St. John's, on through the great defiles of the Rockies and across country to the headwaters of the Fraser River, thence by boat and stage-coach to the Pacific coast, Butler told in his book, *The Wild North Land*, published in 1873. Butler was himself the first to recognize the difficulty—which he was not entirely able to overcome—of avoiding monotony in a chronicle of experiences in themselves monotonous. 'To recount the events of each day's journey, to give minutely starting-point, date, distance and resting-place, is too frequently an error into which travellers are wont to fall', he wrote a little pontifically.

I have read somewhere in a review of a work on African travel that no literary skill has hitherto been able to enliven the description of how the traveller left a village of dirty negroes in the morning, and struggled through swamps all day, and crossed a river swarming with hippopotami and approached a wood where there were elephants and finally got to another village of dirty negroes in the evening. The reviewer is right; the reiterated recital of Arctic cold and hardship, or of African heat and misery, must be as wearisome to the reader as its realization was painful to the writer.[2]

Butler does not spare the reader 'the reiterated recital of Arctic cold and hardship', but what redeems *The Wild North Land* from dullness is his passionate interest in the world around him (the origin of the Indian, the role of the buffalo in the native economy, the history of the marten from the time of its death in an Indian deadfall trap to its reappearance on the shoulders of a London dowager, the size of noses as a limiting factor in imperialist expansion—'the Roman nose could not have withstood an Arctic winter, hence the limits of the Roman Empire'—and by his portraits of the men whom he met in the lonely posts lying thousands of miles beyond the boundaries of civilization. The work of these men—particularly the wintering agents of the Hudson's Bay Company, many of whom spent their entire adult lives in the gloom of the great northern woods—fascinated and appalled him:

God knows their lives were hard. They came generally from the remote isles or highlands of Scotland, they left home young, and the mind tires when it thinks upon the remoteness of many of their fur stations. Dreary and monotonous beyond word was their homelife, and hardship was its rule. To travel on foot 1000 miles in winter's darkest time, to live upon the coarsest food, to see nought of bread or sugar for long months, to lie down at night under the freezing branches, to feel cold such as Englishmen cannot even comprehend, often to starve, always to dwell in exile from the great world. Such was the routine of their lives. Who can tell what memories of early days in the far away Scottish isles of Highland glens must have come to these men as the tempest swept the stunted pine-forest, and wrack and drift hurled across the lake—when the dawn and the dusk, separated by only a few hours' day-light, closed into the long dark night. Perchance the savage scene was lost in a dreamy vision of some Scottish loch, some Druid mound in far away Lewis, some vista of a fireside, when storm howled and waves ran high upon the beach of Stornoway.[3]

The old men of the north held the same fascination for Butler as the army veterans he had listened to in youth. They were full of good stories, they had seen strange things in the long ago, they formed living links with the past. Men like M. Jean Batiste St. Cyr, descendant of one of the old Nor'-Westers set adrift by the merger of the two great fur-trading companies, himself a faithful servant of the Hudson's Bay Company who still preserved the manners and observed the courtesies, inherited from his fur-trading forebears, which Butler looked upon as instinctive with the French people; or like the aged pensioner of the Company living out his last years at Fort Vermilion, who had come to the North-West seventy-odd years before and had looked in boyhood on the great explorers of the west—Alexander Mackenzie, Simon Fraser, David Thompson.

But of all the men whom Butler met in the North-West none proved a more interesting—or embarrassing—acquaintance than Dan Williams, commonly called 'Nigger Dan', a negro suspected of at least one murder, and greatly feared throughout the Peace River Country. Dan claimed squatter's rights to a piece of land on which the Hudson's Bay Company factor of Fort St. John's had begun the erection, in Dan's absence, of a new Company building. On his return Dan threatened to defend his property with a rifle. To Butler's acute embarrassment both the factor and Dan Williams appealed to him, in his capacity of Justice of the Peace for Rupert's Land and the North-West Territories—a commission never revoked—to settle the dispute between them. Butler's adjudication is a masterpiece of diplomatic evasion and deserves to be quoted in full:

JUDICIAL MEMORANDUM

Various circumstances having occurred in the neighbourhood of the Hudson's Bay Fort, known as St. John's, on the Peace River, of a nature to lead to the assumption that a breach of the peace is liable to arise out of the question of disputed ownership in a plot of land on the north side of the river, on which the Hudson's Bay Company have erected buildings to serve as their future place of business, and on which it is asserted one Daniel Williams, a person of colour, formerly lived, this is to notify all persons concerned in this question, that no belief of ownership, no former or present possession, will be held in any way to excuse or palliate the slightest infringement of the law, or to sanction any act of violence being committed, or to occasion any threats being made use of by any of the said parties which might lead to a breach of the peace.

Executed by me, as Justice of the Peace for Rupert's Land and the North-West, this 22nd day of April, 1873.

SIGNED, ETC. ETC.[4]

Butler admitted that his judgement 'bore a striking analogy to diplomatic documents for which of late years the British Government has been conspicuous in times of grave foreign complications', with the difference that, whereas the government documents were usually treated with contempt by those to whom they were addressed, his judgement was received with every mark of respect. The word 'executed' seemed to make a profound impression on Dan Williams, and when Butler left Fort St. John's relations between the contending parties were verging on the amicable.

In a springtime of rare beauty permeated with a sense of renewed life all the more intense because of the ice-bound winter death preceding it, Butler toiled westwards through the immense defiles of the Peace and Ominica Rivers. For three days he and his companions, two half-breeds and a lively little French miner named Jacques, struggled unsuccessfully to surmount two miles of mad rapids in the sinister Black Canyon of the Ominica. By a stroke of good fortune they met in the Canyon a gold-miner, Pete Toy, who had left his boat at the head of the rapids and was portaging a load of supplies, bought at an inland mining town, downstream to his permanent wilderness camp. Toy treated Butler and his party to a mighty dinner consisting largely of delicacies drawn from the newly bought load of supplies—bacon, beans, and best of all the bread, dried apples and sugar for which Butler had developed a positive craving.

With the grocer in the neighbouring street and the baker around the corner [he explains] we can afford to look upon flour and sugar as very commonplace articles indeed; but if any person wishes to arrive at a correct notion of their true value in the philosophy of life let him eliminate them from his daily bill of fare, and restrict himself solely to moose meat, grease and milkless tea. For a day or two he will get on well enough, then he will begin to ponder long upon bread, cakes and other kindred subjects, until day by day he learns to long for bread; then the Bath buns of his earlier years will float in enchanting visions before him, and like Clive at the recollection of that treasure chamber in the Moorshedabad Palace, he will marvel at the moderation which left untouched a single cake upon that wondrous counter.[5]

After the meal Toy talked at length of the home in far-off Cornwall which he had left many years before. Some day, of course, he would go back. After he had made his pile. In the meantime—'You're really going to see the old land? Maybe you'll go to Cornwall, too? Well, if you should meet an old couple of the name of Toy down there, just say to them that you saw their son Pete, him as left them twenty years ago, out on the Ominica, and that they were as fresh in his mind as the day he saw them last.'

Butler knew that Pete Toy would never go back to Cornwall. He recognized in him the archetypal treasure-hunter whose purpose in life is not finding but seeking—whose El Dorado lies always just beyond the nearest mountain range.

Since Toy's boat was at the head of the boiling rapids and Butler's at the foot, the two men hit upon the expedient of passing the dangerous stretch of river by exchanging boats. On parting, Butler took from his scanty stock of personal belongings a heavy winter coat and offered it to the miner. Toy's face flushed. 'As payment for what I've done for you?'

Butler answered with the tact he was always capable of, but did not always exercise. 'No, as a token of your meeting a stranger in the wilderness and being kind to him.'

Toy, with matching courtesy, accepted the gift. It is an oddly moving little episode as Butler describes it, and its pathos is intensified by the knowledge that a year later Pete Toy was drowned in the same Black Canyon where he had greeted Butler and his party with the warmth and practical assistance which for Butler epitomized the hospitality of the wilderness man.

The story of Butler's subsequent journeyings is the story of a man and his dog. Following the spring break-up Butler had left all his dogs behind at Fort St. John's except Cerf Volant, from whom he could not bear to part. Thereafter the great husky ran free through the woods, leaving innumerable caches of bones and moosemeat along the way, pursued forest birds and animals with unquenchable zest and little success, guarded his master against the perils of the dark hours, and adjusted after some misgivings to water transport:

It was a completely new life to the dog. He lay in the bottom of the canoe at my feet, unable to persuade himself by any process of dog thought that he had a share in the locomotion of the boat; he saw the shore drift slowly by, and whenever an opportunity offered he showed unmistakable symptoms of a preference for the land; but on the whole he sat a quiet spectator of these new scenes, and under the combined influences of rest, genial atmosphere and good food, became rapidly rotund and philosophic.[6]

In June, Butler reached Quesnel, a mining town on the banks of the Fraser River 400 miles north-east of Vancouver. By 1873 the once-booming goldfields of the Cariboo were nearly played out; but gold-seekers still swarmed through the region and kept half alive the communities that had flourished a decade earlier and were doomed shortly to become lonely ghost-towns among the lonely mountains. (Quesnel, luckier than most, has survived.) Here Butler gave away to the wilderness men items of baggage which over the preceding months had become infinitely precious to him—'an iron cup and saucer, sacred to the memories of hot delicious tea-drinks in icy bivouacs; a copper kettle, black with the smoke of a thousand camp fires and dinted with blow of tree-stump and sled upset; blankets burnt and scorched by pinewood sparks on many a freezing night in far-away Athabasca'—and with his remaining goods packed in a small handbag boarded the river steamer heading south.

The Fraser is navigable for only a short distance at either end, and Butler and his dog were soon compelled to transfer from steamer to stage-coach. Cerf Volant disliked the stage-coach, on which he usually rode as excess baggage, but once hoisted to the top conducted himself with his accustomed dignity and decorum. So the two rode together, the man and his dog, from the goldfields of central British Columbia over the recently built and perilous Cariboo Trail that snaked along the wild and forbidding Fraser River Canyon to the mining town of Yale, near the Canyon's southern end, thence by steamer to New Westminster and Vancouver. From Vancouver, Butler crossed over to Victoria, where he was charmed less by the inhabitants than by the humming-birds which swarmed in their gardens. From Victoria, still accompanied by Cerf Volant, he made his way by steamboat and stage down the Pacific coast to San Francisco.

The summer of 1873 was drawing to a close when Butler, having parted from Cerf Volant in Boston, found himself again on Canadian soil. He was undecided what to do next. His journeyings had consumed most of the thousand pounds he had made from his oil-well speculation, but he did not want to return to England, for he still hoped against hope that the Canadian Government might offer him congenial employment in the North-West.

Once again, as had happened three years earlier, a newspaper dispatch which he read by chance determined his course of action. From the dispatch he learned that a military expedition under the command of Sir Garnet Wolseley was being sent from England to West Africa to punish the powerful Ashanti tribesmen for a variety of unspecified offences committed against their neighbours and the British traders on the Gold Coast. At once Butler sent off a characteristic telegram to Wolseley—'Remember Butler. Will sail by first steamer.'

When he went aboard the *Russia*, sailing from Montreal, he carried with him in his handbag the manuscript of *The Wild North Land*. It smelled not of the lamp but the campfire, for it was written in wilderness camp, in lonely Hudson's Bay Company posts, in hotel rooms and on trains—anywhere that it was possible to hold a pen and make an entry in a notebook. The *Preface* concludes with a note which is ostensibly an apology to prospective readers—'in truth there has been time for neither revision nor correction'—in reality an expression of Butler's wild enthusiasm at the prospect of military service now opening out before him, of an almost arrogant confidence in his ability to carry through whatever tasks might be assigned him, and of his passion for bad puns:

Long ere this story finds a reader I hope to be on my way through the mangrove swamps which lie between the Gold Coast and Coomassie. To others must fall the task of correcting proofs, while I assume my part in the correction and revision of King Koffi Kancalli, and the administration to his subjects of that proof of British prowess which it has been deemed desirable to give them.[7]

Happily for his peace of mind, Butler could not foresee that his next book would be sub-titled *The Story of a Failure*.

CHAPTER EIGHT

The Story of a Failure

PORTUGUESE MERCHANT ADVENTURERS opened up the Gold Coast of West Africa to trade in the fifteenth century. By 1750 half the countries of Europe had established depots along the coast where they traded guns, gunpowder, knives, trinkets and rum for gold, ivory and slaves. The coastal tribes of Elmina, Accra and the Fante Confederation traded directly with the European agents and acted as middlemen for the tribal empires of Denkyra and Akim, lying immediately inland, which supplied gold and slaves drawn by various routes from the interior. But by the eighteenth century the real power among the Gold Coast tribes lay still farther inland with the Ashanti Confederation—the creation of a handful of native leaders of military and political genius. The boundaries of the Confederation were vaguely defined by the branches of the Prah River on the south, the Volta River on the north and east, and open country lying to the west. The capital of the Confederation was Kumasi (in the nineteenth century commonly spelled Coomassie), a jungle city lying more than a hundred miles inland and rarely seen by white men.

The Ashanti were the Spartans of the Gold Coast. While the coastal tribes were being corrupted by glass beads and rum the Ashanti were building up a military force and a discipline which by the mid-eighteenth century made them the most formidable fighting force in the land. Every male Ashanti had his place in the machine, and when the call to arms went out he took that place with a precise knowledge of what was expected of him. The standard military formation of the Ashanti was complicated, but because of the superb discipline of its units highly efficient. Scouts led the way, followed by an advance guard, central column and rearguard, with flanking wing formations of five groups on either side, each group in the interests of unity and *esprit de corps* made up of warriors from the same tribe. The king invariably took the field with his army, but wisely left the direction of operations to a professional commander-in-chief.

By the beginning of the nineteenth century the Ashanti were the acknowledged overlords of the Gold Coast. Hitherto the British had experienced little difficulty in dealing with tribes who were reluctant to acknowledge the benefits of 'protection'. Now things were different. 'Whenever a village on the coast became bumptious', Butler wrote, 'the inevitable frigate cast the inevitable shell among the everlasting coconuts; the natives rushed out on the sands, then again rushed back into the forest; the marines landed; four goats and twelve fowl were captured, and the war was over.

> But it was a different story whenever the army of the Ashanti-foo came seawards from Coomassie. . . . Constant conquest gave to these negro hordes a bravery which is foreign to the African character. . . . To disobey the mandate of a chief, to run away in battle, to fail in the transmission of an order, were crimes punishable with death. 'If I go back in fight,' sang the soldier of the Ashanti as he went into battle, 'I die. If I go on I die, It is better to go on and die.'[1]

Tribal warfare on the Coast followed a predictable pattern. In time of peace the Elminas, Fantes and Akims were insolent to the Ashanti. They hindered Ashanti emissaries on their way to the coast, sometimes refused to surrender prisoners they had no right to hold in the first place, and sooner or later defaulted in the payment of tribute. Then the Ashanti war-drums would beat through the jungle, the mighty machine assemble and rumble down on the coast. The Ashanti would burn a few villages, carry off such women as took their fancy, exact heavy tribute from the coastal tribes and return home to live quietly until the next punitive expedition was called for.

The Ashanti did not always confine their raids to the native villages. Several times they had the temerity to attack British soldiers and marines garrisoning the coastal forts, and what was worse, defeat them by sheer force of numbers and complete disregard of casualties. But their most notable victory they scored fighting on their own ground. In 1825 Governor Sir Charles Macarthy, a stately, bearded and pig-headed Irishman who flatly refused to believe that the Ashanti would dare to oppose real soldiers, led an expedition consisting of a handful of British troops supported by a brass band and levies of coast natives into the jungle to punish the Ashanti for raids on tribes theoretically under British protection. The native levies all ran away at the first sound of gun-fire and what was left of Macarthy's force was quickly surrounded and all but annihilated. Macarthy himself was killed, his head cut off and his skull paraded once a year for many years thereafter through the streets of Kumasi. The Ashanti were seldom happier about the spoils of war than on this occasion; they were fond of music, and the band instruments delighted them.

The British Gold Coast Protectorate was not, however, entirely a fiction. When in 1871 the Ashanti, angered by the transfer to the British of the Dutch trading rights in Elmina and the loss of the substantial tribute paid them by the Dutch, threatened an attack on the city of Elmina itself, Mr. Robert Keate, the Governor of the Protectorate wrote that 'the wars in which they [the 'protected' chiefs] engage are their wars, and not the wars of Great Britain. . . . They must rely upon themselves for success in their wars and . . . the British Government is unable to make itself responsible for their defence in case they should prove unable to defend themselves.'[2]

Ninety-nine times out of one hundred Mr. Keate would have been right; this time he was wrong. Prodded by the Press, by innumerable societies concerned about the welfare of the black man, and most effectively by large business interests to whom the Gold Coast trade was immensely lucrative, the Government of Great Britain at last prepared to take strenuous punitive action to put the Ashanti in their place.

Many other factors, none of them easy to define in specific terms, helped to prompt the Government's decision. Undoubtedly the conscience of Victorian England was seriously disturbed by stories of Ashanti atrocities and the knowledge that the slave trade still flourished along the Gold Coast and indeed within the limits of the alleged protectorate itself. ('When sin ceases to pay', Butler wrote, 'we have a happy knack of finding out that it is wrong.') There was, too, a feeling on the part of many people, few of whom knew where Ashanti was, that the Ashanti were getting too big for their breechcloths and should be taught a lesson. British prestige was at stake; and, as Stephen Leacock has observed, nothing outraged the people of Victorian England so much as a blow in the prestige.

It was, of course, understood that the expedition to the Gold Coast should not constitute a burden to the taxpayer, whose conscience could not always be counted on to survive a conflict with his pocket-book. The original Government plan called for the dispatch to the Gold Coast of a select group of officers under the command of Sir Garnet Wolseley to organize the local tribesmen into appropriate military units, put some backbone into them and lead them to victory against the Ashanti. There was, however, the proviso that should the native tribesmen fail to develop the required backbone not more than two regiments of British troops would be sent to the Gold Coast to provide the essential hard core of trained fighting men. Mr. Edward Cardwell, the progressive and far-seeing Secretary of War, and Sir Garnet Wolseley understood one another perfectly. From the outset both men knew that the British regiments would be required and shaped their plans in that knowledge.

Wolseley's first step was to gather round him the group of brilliant subordinates who formed the Wolseley Ring—most of them radical military theorists and some already distinguished by their success and daring on the battlefield. Several of the men—Lieutenant-Colonel McNeill and Captains Buller, McCalmont and Huyshe—had served with Wolseley on the Red River Expedition, of which Huyshe had written an excellent account. Others of the Ring included Colonel Evelyn Wood, Major George Colley, Captain Henry Brackenbury, Major Baker Russell and Lieutenant Lord Gifford, all of whom were to survive the hazards of war and disease long enough to win high rank and many decorations.

In a sweat of excitement and impatience Butler reached London a few days after Wolseley and his staff had sailed for the Gold Coast. In accordance with Wolseley's instructions he followed at once aboard the merchant ship *Benin*, and was fortunate to survive the voyage. The *Benin* was a foul-smelling fever-infested death-trap, typical of many of the ships engaged in the Gold Coast trade; the liberal supply of round-shot she carried was used not for ammunition but burials at sea. Six sailors and the captain died on the voyage that carried Butler to the Gold Coast and were cast overboard in their shot-weighted hammock-shrouds into the Bight of Benin, whose terrors were celebrated in the old sea-song—'Remember, remember, the Bight of Benin—Few come out though many go in.'

The *Benin* touched at several points along the Coast and Butler went ashore at Freetown, Sierra Leone. 'It is by no means a lively place', he noted 'Its principal feature is its graveyard. Whatever may be said of its want of accommodation for the living . . . no exception can possibly be taken to the space allotted to the dead.'

Wolseley had established his headquarters at Cape Coast Castle, a former slave depot and fortress, one of the many studding that dismal coast, and there Butler disembarked, riding through the surf in a rowboat, on October 22, 1873.

At Cape Coast Castle all was bustle and excitement—Wolseley and his officers working with desperate energy to whip the native levies into shape and inspire them with courage to attack the small-pox-riddled Ashanti warriors, who, cowed by an enemy against which there could be no fighting back, were sullenly withdrawing across the Prah River into home territory. A thankless task, for the coastal tribes were not interested in fighting England's war for her. Glowing pictures painted by the British officers of the paradise that would prevail along the Coast once the Ashanti were soundly trounced left the natives unimpressed. Paradise was no good to dead men.

Wolseley's campaign was conducted in an extraordinary blaze of publicity, for the Press was represented in the Gold Coast by the most impressive battery of reporters ever assembled to cover a military campaign and tell the Commander-in-Chief what to do. Chief among the newspaper men was Henry Morton Stanley of the New York *Herald*, then at the very height of his fame. Brave, cunning and utterly ruthless, the man who found Livingstone was ideally suited by training and temperament to cover a jungle campaign certain to test to the limit human courage and endurance. Stanley's associates included Melton Pryor of the *Illustrated London News*, whose numerous sketches were to provide excellent visual coverage of the campaign; George Alfred Henty of the London *Standard*, a huge bearded man whose career as an immensely successful writer of juveniles was just beginning (the Ashanti campaign provided him with material for two books, one adult, the other juvenile); and the most attractive personality of the lot—Winwood Reade of *The Times*. Reade, a one-time medical student, had already made something of a name for himself as an African explorer and botanist. A gentle man whose faintly ironic view of life was tinged with melancholy, Reade observed the war and the men who made it with a clear-eyed detachment that none of his colleagues was able to match; and his *Story of the Ashanti Campaign* is the most reliable account of the war written by an eyewitness.

Wolseley, like Lord Kitchener after him, hated war correspondents and took malicious and childish delight in giving them false information. Butler liked and admired Winwood Reade alone among the correspondents, but took the curious view that his intelligence unfitted him for journalism:

In Africa men usually lose mental power to a greater degree than physical strength; but Reade had preserved intact all the great energies of his brain. . . . But his knowledge was almost too extensive for the work assigned him, and in his case the temptation to overstep the limits of a war correspondent was great. To record and not to teach, to tell what has been done, not to say what should be done; to picture the fight, the march, the bivouac, the life, the death of the soldier; all these are within his province.[3]

In the sinister shadow of the Castle, Butler came across a lonely tomb with the letters L.E.L. outlined on it in light-coloured brick. The tomb and the inscription called to mind the almost forgotten story he had heard many years before of Letitia Elizabeth Landon, a celebrated London beauty of the early nineteenth century and a popular writer of sentimental verse and fiction. In 1830 she married George MacLean, Governor of the Gold Coast, and, dreaming of yellow sands and blue waters and innocent children of nature frolicking beneath waving palm-trees in a kind of Golden Age, sailing with him to Cape Coast Castle. Four months later, broken by the squalor of her surroundings and the blatant infidelities of her husband whose taste ran to native women, she died, almost certainly by her own hand. Sight of the tomb in moonlight moved the tender-hearted Butler almost to tears: 'Here in this desolate wave-beat castle, by this dreary equatorial sea,' he wrote in an excess of emotion, 'was the end of all her genius and loveliness. She had pictured it herself—

A lonely grave
Just where a broken heart might be
With not a mourner by its sod—

and now the clank of guns and tumbrils sounded through the courtyard and the echo of the surf was blended with wilder sounds than the dying girl had ever pictured round her lonely grave.'

Soon after his arrival on the Gold Coast, Butler was ordered by Wolseley to proceed to the kingdom of Akim, 150 miles north-east of Cape Coast Castle, and from among the subjects of kings Kobina

Fua and Kofi Ahinkora—reputed to be the best fighters of the coastal tribes—recruit a force of several thousand warriors to strike at the flank of the Ashanti army as it withdrew across the Prah. It was the kind of independent commission that Butler always coveted, and almost beside himself with excitement and enthusiasm he at once sailed aboard a British gunboat for Accra, the coastal town which he planned to make his base of operations.

What he saw of the Gold Coast during his 150-mile cruise did something to subdue his exuberant spirits:

We rocked all night in the cradle of the deep and at daybreak were off Accra. Another big slave castle was here, and the huge bastions of yet another prison could be seen three miles deeper in the Bight, at Christianburg. The last glimpse seen of the shore after sunset on the previous evening had been of slave castles; and round that fatal coast-line, between the feverish forest and the yellow sand, they stand, now lonely and untenanted, with rusty gates and empty vaults, the mouldering monuments of two centuries of a gigantic injustice.[4]

Butler reached Accra, an evil-smelling town lying 'white and foul under a blazing sun', to find most of the citizens drunk as lords. They were celebrating not the arrival of Butler but the departure of an expedition up the Volta River some sixty miles farther east under the command of Captain Richard Glover of the Royal Navy. Glover, a veteran of the African jungles and administrator for the Colonial Office of the district of Lagos, had at his own request been commissioned by the Foreign Office to raise a force—in effect a private army—proceed up the Volta and from somewhere above Butler's proposed line of march strike west across country towards Kumasi. Nobody in Accra had the slightest intention of fighting anybody, least of all the Ashanti; but Glover, a firm believer in good public relations, had distributed rum in generous quantities; and Butler, as always in a sweat to get on with things, found the men whom he had hoped to recruit as bearers for his journey inland turning cartwheels and firing off their ancient muzzle-loaders while in the air.

It says much for Butler's leadership and powers of persuasion (exercised through an interpreter) that two days later he was able to march out of Accra at the head of a crew of hungover carriers convoying inland the goods he would need for the army he hoped to recruit from the Akim tribesmen ruled by Kings Kobina Fua and Kofi Ahinkora. Two days out from Accra he met a processional moving towards the coast. King Fua had smelled Glover's rum and was on his way to Accra to 'make fetish'—his euphemism for getting drunk. In vain Butler argued, cajoled, scolded, threatened and offered extravagant bribes in an effort to get King Fua moving in the opposite direction. King Fua took a practical view of the situation. He could fight the Ashanti next week or next month or next year, but Glover's treat might be gone tomorrow, and King Fua found the champagne which Butler pressed upon him insipid stuff by comparison with high-powered navy rum.

Butler repeated to Fua the speech he had already made in Accra to whip up the fighting spirit of the natives: 'We will fall upon the Ashanti as they fly across the Prah, driven off by the victorious English General. Let your chiefs and your headmen assemble; let your fighting men come together, let only cowards and women stay at home!' King Fua, a connoisseur of oratory, approved Butler's words and assured him of his co-operation on his return from Accra. In the meantime, why shouldn't Butler go back to the nearest village and wait quietly there until Fua joined him? 'Tell him that I can never go back,' Butler shouted to the interpreter. 'I must go forward. If he returns with me now he will become the greatest king that ever reigned in Akim; if he goes on to the coast he will cover himself with disgrace, and his name will be a byword.'

For the sake of Glover's rum, King Fua was willing to risk his good name. In a fury Butler stormed off into the jungle, determined now to play off his second king, Kofi Ahinkora, against Fua and humiliate Fua in the eyes of his own people.

King Kofi Ahinkora gave serious consideration to Butler's exhortations. He, too, was on his way to the coast to make fetish, but Butler, who was quickly learning the subtleties of jungle diplomacy, had had twenty gallons of rum brought up from his base at Accra. Butler urged upon King Kofi the importance of catching the Ashanti on the flank before they got across the Prah. King Kofi debated with his councillors long enough to make sure he wouldn't catch up with the Ashanti, and then, having recognized in Butler an innocent enthusiast ripe for the plucking, agreed to go along with him and assist in the raising of a mighty army for a march on Kumasi.

With his straggling crew of bearers, King Kofi and entourage bringing up the rear, Butler plodded steadily towards Swaidroo, King Kofi's capital, about sixty miles inland from Accra, which he hoped to use as a base for a subsequent lightning thrust to the Prah. The sooner he got there the better, for Butler had by this time conceived a genuine horror of the jungle; it was a world in all respects at opposite poles from the one he had so lately known and loved in the Canadian north-west:

Set in an eternity of sombre gloom, rests this huge equatorial forest. The day and the night are the same to it; noiseless rivers steal along under dense layers of tangled foliage; huge poisonous fruits fall down from lofty close-set trees, and lie beneath the undergrowth emitting noisome odours; great orchids hang over the pathway, spiral creepers, hundreds of feet in length, twisted like huge serpents, cling from tree to tree, and far down below the mass of foliage, amidst these tangled and twisted evergreens, beneath the shadow of the great grey tree-trunks, man moves as though he slowly picked his way at the bottom of some mighty ocean.[5]

To add to his sense of frustration and misery he came down with a violent attack of fever, and thereafter was plagued intermittently by severe bouts during the three months he spent in the jungle trying to form an army from men who had no intention of going to war. His once-powerful body wasted away; he was at times so weak that to his utter disgust he had to be carried by native bearers; and every fever-ridden night spent in some wretched jungle hut was an interminable delirium of obscene horrors. 'I now dreaded the approach of night, it was so certain to bring with it the fever', he wrote in the chronicle of his lonely campaign.

Oh, the memory of those nights! The sense of utter darkness that came upon one when the long hours rolled by and the hideous noises of the African forest sounded at intervals like echoes from some other world; for this grim labyrinth of trees, so silent under the sun, gave forth strange sounds at night; and as the small hours drew on, the shrieks of the sloth rang with dismal distinctness from the echoing vaults and mighty aisles of the forest, until over the fog and vapour the light of day struggled upward, the dripping trees seemed shrouded in smoke, and the night was at an end . . .

A year has gone by since that time, and yet the hideous reality of these nights of fever seems sometimes to live again. When the eyes closed in utter weariness the brain still saw; the gloomy arches grew to endless length; the fog hung over a vast dreary landscape; an endless, all-tiring toil oppressed the mind, and one woke to hear the scream of the sloth, the drip of rain on poisonous leaves, the rustle of rats in the palm-thatched hut . . .[6]

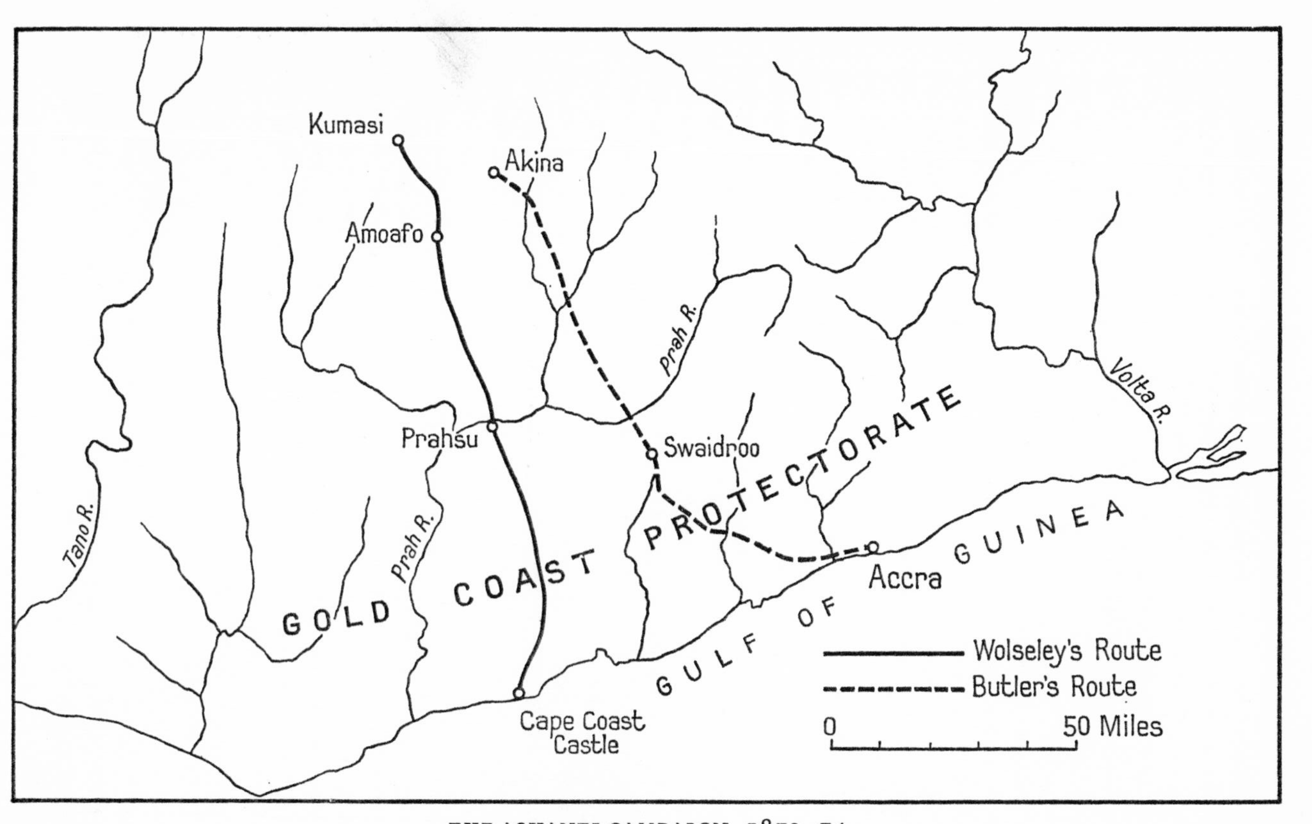

THE ASHANTI CAMPAIGN, 1873–74

But there was never any thought in his mind of giving up, or asking for help. Indeed, Butler's chief concern when the fever was at its worst was to conceal his condition from Headquarters, as Colonel Evelyn Wood was able to testify. While at Prahsu, Wolseley's advance base, Wood received a message from Butler asking him to investigate the alleged kidnapping of a tribal queen, an incident almost sure to cause serious dissension between the tribes involved: 'My Dear Colonel—The King of Accassi's Queen has been carried off by the Haussas and her chastity is in danger. Express messengers have arrived to announce her detention at Prahsu when tending plantains. Please do what you can to save her Majesty's honour—or the plantains, for I cannot make out which is rated at the highest figure by the King.' Reporting the episode, Wood adds, 'The messenger who brought me (the letter) handed me a slip of paper with the significant words, 'Please send me more quinine.' This was the only indication Butler gave of his being very ill.'[7]

No thought of giving up. Butler was under orders to try to intercept the Ashanti at the Prah and to the Prah he was determined to go. He reached the river after a month of agonizing toil through the jungle with a following of one chief, three scouts and twenty-six Akim soldiers. King Fua was still drinking rum at Accra and King Kofi Ahinkora had gone lame and was twenty miles to the rear. Fortunately the Ashanti had long since crossed the river and were deep in their own territory.

After enjoying a brief rest period at Headquarters, Butler returned to the jungles of Akim-foo to prepare for a final all-out assault on the kingdom of the Ashanti. Wolseley's plan of invasion called for a four-pronged attack to be delivered from widely separated points in varying degrees of strength. From the Volta River country far to the east Captain Glover was to advance with his army of Haussas which he confidently predicted would number many thousands; Butler, still hopeful of raising a strong force from among the Akims, was to move up from the south-east and cross the Prah at a point some thirty miles above Wolseley's line of advance; Wolseley himself proposed to lead the main attack with the British troops in a direct line from Cape Coast Castle to Kumasi; and on Wolseley's left Captain Dalrymple would advance with a native force on Kumasi from the south-west.

For thus splitting his forces Wolseley was afterwards taken to task by Winwood Reade, the *Times* correspondent:

A weak auxiliary force may be of use if added to the main body [Reade wrote] but can be of no use if separated from it. Either it will not draw a large body from the enemy, in which case it might as well be at home; or it *will* draw a large body, and in that case would be destroyed. . . . Sir Garnet's method was the worst that could be conceived. His main body was quite strong enough to fight all the Ashantis in the kingdom; and by dangling a weak body of men as bait to draw off part of the Ashanti army he imperilled the lives of the officers employed.[8]

Butler naturally approved Wolseley's plan, since it gave him an opportunity to redeem his earlier failure. Partially restored to health and this time accompanied by three fellow officers, he plunged back into the jungle. His companions came down at once with fever and Butler was left to carry on almost single-handed. Once again he exhorted, bullied, bribed—with little more success than before. But in one sense at least he could claim to be foremost in the fight. Wolseley had fixed January 15 as the date on which the four armies converging on Kumasi should cross the Prah River. On January 15 Captain Glover was floundering in the jungle many miles to the east with an army of a few hundred natives rather than the many thousands he had expected to lead; Wolseley was still thirty miles south of the Prah, and Captain Dalrymple had been unable to make a move of any kind. Only Butler kept the appointed date. On January 15 he stood on the south bank of the Prah at the head of an army of two hundred Akim warriors. He delivered a congratulatory address, then gave orders to cross the river into Ashanti territory. No one moved. No one had any intention of moving.

'Then we shall cross alone,' Butler roared. 'It is the day named by the English general; his orders must be obeyed.'

Solemnly Butler and his two fellow officers, Lieutenant McGregor and Surgeon Lowe, stripped to their pelts and waded into the river. The water rose to their chins, but no higher, and presently the three stark naked officers emerged from the river and scrambled up the north bank. The Akims stared and stayed where they were.

'The sight was certainly a curious one,' Butler commented. 'Three white men and six native policemen carrying baggage had invaded Ashanti.'

Almost immediately after the crossing recruiting picked up, and Butler dared to hope that the Akims had been sufficiently impressed by the resolution of the British officers to risk following them on the road to Kumasi. Within a few days he had assembled on the north bank of the Prah an army numbering several hundred men and no fewer than three kings—including Fua who had heard that Butler was carrying a keg of rum. The soldiers were not a warlike-looking lot. One of them was prepared to take the field armed with an old flint-gun and dressed in an empty gin-bottle—'The gun was balanced upon his head; the bottle was worn after the manner of the old Hussar jacket, suspended from the left shoulder'—but everyone showed such a lively spirit that Butler allowed himself to dream of marching into Kumasi at the head of his own little army, which he was sure would shortly number at least two thousand men.

A small party given by the British officers for the three kings was a roaring success. Butler broached a demijohn of rum and Surgeon Lowe played 'Love is Like a Cup of Tea'—the one piece he knew—several times on his banjo.

While Butler was busy recruiting warriors on the banks of the Prah, Wolseley was moving up fast from Cape Coast Castle. His staff officers had worked with extraordinary energy to establish an advance base at Prahsu, sixty miles from Kumasi, and by the time the troops from England were ready to march through the jungle a parade ground, Headquarters building, staff huts, hospital, mess, press office and flower-garden stood on the south bank of the swift-flowing muddy Prah. Getting supplies up to the advance base and keeping them coming once the troops were on the move were among Wolseley's most serious technical problems. He solved them by the use of impressed labour. Able-bodied natives of both sexes, including 150 women and girls from the Cape Coast Wesley-an Mission, were forced into service, if need be at gun-point. Villages housing deserters were burned, and the punishment in-flicted on the deserters themselves was often brutal. It is difficult to escape the conclusion that many of the coastal tribesmen must have longed for the good old days when they had from time to time faced the threat of violent death, but never from overwork. Wolseley was further inspired to place Major George Colley in charge of transport. Colley was perhaps the most talented officer of the Ring, and the success of the campaign owed more to his work than to that of any other man except Wolseley himself.

The British troops—two battalions of the 1st West India Regi-ment, one battalion each of the Royal Welch Fusiliers, Black Watch and Rifle Brigade, units of the Royal Engineers, Royal Artillery and Royal Marines, and a small naval brigade from the Cape Coast Squadron—reached Prahsu in good heart and health, but almost immediately the jungle climate began to take its toll. Five of Wolseley's officers, including Captain George Huyshe, author of *The Red River Expedition*, were already dead, others had been invalided home, and now the newly arrived troops were going down like nine-pins. Since the Ashanti king, Kofi Karikari, had shown no interest in the terms Wolseley offered him (withdrawal of the British troops and the signing of a peace treaty upon the payment by the Ashanti of an indemnity of 50,000 ounces of gold, the release of all prisoners and the delivery to Wolseley of a number of hostages of high rank), it became imperative to drive with all speed along the ancient jungle track to Kumasi before illness crippled the white battalions.

On January 31 Wolseley's little army—native scouts under Lord Gifford leading the way, the Black Watch in the place of honour immediately behind the scouts—joined battle with the Ashanti at a village called Amoafo about twenty miles short of Kumasi. In all respects but one the odds heavily favoured the Ashanti. They were fighting on home ground; their battle formation was ideally suited to the jungle environment, and they outnumbered Wolseley's men by at least five to one. But the one respect in which the odds were against them easily outweighed all the others. The British fought with rockets, artillery and breech-loading Snider rifles, the Ashanti with muzzle-loaders almost totally ineffective except at close range. During the campaign nearly every British soldier was hit by one or more Ashanti slugs (Wolseley himself was bowled over at Amoafo), but the loss of life was negligible. At Amoafo two Highlanders were killed and no fewer than 105 wounded. So long as the British troops were able to maintain a semblance of discipline, so long as they followed Wolseley's celebrated injunction, 'Fire low, fire slow', victory was certain. The Ashanti fought with skill and great bravery; they tried to employ their usual tactics, 'ambuscade after ambuscade with ever-increasing numbers and a constantly decreasing pursuit', but this time the pursuit constantly increased, the Ashanti died in hundreds and in the end left the enemy master of the field.

It is significant that both sides in the Ashanti war fought with weapons supplied by British armament-makers. During the actual course of the war itself, guns and gunpowder were delivered from British merchant ships to the Ashanti. An attempt to prohibit such deliveries was dismissed as a proposed 'restriction upon the commerce of this country entirely new in international law and most difficult to carry out.'

Amoafo was a wild and confused conflict. Even the war correspondents took part in it, Winwood Reade at the front with the Highlanders, and Stanley in Amoafo itself when the village was under attack.

A thoroughly good man [Wolseley wrote of Stanley in an excess of good fellowship and clichés]. Time after time as I turned in his direction I saw him go down to a kneeling position to steady his rifle as he plied the most daring of the enemy with never-failing aim. . . . I can still see before me the close-shut lips and determined expression of his manly face, which—when he looked in my direction—told plainly I had near me an Englishman in plain clothes whom no danger could appal. Had I felt inclined to run away, the cool, firm, unflinching manliness of that face would have given me fresh courage.[9]

But the eyewitness accounts of the correspondents are as confused as the fighting itself; in truth no man could give a clear picture of a battle which quickly became a series not of conventional military manouevres but of group or individual conflicts in which every man fought for himself.

The Ashanti were badly hurt but far from beaten. Almost immediately after the battle they began re-forming in strength between Amoafo and Kumasi, and large bands were detached from the main body to slip in behind Wolseley's army and harass his precious supply line from the coast. Food was running low, but ammunition was in good supply, and for once Wolseley decided to gamble. Without waiting for further supplies to come up from the coast, he placed his troops on short rations and prepared to drive with all speed to Kumasi, now only fifteen short miles away, and trust to the fall of the city to break the spirit of the Ashanti.

In the meantime Butler was making excellent progress towards Kumasi with his little force, in a line running almost parallel with that of Wolseley's advance. At a village nearly thirty miles north of the Prah and deep in Ashanti territory his men beat off a night attack, killing three of the enemy with no loss to themselves. It was later revealed that the attackers were not Ashanti at all but part of Glover's army of natives advancing from the east. Butler, unaware of the mistake, was delighted with the way his men had behaved under fire. The three kings seemed braced, too—even Fua, who now 'wanted only a demijohn of rum to set up his standard within four miles of the nearest skirmish'.

By January 30 Butler had hustled his army as far as the village of Akina fifteen miles south-east of Kumasi and less than ten from the advance units of Wolseley's force. A party of scouts brought him word of a strong concentration of Ashanti between Akina and Kumasi, and like the warhorse in Job he scented battle from afar and figuratively pawed the ground. At this point the three kings, who had also learned of the presence of the Ashanti in the jungle just ahead, decided that it was time to go home. They had got everything possible out of their young white friend—the rum had run out a day or two earlier—and they were lonely for their wives. On the afternoon of January 30, the day before the battle of Amoafo, Butler sat on a hill outside Akina, his head in his hands, and watched his Akim warriors do an about-face and go quietly back to where they had come from.

It was the bitterest hour of his life. All his devoted if sometimes misdirected work of the past three months, work carried on in ill health and loneliness and sometimes great peril, was in an hour cancelled out as if it had never been; and now there was nothing left for him to do but make his way to Prahsu and report to Headquarters his humiliating failure.

It does not seem to have occurred to him—as it certainly did to the three kings—that had he and his Akims actually taken the field against the Ashanti neither he nor the Akims would have left it alive.

At Prahsu he learned that the battle of Amoafo had been fought and at once hurried north along the line of Wolseley's advance, hoping to be in at the death. But Kumasi had already fallen, and Wolseley, having plundered and burned the city, was already moving back towards the coast. King Kofi Karikari had declined to make terms, and Wolseley's withdrawal from Kumasi might have become a desperate retreat except for an extraordinary stroke of luck which made Captain Richard Glover, R.N., one of the heroes of the campaign and forced the Ashanti to sue for peace.

Glover's march through the jungle from the east at the head of a small army of tribesmen from the Volta River country had been even less impressive than Butler's. But the day after the fall of

Kumasi, Ashanti warriors lurking in the jungle east of the burning city made contact with Glover's scouts, and King Kofi, leaping to the wholly erroneous conclusion that a second great army was advancing against him from the east, informed Glover that he was ready to make terms. Glover immediately dispatched Captain Reginald Sartorious to Headquarters, and Sartorious, after a hazardous jungle journey, communicated to Wolseley the information which enabled him to bring the Ashanti campaign to a triumphant conclusion.

Poor Butler's cup of bitterness was full. A fluke had given to Glover—whom he didn't like very much—a most extraordinary success, made him the hero of the hour. At Headquarters, Butler and the officers who had been with him during his last weeks in the jungle emanated gloom in the midst of general good cheer. 'For several days not one of them smiled, or made a good-natured remark of any kind', Winwood Reade, an amused and sympathetic observer, reported. 'And it certainly was most mortifying to be so near success, and then to be thrown back into failure by these useless savages.'[10]

Among the Ashanti it was customary for a war-chief defeated in battle to sit on a keg of gunpowder and blow himself up. Fortunately no keg of gunpowder was available at Headquarters or Butler might have been tempted to follow the Ashanti custom.

The tawdry little war was over, but not Butler's sufferings. Indeed, for him the worst was yet to come. Hardly had he reached Cape Coast Castle preparatory to embarking for home when he was stricken by an attack of fever far more virulent than anything he had suffered in the jungle. He was at once taken on board an ancient ill-ventilated steamer doing duty as a hospital ship and bedded down in a swing-cot in a steaming hot room already overcrowded with the sick and dying.

After ten days of raging fever and delirium he fell into a coma and was pronounced dead. Although unable to move or make a sound he was dimly aware that the pronouncement was premature. 'All the time', he reports, 'there was a curious indistinct idea in my brain that it was not as people supposed; that I was still conscious and even that I was being carried by invisible hands, or being floated on towards a great cloud-veil, the passing through which it seemed was to be the final passage out of life.' He did not pass through the cloud-veil; instead he lay listening in horror to the talk of the men who had come to wrap him in his hammock-shroud. One of the men, to whom the bodies of fever victims were by now a familiar sight, noticed something odd about the alleged corpse and insisted that a doctor be called. Signs of life were detected and Butler was at once hurried back to the sickbay. But for a long time the fever and delirium persisted, and he arrived back in England a ghastly caricature of the superbly conditioned athlete who had gone into the jungle five months before.

In Netley Military Hospital, where he lay for the next two months, Butler was nursed back towards health by his sister Frances. Fanny Butler was eccentric and devout, and according to a family legend swore, at a time when Butler's condition was still grave, that she would gladly give up her hearing in exchange for her brother's life. The offer met favour in the eyes of the Almighty. Butler recovered and Fanny was struck deaf.

Butler was greatly aided in his fight to live by the knowledge that his services on the Gold Coast had not been overlooked. He was given a majority and a C.B. and Queen Victoria herself visited him in hospital. Most gratifying of all was the honourable mention given him in Wolseley's dispatches: 'So far as the interest of the expedition under my orders are concerned,' Wolseley wrote immediately after the fall of Kumasi, 'Captain Butler has not failed, but most successfully achieved the very object which I had in view in detaching him for the work he so cheerfully and skilfully undertook. He has effected a most important diversion in favour of the main body, and has detained before him all the forces of one of the most powerful chiefs.'

The *Illustrated London News* reflected the general feeling of the Press towards Butler and his work:

The General's candid and considerate remarks . . . upon the merits of Captain Butler . . . should go to the hearts of all who desire justice above every other quality, in a superior commander. The Duke of Cambridge, in his express mention of Captain Butler in the House of Lords on Monday, proved that this beneficial spirit of fair appreciation is cherished at the Headquarters of our noble Army. The unsuccessful, indeed, are not always the least deserving, or the least competent to achieve high success with more favourable conditions. It is a most encouraging sign for the public service, and an agreeable trait of character in one so fortunate, while so prudent and skilful as the General commanding this Ashanti Expedition, that the services of Captain Butler should have been thus frankly acknowledged. We have been the more inclined to dwell upon the case of this officer, because the home staying and reading English public is indebted to him . . . for two delightful books, *The Great Lone Land* and *The Wild North Land*, which, we hope, will not be his last narrative of adventurous travel.[11]

Butler deserved no less honour than he received. In his dealings with the Akims he had made many mistakes. He had been over-confident, he had absurdly underestimated the shrewdness and intelligence of the natives, and he had made promises to them which could not possibly have been fulfilled; but under the most wretched conditions he had displayed qualities of courage and perseverance and imagination deserving of better things than the wreck of all his hopes. Winwood Reade, who was not given to praising indiscriminately, said of Butler, and said truly, 'No man could have done more than he did; few men could have done so much.'

From Netley Hospital, Butler, still barely able to walk, went to the west coast of Ireland, and among the Kerry Hills felt the quickened renewal of life in the almost burnt-out shell of body. A Ballycarron tenant who was an old fishing companion came to see him and urge his return to Tipperary that he might breathe again the glorious life-giving air blowing down from the Glen of Aherlow —'Had not Father Maher, the Coadjutor, been to Rome and Asia Minor and them northern parts, and didn't he give it up, for goodness, to the air on Ballycarron Bridge?' Butler chose, however, to remain in Kerry. There, during his long convalescence, he read a great deal, followed with interest the newspaper accounts of the spectacular successes of a young lady named Elizabeth Thompson whose painting, *The Roll Call*, was the sensation of the 1874 Academy, wondered idly if Miss Thompson would marry him supposing he ever had a chance to ask her—and when his hand was steady enough began the writing of another book.

Akim-foo: The Story of a Failure was published in 1875. The sub-title anticipates not only the contents of the book but its publishing history, for it was much less successful than either *The Great Lone Land* (by 1875 in its fifth printing) or *The Wild North Land*. The truth was that by the time *Akim-foo* appeared the reading public were sick to death of the Ashanti war. During the actual campaign the newspaper coverage had been immensely detailed; and by 1875 Wolseley had written voluminously of the campaign in various military and popular journals, Major Brackenbury had written a semi-official two-volume history, and the correspondents, Stanley, Reade and Henty, had published their eyewitness accounts. Besides, no one in the optimistic Victorian era was much interested in the story of a failure.

None the less, *Akim-foo* was the best book to come out of the war. It is an intensely personal document; and the author's concentration on himself at the centre of his jungle world gives the book an artistic unity and a compression which communicate with genuine power his hatred of the jungle environment and his bitterness towards the natives whom he felt had betrayed him.

Akim-foo is not the history of a military campaign; it is a vivid and passionate account of one man's journey through a private hell.

For his ferocious indictment in *Akim-foo* of the African negro Butler later made handsome apology. In his autobiography he wrote:

Looking back now upon that big forest, with its days of disappointment, its nights of sickness . . . I can perceive much that I did not discern then. I see much that was good and human in these poor black savages—true and faithful service, patience, honest dog-like fidelity. After all, we were expecting too much from these Coast negroes. Firstly, we expected that they would accept as truth everything we told them, but why should they? For three or four hundred years the white man had robbed, tricked and enslaved them. . . . What reason was there now that they should think honest, truthful men had all at once come among them, whose words they were to believe at the first sound? . . . Secondly, we expected to find among them habits of punctuality, obedience to command, order and even discipline, which we had been accustomed to at home; but surely this was wrong. It was our drink, our trade, our greed, which had hopelessly demoralized the native African. We wrung our wealth out of his sweat, we drugged him with our drink; we shot him with our guns; we sold him powder and lead, so that he might shoot and enslave his fellow-blacks. These castles along the coast were the monuments of our savage injustice to him.

Thirdly, we were wrathful with the tribes of the coast because they did not at once turn out and fight the Ashanti at our bidding. In this, too, we were looking for more than we had a right to expect. When the Ashanti had come down upon the tribes six months earlier, the help we had been able to give those tribes against their enemies had been of the feeblest sort. . . . Why, then, should they have rushed at our bidding into a fray which had already proved disastrous to them?[12]

There is a pleasing little footnote to the story of Butler's Gold

Coast adventure. A few years ago several young gentlemen from the Ghanaian Embassy in London, all speaking impeccable English, paid a call on Butler's son, Lieutenant-Colonel Patrick Butler, himself a distinguished soldier. They were the descendants of the savages whom Butler had cursed and hated and eventually forgiven almost one hundred years earlier.

The young men from the Embassy borrowed Colonel Butler's copy of *Akim-foo*. They read it, they said later, with great interest and pleasure.

CHAPTER NINE

South African Interlude

FOR EIGHT MONTHS Butler lived among the Kerry hills. His convalescence was slow and painful, but there came the day when he ventured to leave the hotel in which he had been an armchair-ridden guest for several weeks to go snipe-shooting in a near-by bog. The tramp into the bog exhausted him, and when a snipe rose almost at his feet he was barely able to raise his gun to his shoulder. Somehow he got it into position, staggered back against a bank and fired. The snipe fell, and Butler knew himself to be a man again. Not because he had killed an unfortunate bird, but because he was once more a part of the world from which, ever since the end of the Ashanti war, he had felt strangely detached—more than once to the point of leaving it for good.

In February 1875 a telegram from Sir Garnet Wolseley reached Butler in Kerry: 'Come at once, and be ready to start with me for South Africa on Thursday.' Butler, true to his old form, was in London the next day. There he learned from Sir Garnet himself what was afoot. No campaigning this time in some dank and dismal corner of darkest Africa but a diplomatic mission to sunny Natal, where Sir Garnet was to assume office as Governor and High Commissioner of the Crown Colony. He had been allowed a staff of four of his own choosing to assist him in his new duties. The men he chose were all members of the Ring—Colonel George Colley, whom he regarded as 'the ablest officer in the Army'; Major Henry Brackenbury, impossible socially but a tremendous worker, a shrewd business head and a sound historian; Lord Gifford, a dashing hero of the Ashanti war to add glamour and social tone to the party; and Major William Butler.

Wolseley's appointment—which he accepted reluctantly, for he had no taste for politics—stemmed from the determination of Lord Carnarvon, Disraeli's Colonial Secretary, to unite the British colonies in South Africa, hitherto left much to their own devices, into a federation which would assure uniformity of government for all, simplify problems of administration and strengthen the authority of the Colonial Office. As a first step towards confederation Carnarvon sought to reduce the power of the Natal Legislative Council, which had recently passed a resolution calling for responsible government after the model of Cape Colony. It was, of course, theoretically within the power of the British Government to suspend the Colony's existing constitution, but to do so would be to make bitter enemies of the colonists, and Carnarvon preferred to gain his ends by guile rather than force. Hence the appointment of General Sir Garnet Wolseley, the Empire's hero of the hour, to the governorship of the Colony. His immense prestige was bound to make easier the delicate and complex task he had been appointed to carry out—that of persuading the Legislative Council of Natal to withdraw its resolution calling for responsible government, reduce drastically the scope of the powers it already held and place itself more completely under the control of the Colonial Office.

The Legislative Council of Natal was made up of fifteen members elected by 4,000 white voters (the 300,000 natives of Natal were, of course, without representation of any kind) and five members nominated by the Colonial Office. The five nominated members together with the Chief Justice and the local army commander comprised the Executive Council, presided over by the Governor. Wolseley quickly gained control of the Executive Council by the arbitrary tactic of giving certain sitting members compulsory leave of absence and replacing them with his own nominees. Colonel Colley thus became Treasurer and Postmaster-General, and Butler Protector of Immigrants. Butler had at first no difficulty reconciling himself to the work which lay ahead—that of stripping the Colony of much of its independence. The Natal Legislative Council had recently passed 'certain repressive measures against the natives which the secretary of state considered had been hostile to the spirit as well as the letter of English law'. Butler persuaded himself that one of the chief purposes of the Wolseley mission was to see that these repressive measures were modified or withdrawn.

Unfortunately for Wolseley, the fifteen elected members of the Legislative Council, representing the interests of the white colonists, could reject by a majority vote any resolution introduced by the nominated members. Wolseley, an autocratic dictator to his finger-tips, was inclined to tear up the old constitution and write a new one, but on being told by Carnarvon that such procedures would be neither legal nor wise, undertook to persuade the Council to raise the number of nominated members to fifteen, thus providing for a balance of power in the Council between nominated and elected members, the balance to be tipped, in the event of a tie vote, by the Governor himself.

It was then that Government House in Pietermaritzburg, the capital of Natal, became the centre of a dizzy social life such as the colonists, and particularly the legislators, had never before enjoyed or witnessed. Wolseley had decided that if he could not win over the hard-headed members of the Legislative Council by argument he could soften them up with champagne—and even more important, through the exertions of himself and his staff win the ladies to the cause. The London season at its giddiest, so one delighted matron affirmed, was drab by comparison with the goings-on in Government House; and even the Viennese might have envied the grace with which Wolseley and his aides whirled the ladies—particularly the legislators' wives—through the intricacies of the waltz.

Wolseley's tactics involved certain complications which he had not foreseen. Many wives and several of their daughters fell violently in love with the dashing young officers of the Governor's staff and this was fair enough. What Wolseley had not anticipated was that the officers should feel a reciprocal emotion, and his agitation was great when he learned that Brackenbury was carrying on half a dozen affairs concurrently (a gentleman arranged his affairs successively), and that Lord Gifford was actually proposing to marry a Jewish girl whose mother was 'a drunk'. Wolseley reported to Louisa that 'Major Butler has also another affair on his hands', but there is no evidence to suggest that Butler was at any time in danger of losing his head or heart. Wolseley himself was careful to avoid any sort of involvement beyond the purely social. Caesar himself, rather than Caesar's wife, must be above suspicion, and his behaviour was impeccable. But occasionally when a pretty woman behaved towards him in a 'demonstrative manner' he seems to have envied the liberty enjoyed by his staff. 'Indeed, grey-headed as I am,' he wrote wistfully to Louisa, in one of the few authentic flesh-and-blood utterances he ever set down on paper, 'I might have had a *rare high time* of it here.'

The Bill designed to bring the number of nominated members of the Legislative Council up to fifteen was passed by a small majority and Wolseley breathed more easily. He now prepared to carry out a second and more agreeable commission for the Colonial Office, that of visiting the hinterland of Natal to investigate local conditions, particularly among the natives, and make recommendations regarding taxation, defence, the administration of justice—indeed, all matters of interest and concern to both local and imperial governments. Wolseley took with him Gifford, Brackenbury, Butler, and, in the interest of public relations, a wagonload of champagne.

Gifford and Brackenbury were still in the throes of love-sickness, but Butler, whose succession of genial flirtations had left him entirely heart-free, was delighted to be on the move. Although he had spoken eloquently and wittily in the Legislative Council in favour of Wolseley's Bill—dismissing Mr. Winter, the editor of the leading opposition newspaper, as 'the Winter of our discontent'—he had later experienced some misgivings about the justice of depriving the colonists of most of the limited power they possessed. The journey into the hinterland in a great wagon drawn by nine yoke of oxen was an escape from a stultifying world of petty intrigue and corrupt diplomacy. And the landscape, like that of western Canada, moved him by its emptiness, its immensity, its previsionings of eternity:

The weather was perfect, the scenery not to be surpassed. Tower-topped mountains, ten and twelve thousand feet in height, snow-crowned and purple, rose as Natal's western boundary wall. Along the feet of these we travelled, each night's camp measured from the last night's one by the 'trek' of the oxen—sometimes ten miles, sometimes five, for there were many drifts to be crossed and hours were lost at some of them. But with our horses to let us rove in front or on the flanks of the transport wagons, the shortest day's trek often gave us the longest day of sport or rambling. June is South Africa's mid-winter, a season of brilliant sunshine and clear frosty nights; sunrises of great beauty, with snow-white mists rising from unseen river beds, and climbing slowly up the mountain's eastern face, thinning and dissolving as they ascend; evenings of still more perfect lustre when the sun has gone down behind the many domes and turrets of the Drakensberg, and the western sky above the serrated snow is one vast green and saffron afterglow.[1]

The best time of all came when Butler left the main party and rode off alone on a diplomatic and exploratory mission that took him to Bloemfontein, the Kimberley diamond fields and Basutoland. He was a man who enjoyed companionship but did not need it, to whom periods of solitude were essential, a withdrawal into the wilderness a means to physical and spiritual rejuvenation. There was, too, perhaps some sense of relief in being separated for a time from Sir Garnet Wolseley. To the end of their lives both men professed, in public, the utmost admiration for one another; but they were poles apart in temperament and thought, and here in Natal their views on the solution of the native problem differed widely. Wolseley recommended the immediate annexation of Zululand, the territory lying north of Natal; he approved the Boer method of coping with the natives by 'reducing them to manageable proportions', and denounced Bishop Colenso, the militant champion of native rights, as a meddlesome prelate who ought to be locked up. Butler believed that the Zulus should be left to themselves; he considered the white man's treatment of the South African native a crime against humanity, and he regarded Bishop Colenso as a 'brave and devoted soldier fighting an uphill battle against the greeds and cruelties of man'.

Butler rode through the defiles of the Drakensberg into the Orange Free State and on by post-cart to Bloemfontein, a five days' journey across a great rolling veldt dotted with herds of antelope. At Bloemfontein he had several long talks with President Brand, explored the town—then hardly more than a primitive rural village—and took particular pleasure in market-day, when the burghers for many miles around drove into the capital in their Cape carts and huge wagons drawn by many yoke of oxen. He was impressed by the physique of the Boer farmer and the astonishing number of children he produced. Ever since that night in the North-West Territories when he had surrendered his precious sleeping-bag to a mother and her eight-months-old child Butler tended to view all babies with apprehension.

From Bloemfontein, Butler continued his travels in a post-cart driven by a full-blooded Bushman with two half-caste Bushman girls as passengers. The first night out from Bloemfontein a savage storm broke over the veldt—thunder, lightning, dust, rain and at last snow. Butler had with him a heavy sheepskin cape called a 'karrosse', but characteristically he did not use it for himself. 'I could not allow the two wretched Bushman girls in the back of the cart to be cowering in the wet snow,' he explains, 'and the karrosse made them less miserable.'

Kimberley, in 1875 the centre of the diamond-mining industry in South Africa, at once fascinated and repelled Butler. It was a hideously ugly town built of corrugated iron and canvas, standing on a bleak plain in the angle between the Orange and Vaal Rivers and dominated by the great clay mounds surrounding the famous Colesberg pit. Twelve thousand negroes worked the Colesberg pit—twelve acres in area and 200 feet deep. All the violence, excitement and tensions of a typical mining-town were here; but nothing in Butler's previous experience of mining towns had prepared him for the variety of nationality swarming through the dusty sun-baked streets and crowding the bars. Englishmen, many wearing Old School ties, predominated—one of whom gave weekly poetry readings, mostly from the works of Alfred Lord Tennyson, to enthusiastic audiences in the tin-roofed ramshackle town hall. Cecil Rhodes, still in his twenties and already a millionaire, was in Kimberley at the time of Butler's visit, but the two men did not meet. Had they done so it is unlikely that they would have found any common ground, for Rhodes was the kind of ruthless entrepreneur whom Butler hated.

Although he found much of interest in the raw towns and cities of the Free State, Butler's chief pleasure lay in riding over country which, although young in European eyes, was already rich in history and folklore and in odd characters to be met with in odd places. In Basutoland, Butler crossed the table mountain called the Berea, once a native stronghold, where in 1852 the great chief Moshesh defeated a British force led by General Cathcart. A day or two later, after a nerve-racking ride on a tough Basuto pony up a narrow mountain trail, he found food and entertainment in the hut of a young Basuto chief named Letsika. He feasted on freshly killed kid, followed by the cakes and coffee which Letsika, on hearing that a white man was on his way to the kraal, had ridden ten miles to buy. After the meal Butler, Letsika and his young wife settled down to a literary evening inside the Basuto hut:

They had a Basuto Bible, printed in English letters; I had a story of Bret Harte's.

To Letsika's astonishment I read, letter by letter, his Bible, my pronunciation evoking frequent laughter; and to my own astonishment

Madame Letsika spelt out Bret Harte in the same manner, the . . . clergyman's wife having taught her at the mission school.

As the night closed, the literary entertainment continued by the light of a fibre wick floating in the grease of the fatted kid.[2]

And once, early in the morning, Butler came upon a lonely house in the foothills of the Drakensberg where an old man invited him to dismount and off-saddle. From the old man Butler heard the story, told by one who was himself a part of it, of the Great Trek of the eighteen-thirties, when thousands of Boers, dreaming of a promised land lying somewhere beyond reach of the outside world, moved up in their great covered wagons from the Cape to northern Natal and there came into contact with the Zulus. The old man had survived the time of blood when the Zulus had swept down on the scattered Boer laagers and killed hundreds of men, women and children—a time that earned for northern Natal the name 'Weenen' —a place of weeping. The unaffected kindness of the old man and his wife (who had been a child in one of the laagers at the time of the Zulu war) won Butler's heart. About the old Boer couple and the young Basutos there was a kind of Biblical simplicity and innocence perfectly attuned to the pastoral life—the kind of life Butler dreamed of for the displaced peasants of his own land.

But in spite of his warm feeling for many of the individuals whom he met and talked with in his wanderings through Natal and Basutoland, Butler was no great admirer of the Boer, His observations on the future of South Africa and the nature of her peoples, voluminously recorded in the notebook which was more precious to him than food and drink, are frequently pointed and perceptive. He recognized in the Boer a formidable fighting man, and in this he stood almost alone among officers of the British Army. A superb horseman, a crack shot, able to live for long periods on the scantiest of rations, the Boer, fighting on his own ground in mobile units, would be tough to beat. The Boer in peacetime was a less admirable being—lazy (to Butler sloth was the deadliest of the seven deadly sins), wasteful of land, unimaginative, often brutal to the natives under his authority. It was not love of the Boer that impelled Butler to do all in his power to avert the Boer War of 1899, but hatred of the forces which sought, so he believed, to dominate a free people.

In the long run, though, any clash between the white peoples of South Africa would be of little significance. 'The eternal black man is the only reality', Butler wrote—who even then foresaw the gradual unification of hitherto hostile African tribes, drawn together by community of suffering in utter hatred of the white man. And for this the white man alone was to blame:

When the wild man or the negro gives up his Great Spirit, his fetish, or his idol, and adopts the teaching of Christianity he also adopts the social standards of what we call civilization. Where does he find himself in that new scale? At the very lowest point, somewhere between the beggar and the pauper.

In nine cases out of ten we have taken, or bought, or tricked his land away from him; we have killed or chased away the wild animals that roamed over it; we have shouldered him out into the remote mountains or regions unfitted for our present wants. He learns our knowledge after a time; but it is only as a light held out to show him how miserable is the position he has accepted—the position of a Christian pariah.

He has been told a hundred times that this new religion meant brotherly love; that before God colour vanished and race was not known; and if he has believed the teaching how bitter must be the sense of disappointment with which he learns the real nature of the role he has accepted in the new creed and social state; how startling the discovery that this beautiful theory of the white man's love and brotherhood and charity to all men means, in the hard logic of fact, the refusal of a night's shelter under the same roof; means the actual existence of a barrier between him and the white race more fatally opposed to fusion, more hostile to reciprocity of thought, mutual friendship, or commonest tie of fellowship, than that which lies between civilized man and the dumb dog which follows him.[3]

Butler's plan for making the African negro—who, unlike the North American Indian, 'refused to die or disappear'—an independent unit in a civilized community was one recommended earlier by Sir George Grey—the breaking-up of the tribal system and the introduction of individual small-scale ownership of land. He acknowledged that the cost in the cause of humanity and progress might be heavy, but still much less than the millions already lavished on 'the old hopeless lines of punishment and repression'.

In his more pessimistic moments Butler was prepared to concede that any dream of a united South Africa, Boer, Britisher and native living peacefully side by side, must remain a dream to the end. An entry in his journal for 1875 strikes a chill note of warning: 'Thus far the white man's course has been marked with blood, and with blood must it be traced to its termination, either in their own destruction or in that of thousands of the population of South Africa.'

In 1875 such moments of pessimism were rare. South Africa gave little evidence, on the surface at least, of the evil times that lay ahead. With one significant exception. Already the diamond mines were bringing into South Africa the hustler, the sharper, the entrepreneur, the exploiter of the weak—men and forces whose presence was inimical to the old isolated pastoral way of life, and which in the long run were to render useless the work of all the eager young idealists like Butler, Colley and a score of others who were busy with their plans for confederation, native self-government, schools, roads, railways, hospitals—all the benefits of civilization and none of its complications. It was a time of hope—to be looked back upon with a wry smile and a pang of regret for the vanished illusions of youth.

Butler returned to Pietermaritzburg after an absence of nearly two months to find all the members of Wolseley's staff reassembled and working like mad on their reports: although Brackenbury and Gifford, much to Wolseley's disgust, still found time to pursue their favourite game. 'I do not know what the husbands will feel when we all leave.' he wrote to Louisa, 'but I am sure that several pretty wives will wipe their eyes.'

James Anthony Froude, the historian, was a guest at Government House in the course of a semi-official tour of South Africa on behalf of the Colonial Office. Froude found Butler a particularly lively and congenial companion; and Brackenbury reported, with some chagrin, that Butler got more into Froude's confidence and intimacy in a day than he himself did in six months. He offered the not-very-convincing explanation that 'in the woes of Ireland they had a subject of deep common interest to them both'.

At the end of August Sir Henry Bulwer arrived in Durban to take over from Wolseley as Governor of Natal. Only just in time, so Wolseley felt. 'I seem to be living on a female powder-keg', he reported to Louisa. He was appalled by what he saw of Sir Henry Bulwer's staff, which consisted of 'a leggy-looking youth not long, I should say, from school, who seems the picture of weakness and dullness. (Sir Henry) little knows what is before him if he thinks he can get on in Natal with such help alone.'

Fifty years later the leggy youth recorded his impressions of Sir Garnet's staff: 'Those of the staff whom I recollect are, or were—for I think they are now all dead—Lord Gifford, Colonel (afterwards Sir Henry) Brackenbury, and Major (afterwards Sir William) Butler. Of these the one who impressed himself most deeply upon my mind was Butler. He was a most agreeable and sympathetic man, who took the trouble to talk a good deal to me, although I was but a lad.'[4]

The name of the youth was Rider Haggard.

On his return from South Africa in September 1875, Butler went to the War Office as Deputy Assistant Quartermaster-General. His natural inclination was for a more active life, but the change of scene 'from the extremity of the circumference . . . to the exact centre of the system' was of immense value and not without interest. There Butler discovered the enormous complexity of the system which set men in motion over half the earth's surface, and the seeming futility of any individual effort, however intelligently directed, to simplify its operation. The War Office, Butler concluded, was 'a vast wheel . . . going round, and all men, big and little, were pinned upon it, each one bound to eat a certain set ration of paper every day of his life'.

The War Office building in Pall Mall reflected the confusion within its walls. It consisted of half a dozen ill-matched, ill-ventilated houses linked haphazardly together by dark passageways, doors cut in adjoining walls, and steps leading up or down to floors on approximately but never precisely the same levels. The interiors were as diversified and ill matched as the houses. They ranged all the way from 'the fine room of a ducal residence, where one saw walls and ceilings with medallions by Angelica Kauffman and Italian mantelpieces of the finest sculpture to the mean-looking lobbies and by-rooms of a silk-mercer's establishment'.

In this tangled warren Butler became aware, after one or two abortive efforts to encourage the simplifying of army kit, of those mysterious forces which in the face of enthusiastic committee reports, urgent board recommendations and vigorous advocacy by far-sighted reformers, defeated every effort to interfere with the *status quo*. One of these forces Butler soon identified as the army contractor, and it was then that he began his lengthy campaign 'to expose the evils of the contract system as it was practised and sustained by our army administrators'.

There was some compensation for the frustrations Butler experienced working in an institution as reactionary as the War Office.

His associates he found generally congenial. Several were boon companions of the Wolseley Ring—Herbert Stewart, Redvers Buller, Brackenbury and half a dozen others—but the colleague who attracted him most strongly was Colonel Robert Hume of the Royal Engineers. Hume in Butler's view was the real head of the Intelligence Department. He received a meagre salary, he had a large family to support and no private means; and his early death, so Butler believed, was the result of overwork: 'At the moment when Colonel Hume was finding brains and knowledge, geographical and other, for ministers and statesmen whose names figured largely in the European congresses that preceded and followed the Russo-Turkish war, he frequently sat late into the night at home working a sewing-machine to keep his children in clothes.' And Butler added bitterly, 'What a lot of splendid human steel I have seen cast on the scrap-heap in my time, in the fulness of its strength and usefulness, through the selfish stupidity of a system which never seemed to know the worth of any human material it had to deal with.'[5]

In the winter of 1876 Butler met Colonel Charles Gordon of the Royal Engineers, recently returned from the Sudan after two years in the service of the Khedive Ismail of Egypt as Governor of Equatoria. Recognition was instantaneous. Here, in the flesh stood the authentic Hero. The eyes alone were enough to suggest to Butler the quality of the man:

On the ocean one is able at a glance to discern the difference between the surface that has the depth of the Atlantic under it, and that other surface which has the mud of the English Channel only a few fathoms below it. A depth like that of ocean was within Gordon's eyes. I never saw thought expressed so clearly in any other man's.[6]

From the moment of that first meeting Butler's faith in Gordon's greatness never wavered. The two men dined together that night and afterwards talked for hours in the club smoking-room. Most of the talk was of the East. Gordon had that day received a letter from the Khedive Ismail urging his return to Egypt—and he did most of the talking. Of the Nile, the desert, the races of the lower Danube, the Far East where he had first won fame, the iniquities of the War Office and the ignorance of politicians. It was talk that was humorous, pungent—a new fever prophylactic would 'make a sack of sawdust sweat'—and phrased with such exquisite precision that Butler straightway conceded first place to Gordon among all the brilliant conversationalists he had ever listened to:

I never heard human voice nor looked into any man's eye and found similar tone and glance there [he wrote many years after the meeting], nor did I ever meet a man who had equal facility for putting into words the thoughts that were in his brain. You never had to ask for an explanation; the thing, whatever it might be, was at once said and done. That night was the only one in my club life in which I saw the man with the bull's-eye lantern come to say that the hour of closing had come and gone.[7]

In Butler, Gordon must have recognized a kindred spirit. Both men shared an individualism bordering on the eccentric, and a passion for social justice frequently expressed in words and deeds which in the eyes of the world were at best quixotic and at worst absurd.

Butler and Gordon never met again. But the most heroic efforts of Butler's life were to be expended eight years later in the effort to rescue Gordon from the death-trap of Khartoum.

In one important respect the two men were unlike. Gordon was by inclination and choice a lifelong celibate. Butler was not. On June 11, 1877, he married Miss Elizabeth Thompson, the painter of *The Roll Call*. Cardinal Manning performed the ceremony in the little London Church of the Servite Fathers. Sir Garnet Wolseley and half the brotherhood of the Ring were present; and Miss Thompson's fellow students from the near-by South Kensington School of Art scattered flowers in the path of the couple as they left the church.

CHAPTER TEN

Painter of Heroes

AH! THEY SHALL HEAR OF ME SOME DAY!' Elizabeth Thompson, aged twenty, wrote in her diary—prompted by the confidence of youth and the assurance of her teachers at the South Kensington School of Art that she was to an uncommon degree talented. But not even in her moments of most extravagant dreaming could she have envisioned the shape of the extraordinary success that was to come to her early in life, before she was out of her twenties—a success which by reason of its immensity, its completeness, was to imprison a genuine talent within a mould from which it was never able to break out and so prove, as early successes have so often proved, an agent of destruction. In 1874 Elizabeth Thomson, then aged twenty-eight, was the most talked-about woman in England. When she died in 1933 at the age of eighty-seven she was remembered in her obituary notices as a once-popular painter of war pictures whose work was without significance except as a reflection of the taste of a bygone age.

If freedom from convention is indeed a factor in the development of the artist, then Elizabeth Thompson and her younger sister Alice were blessed from the cradle. Their father, Thomas James Thompson, inherited a modest fortune, married Christina Weller, a young lady of some artistic talent—she played the piano brilliantly if not altogether accurately, painted what she called 'arts' and wrote verses—and after the birth of his two daughters devoted his limited energies to their education. The family led a pleasantly nomadic existence wandering about Italy on an extended Grand Tour, living wherever Thomas Thompson's wayward inclinations led—in pensions, villas, hotels, palaces, boarding-houses. Christina, who had little taste for domesticity, struggled inadequately with the housekeeping and let the children, who adored her, do as they pleased. Charles Dickens, a friend of Thompson's and a devoted admirer of Christina's, whom he had known when she was Miss Weller (and to whom he had once written some abominable verses), visited the family *ménage* in Italy and was shocked by what he saw.

I found them in a beautiful situation in a ruinous Albaro-like palace. Coming upon them unawares I found Thompson with a pointed beard, smoking a great German pipe, in a pair of slippers; the two little girls very pale and faint from the climate, in a singularly untidy state—one (heaven knows why!) without stockings, and both with their little short hair cropped in a manner never before beheld, and a little bright bow stuck on top of it. C. said she had invented this head-gear as a picturesque thing, adding that perhaps it was, perhaps it was not. . . . We had disturbed her at her painting in oils, and I have rather received an impression that, what with that and with music, the household affairs went a little to the wall. T. was teaching the two little girls the multiplication tables in a disorderly old billiard room, with all manner of maps in it.[1]

The letter is Dickens at his most conventional, but judged by even the most liberal standards the Thompsons were an oddly assorted household—Thomas James a dedicated dilettante ('loving literature he never lifted a pen except to write a letter', his daughter Alice wrote of him after his death; and added in what is surely one of the most innocently double-edged tributes in literature, 'the things he refrained from were all exquisite')[2]; and by contrast Christina, who refrained from nothing—overflowing, exuberant, a little blowsy both in appearance and talent, and, one suspects, doomed to suffer the tortures of frustrated ambition. If she herself did not suffer thus, one of her daughters suffered for her. 'Often I cried my heart out,' Elizabeth Thompson recalled, 'when through the open window, I could hear my mother's light soprano drowned by the strong tenor of some Italian friend in a duet. . . . It seemed typical of her extinction, and I felt a rage against that tenor.'[3]

Thomas James Thomson might himself refrain from all things exquisite, but he saw to it that his daughters were encouraged to develop their talents to the full. Alice from an early age wrote sensitive verses (she was to become the best-known English poetess of the late nineteenth century), and Elizabeth's peculiar skill lay in drawing. Thomas Thompson, whose knowledge of literature was extensive, could himself supervise Alice's development, but for

Elizabeth there were private teachers—a wide variety, for Thomas's nomadic inclinations died hard—and eventually the South Kensington School of Art where Elizabeth's chief rival for first place in various school competitions was a girl named Kate Greenaway. After Kensington Elizabeth studied in Florence and Rome, and gradually made a modest reputation for herself as a competent painter of animals and military subjects. The delightful flashes of humour which animate her early sketch-books she seems unfortunately to have repressed as she grew older.

In 1874 Elizabeth was commissioned by a Manchester industrialist to do a painting of a war scene for £100. She completed the painting, which depicted the roll call of a decimated British battalion after the Battle of Inkermann, and submitted it to the Royal Academy. It was accepted by the Academy and proved the sensation of the 1874 showing. Policemen were called in to control the throngs fighting elbow-to-elbow for a view of *The Roll Call*, and Royalty competed for permanent possession of the work. Edward, Prince of Wales, was a would-be purchaser, but lost out to his mother. The Queen, having had the picture abstracted for a few hours from the Academy so that she might study it in private, found that she could not bear to part with it, and the Manchester industrialist was persuaded to cede the right of purchase to Her Majesty.

He stipulated, however, that Miss Thompson must paint him another picture just as big as *The Roll Call.*

To crown Miss Thompson's success, *Punch* ran a cartoon showin the President of the Royal Academy remarking to the Academy banqueteers (all male), 'Shall we join the lady?'

Other popular successes followed—*Quatre Bras, The Dawn of Waterloo, The Defence of Rorke's Drift, Floreat Etona, Listed for the Connaught Rangers*, and a score of other once-familiar canvases dear to the hearts of the Victorian middle class, who loved pictures that 'told a story'. Even John Ruskin, in his Academy notes of 1875 (his first in fifteen years), joined the popular voice in praise of Miss Thompson's second big Academy success, *Quatre Bras:*

I never approached a picture with a more iniquitous prejudice against it than I did Miss Thompson's; partly because I had always said that no woman could paint; and secondly, I thought what the public made such a fuss about *must* be good for nothing. But it is Amazon's work this, no doubt about it; and the first fine pre-Raphaelite picture of battle we have had; profoundly interesting and showing all manner of illustrative and realistic faculty. . . . (It exhibits) gradations of shade and colour of which I have not seen the like since Turner's death.[4]

The Poet Laureate insisted that he must meet Elizabeth Thompson and her sister (Alice, now Mrs. Wilfred Meynell, had published her *Preludes* in 1875), and early in 1876 the two girls paid him a visit at his home in Aldworth. Elizabeth did not feel that the meeting was a success:

We first saw Mrs. Tennyson, a gentle invalid lady, lying on her back on a sofa. After some time the poet sent down word to ask us to come up to his sanctum, where he received us with a rather hard stare, his clay pipe and long black straggling hair being quite what I had expected. He got up with a little difficulty and when we had sat down—we two and his most deferential son—he asked which was the painter and which was the poet. After our answer, which struck me as funny as though we ought to have said, with a bob, 'Please, sir, I'm the painter,' and 'Please, sir, I'm the poet,' he made a few commonplace remarks in a sepulchral bass voice.[5]

Tennyson offered to read to the girls, and Alice annoyed him by asking for *The Passing of Arthur* instead of one of his more recent poems. Afterwards he walked with the girls in the garden and poked heavy-handed fun at Elizabeth's fashionably tight skirt. Elizabeth was not amused, least of all when Tennyson explained her enthusiasm for military subjects on the grounds that she was just as eager for the sight of a handsome officer as any of Miss Jane Austen's giddy young ladies.

Great popular success in the arts almost invariably provokes an equally great reaction; and today Elizabeth Thompson's paintings gather dust in army messes, gallery store-rooms and lonely palace corridors. But the naïve romanticism of her subject-matter should not obscure her technical skill—Millais cited her draughtsmanship as a glory of the British school—and it is possible that a re-examination of her work might lead to the conclusion that Wilfred Meynell was not far wide of the mark when he wrote, in 1898, 'Lady Butler has done for the soldier in Art what Rudyard Kipling has done for him in Literature—she has taken the individual, separated him, seen him close, and let the world so see him.'[6]

The most significant entry in Miss Thompson's diary for 1876 is dated April 22: 'Went to lunch at Mrs. Mitchells', who invited me at the Private View, next door to Lady Raglan's, her great friend. Two distinguished officers were there to greet me, and we had a pleasant chat. . . . One of the officers was Major W. F. Butler, author of *The Great Lone Land.*'

When, a year later, Elizabeth Thompson—Mrs. William Butler now—walked down the flower-strewn path from the Church of the Servite Fathers she was at the very height of her fame. And here surely, was one marriage made in heaven—a union of two human beings ideally suited to one another in talent and temperament and aspiration. 'By her marriage the painter of heroes became the wife of a soldier of experience in every quarter of the earth,' Wilfred Meynell exclaimed, and John Ruskin wrote to Butler in a positive ecstasy of sentiment, 'I am profoundly thankful for the blessing of power that is now united in your wife and you. What may you not do for England, the two of you!'

And yet few of Butler's friends, least of all, one suspects, the most influential among them, General Wolseley himself, whole-heartedly approved his marriage. Ideal marriages may be made in heaven, but wise ones are made on earth. Elizabeth Thompson brought to her marriage no family influence; she had no friends in the right places (if she had she wouldn't have used them), and in spite of the popularity of her paintings very little money. Besides all these handicaps there was another even more serious; Elizabeth Thompson was a distinguished professional painter, and to many of the Victorians there was something not quite wholesome about a woman who earned a high place for herself in any of the creative arts. True, Elizabeth Thompson's pictures were in impeccable taste; but she was connected through her art with all sorts of queer and Bohemian people—like the Meynells and Wilfred Scawen Blunt and later on the dope-addicted poet Francis Thompson. In short, she was not the kind of person one could ever feel entirely at ease with.

There was a further practical reason why Butler's marriage to Elizabeth Thompson must have appeared in the eyes of the world to be less than wise. In the course of time Butler would almost certainly be called upon to assume important peacetime commands at home and abroad. The average wife of a man so placed found the roles of chatelaine and mother sufficiently exacting to occupy her time to the full, but Elizabeth Butler was inevitably the slave of her genius and at no time did it occur to her to give up her painting. To Butler's credit it did not occur to him either. During the years of her married life Elizabeth Butler was to demonstrate a remarkable capacity for doing several jobs simultaneously and doing them all well. She was eventually the mother of five children to whom she gave far more attention than was usual from the average mother of her time and place; she continued to paint with skill and assiduity, and in spite of waning popularity—in part the consequence of her inability to escape from the pattern established by *The Roll Call*—never lost her sense of joy in the act of creation. As well she looked after a husband who was by no means an easy man to keep in order—Butler was an autocratic figure in his own domestic domain, who from time to time imposed his eccentric notions of kitchen routine and child-rearing on the household with devastating results—and carried out her duties as hostess with tact and charm and only an occasional anguished protest against the social formalities which at times assumed for her the characteristics of an endurance test. 'The professional painter and the social personality did not combine in unruffled serenity', a friend reported. 'There were moments when Lady Butler, having behaved with exemplary politeness, would suddenly and violently break down, as when faced with one final introduction, she cried, "I can't—I can't!" and fled from the house.'

For the honeymoon Butler had offered Elizabeth the choice of a visit to the Continent or the west of Ireland. Elizabeth, tactful woman, unhesitatingly chose Ireland. In part her choice was no doubt dictated by eagerness to please her husband, in part by a very real desire to know something of the land and the people from which he had sprung. So to Ireland they went; and travelling the last twenty miles or more by horse and carriage—Butler holding the reins—made a triumphal entry into Glenaragh in the heart of the Kerry hills—hills dear to Butler, for among them three years earlier he had won his way back to health after the frets and fevers of the Ashanti campaign.

Wild strange birds rose from the bracken as we passed [Elizabeth wrote in her diary] and flew strongly away over lake and mountain torrent, and the little black Kerry cows all watched us go by with ears pricked and heads inquiringly raised. The last stage of the journey had a brilliant *finale*. A herd of young horses was in our way in the narrow road, and the creatures careered before us, unable or too stupid to turn aside into the ditches by the roadside to let us through. We could not head them, and for fully a mile did those shaggy wild things caper and jump ahead, their manes flying out wildly with the glow from the west shining through them. Some imbecile cows soon joined them in the stampede, for no imaginable reason, unless they enjoyed the fright of being pursued, and the ungainly sight of these recruits was a sight to behold—tails in the air and horns in the dust. The troop led the way right into the eye of the sunset. With this escort we entered Glenaragh.[7]

To Elizabeth, Ireland was sheer delight. She had long been innured to the hardships of travel and racketing round from place to place on the Continent—in this respect she was admirably suited to the role of soldier's wife—hence the inconvenience of honeymooning in the primitive west of Ireland left her unruffled; she was much too busy to be concerned about such trivialities, for she was trying to capture with brush and pen the highly individualistic charm of the people and their environment. In this she was at least moderately successful, and it is fair to say that we learn almost as much from Elizabeth's ingenuous notes and sketches about the world which was a part of her husband's heritage as we do from Butler himself. Inevitably she tended to concentrate on the novel, the diverting:

But the chapel! Shall I ever forget the tub of holy water, on my first Sunday, placed before the rickety altar on the mud floor, where the people, on coming in, splashed the water up into their faces? The old women had all brought big bottles from their homes in faraway places to fill at the tub, and nothing could surpass the comicality of their attitudes as they stooped over their pious business, all wearing the hooded cloak that made them look as broad as they were long. One old lady, in her nice white cap, monopolized the tub an unconscionably long time, for, catching sight of her wind-tossed tresses in that looking-glass, she finished her devout ablutions by smoothing her few gray hairs with her moistened fingers into tidy bands, with alternate signs of the cross.[8]

His bride's unaffected enthusiasm for Ireland and all things in it must have warmed Butler's heart. She was even ecstatic about the goat that took part in one church service, pattering purposefully up the aisle to occupy an empty pew.

He lay down with perfect self-complacency and remained quiescent, chewing his cud, while we knelt; but each time the congregation stood up, up jumped the goat, his pale eyes and enormous horns just appearing over the front of the pew. Then as we knelt again he would subside also. . . . Not a single person took any notice of the weird creature or seemed to think him out of place or at all funny; and so he continued to rise and fall with us to the end.[9]

Many of the scenes she witnessed and delighted in Elizabeth Butler recorded not only in her notebook but in a series of water-colours full of charm and light and animation. But her 'big' picture which she projected during her honeymoon was inevitably associated with war. William found her two excellent models for what she called her first *married* Academy picture—*Listed for the Connaught Rangers*—bog-trotters both, one big (raised on potatoes and herring), one small (raised on potatoes only). The painting proved a great popular success. It assured the people of England of the loyalty of the Irish peasant and his continuing willingness to die for the Empire in far-off places.

Elizabeth Butler's best-known painting on an Irish theme, *An Eviction*, now hanging in the Dublin Municipal Gallery, was painted many years later and exhibited at the Academy showing of 1890. An entry in her diary for that year reveals how deeply she had come to feel about scenes which long before had moved her husband to passionate protest: 'I exhibited "An Eviction in Ireland" which Lord Salisbury was pleased to be facetious about in his speech at the banquet, remarking on the "breezy beauty" of the landscape, which almost made him wish he could take part in an eviction himself. How like a Cecil!'

Elizabeth Butler's enthusiasm for Ireland was genuine and lifelong; and it is a pity that her husband could not feel for her own beloved places of earth a similar emotion. But towards continental Europe other than France Butler turned a cold eye—and particularly towards Germany. Like many people—perhaps most—he was unable to separate his feelings for landscape from his feeling for people. So it was that when, to conclude a lengthy honeymoon, he and Elizabeth visited Germany and took a boat trip down the Rhine Valley—Elizabeth's favourite holiday jaunt in all Europe—prejudice triumphed over the desire to please. Rain was falling, and it served Butler as an excellent excuse to retire to his cabin and stay there during the length of the cruise. 'I suspect the natives on board drove him in,' Elizabeth recorded with characteristic perception in her diary, 'rather than his resentment at the come-down from the glowing descriptions in the travel books.'

CHAPTER ELEVEN

Battles and Books

ISANDHLWANA, Ulundi, Rorke's Drift, Brunker's Spruit, Laing's Nek, Majuba. They are names which mean little today, mere identification tags of battles long ago which in terms of the forces involved were hardly more than skirmishes; but in their time the makers and breakers of military reputations and in sum the consequence of Disraeli's dream of a larger Empire, a wider stain of red on the map of Africa. On April 12, 1878, England annexed the Transvaal, the most northerly area of Boer settlement, thereby adding 100,000 square miles of territory to the Empire and preparing the way for nearly a quarter of a century of intermittent warfare between Boer and Britisher and an accumulation of distrust and bitter grievance on the side of the Boer which the passage of time has done little to diminish. Following the annexation of the Transvaal, Sir Bartle Frere, the High Commissioner of South Africa, prepared to annex Zululand, the native territory lying north of Natal. The appropriate charges to justify the move in the eyes of the British public were formally laid against the great Zulu king, Cetewayo, and when he refused to pay the huge indemnity demanded of him and disband his army, four invading columns crossed the border from Natal into Zululand and drove towards Ulundi, Cetewayo's capital. The command of the invading forces was entrusted to Lord Chelmsford, an earnest, slow-witted and unimaginative veteran of the Crimean War. Two of the best-known members of the Wolseley Ring, Colonels Redvers Buller and Evelyn Wood, held commands under Chelmsford.

Meanwhile Wolseley was eating his heart out on the island of Cyprus, Disraeli's 'rosy realm of Venus' acquired from the Turks in 1878, purportedly for use as a bastion to block Russian aggression against Turkey. (The revelation that five days *before* the Turks signed away Cyprus, Great Britain had concluded a secret peace pact with Russia helps to explain Turkey's subsequent hostility to Great Britain. The Turks were unable to distinguish between astute diplomacy and the double-cross.) Cyprus was enthusiastically boosted by Disraeli as the brightest jewel in the Imperial crown, but Wolseley, who had reluctantly accepted the appointment of Governor of the island, did not find it so. He hated the landscape, the climate, the Greeks, the Turks, wanted only to get away. Even Butler, in spite of his passion for new scenes and his inexhaustible curiosity about people, was a little shocked by what he saw when he visited his old commander late in 1878:

I had been a stranger to the East since leaving Burmah and India fifteen years earlier. All the young life of America and the black life of Africa had since been my companions, but here in Cyprus it was the East again, the East with the Turk added on; the ragged squalor, the breast of the earth dried up and desolate, the old glory of Greek, Roman, Norman and Venetian civilization lying in dust and ashes under a thing that was itself a dying force in the world.[1]

On January 22, 1879, two days after crossing the border into Zululand, a force of fifteen hundred British and native troops was overwhelmed by a Zulu impi at a place called Isandhlwana; only a handful of men, including five officers, were able to fight their way through the swarms of Zulus to safety; the rest perished under a shower of assegais, victims of the overconfidence and incompetence of their commanders who, acting on the usual assumption that native warriors could never stand up to modern rifle-fire, had taken no precautions against attack. Their assumption was, in fact, correct; unfortunately communications between rear and firing line broke down completely, no ammunition reached the squares, and when their immediate supply of cartridges ran out the soldiers were butchered. 'At first we could make no way against these soldiers.' Zulu warriors reported after the war, 'but suddenly they ceased to fire, then we came round them and threw our spears until we had killed them all.'

In northern Zululand the invading column under Wood and Buller stood off a furious Zulu attack at Kambula, but suffered such heavy losses it was immobilized. The other columns, on news of the Isandhlwana disaster, had retreated back over the border, and everywhere in Natal rumours spread of an impending Zulu invasion, and men and women lived in terror lest the border country be again a place of weeping.

Butler was on his way back to England from Cyprus when he heard the news of Isandhlwana. His reaction was almost instinctive —he at once hurried off to the nearest telegraph station and sent a telegram to the Quartermaster-General's department offering his services for South Africa. His offer was accepted. Two weeks later, on the last day of February, 1879, Butler sailed for Natal.

He was not given a chance to serve in the field. His work in the Quartermaster General's department inevitably recommended him to similar chores in Natal, and he accepted reluctantly but without demur the staff billet of assistant adjutant-general. For several weeks he ate, slept and worked in a stiflingly hot corrugated-iron shed in Durban, overseeing the disembarkation of troops newly arrived from England and the Cape, the unloading of military supplies and the transporting of troops and supplies upcountry. The regular troops gave little trouble; but the irregular forces of volunteers raised in various parts of South Africa as an emergency against possible invasion soon made themselves anathema to Butler by reason of their extravagant demands for service and supplies and their almost total lack of discipline.

At Pietermaritzburg, where he had gone briefly on business, Butler met in Government House the eighteen-year-old Prince Imperial, son of the late Emperor Napoleon III and the exiled Empress Eugénie. The Prince had wangled a staff appointment with Chelmsford's forces in the hope of obtaining a little real military experience on active service. That the Prince should commend himself to Butler, with whom he held a long conversation, was inevitable. He was an eager unaffected youth—and the blood of the great Emperor flowed in his veins.

One month later it was Butler's melancholy duty to arrange the cortège of the dead Prince, killed when abandoned by a panicky escort of troopers who had been stampeded by a small-scale Zulu ambush. For Butler there was a grain of comfort in the knowledge that the Prince, true to his heritage, had died heroically, all his seventeen assegai wounds in front; and the funeral cortège was invested with a kind of beauty which in turn and for the moment only invested the sordid little tragedy with an element of grandeur:

I think the scene as the funeral cortège wound down the Berea Hill towards Durban was the saddest but most impressive sight I had ever witnessed. It was the sunset hour; the eastern slope of the Berea was in shadow, but the town beneath, the ships in the roadstead, and the deep blue Indian Ocean beyond the white line of shore were all in dazzling light. The regiments that had gone up country had left their bands on the coast, and one after the other they took up the great March of the Dead, until the twilight, moving eastwards towards the sea, seemed to be marching with us as we went. Night had all but closed when we carried the coffin into the little Catholic church at the base of Berea Hill.[2]

It is typical of Butler that he did not blame the captain of the Prince's escort for the tragedy, or the handful of troopers who had left the Prince to face twenty Zulus alone. The men criminally responsible were the staff officers who had permitted the Prince to ride into enemy country without proper protection. And in his eyes it was one more sad example of the fallibility of human justice that following the official investigation 'the unhappy subordinate actor in the tragedy was immolated' and the real offenders were let off scot free.

The Empress Eugénie, in later years one of Butler's most intimate friends, was deeply grateful to him for the immense concern he showed for her dead son; and among the Butler family heirlooms is a diamond stickpin, once belonging to the Prince Imperial, which the Empress gave to Butler as a token of royal gratitude.

In Cyprus, Sir Garnet Wolseley had said to Butler, 'I have put my hand to the Cypriote plough and must hold it till the furrow is finished.' When he heard of Isandhlwana he forgot about the Cypriote furrow and began ploughing his own. He immediately notified the Foreign Office that if a commander in South Africa were to be appointed to replace Lord Chelmsford he would be available for the post. Later, when he learned that such an appointment would definitely be made, he telegraphed Lord Salisbury asking point-blank for the command. He need not have worried. In spite of the opposition of the Duke of Cambridge and the old guard generally, the choice of Wolseley as Commander-in-Chief of the British forces in South Africa was inevitable.

Wolseley did not reach Durban until the end of June, more than five months after Isandhlwana. Long before Wolseley's arrival Lord Chelmsford, with a strongly reinforced army, had plodded back into Zululand, desperate to redeem lost reputation and tarnished honour. He ignored not only all reports that he had been superseded, but also the orders Wolseley bombarded him with from the moment of his arrival in Durban. This time Chelmsford took no chances in the Zulu country and this time he won. The battle of Ulundi lasted just thirty minutes, and when it was over the Zulu war was for all practical purposes over, too.

Wolseley, who had hoped to catch up with Chelmsford in time to assume command and win the decisive victory, concealed his chagrin at Chelmsford's cumbersome *coup* as best he could, and took charge of mopping-up operations in Zululand. Butler remained in Durban supervising the re-embarkation of more than half the army that had been assembled in Natal for the final thrust against Cetewayo. To embark the regular troops without fuss was headache enough; to pay off and get rid of the various irregular corps of volunteers was sheer hell, although even hell had its entertaining moments:

Various units of raffish swashbucklers now came to the port to be paid their reckonings and to pay them again into innumerable public houses of Durban. I devised many plans by which the evil might be lessened. Sometimes I put a pay officer and his pay sheet, with a good guard of regulars, on board a transport in the outer anchorage, and informed the men that they would only be paid on board ship. Another plan was to encamp the corps six or eight miles out of Durban in the vicinity of a railway station, by means of which they could be fed and supplied from the port. The scenes which were daily taking place were often of a very ludicrous description. A battalion of infantry, to whom some five or six thousand pounds had to be paid, would reach the wharf ready for embarkation, having been the recipients on the march through Durban of a public luncheon and innumerable quantities of large watermelons—the latter a most innocuous fruit on ordinary occasions but somewhat embarrassing when presented to a man after a hearty meal and many libations *en route*. I had prepared, however, for the dangers of embarkation from the wharf in the large flat boats, and a dozen steady men with boathooks stood ready to gaff the men who fell into the water—a precaution which bore fruit in more senses than one, for many of the men deemed it a point of honour to hold on by these watermelons even when they were in the sea.[3]

Here, too, at Durban, during the weary weeks of embarkation, Butler came for the first time into direct conflict with the army contractors, whose peculiar business he was to expose more than twenty years later in a sensational War Office Committee report. At Durban enormous stockpiles of surplus foodstuffs and miscellaneous goods no longer needed for the Army had to be disposed of, in theory to the highest bidder. But instead of bidding against one another the contractors seeking to buy the goods at once formed a combine in accordance with a time-honoured tradition, and submitted tenders at a fixed price—according to Butler's calculations about one-twentieth of the real value of the goods offered for sale. (Sixpence per hundred-weight was the bid submitted for corn meal.) Butler, infuriated by what he rightly regarded as a racket, thereupon recommended to the responsible government departments of supply that the goods be shipped back to England—at no cost, since plenty of empty cargo space was available on the troop transports—and sold in the London open market. The contractors were indignant, the departments concerned confused and shocked—surplus supplies were customarily disposed of at point of stockpiling and there was no precedent for Butler's proposal—but in the end Butler had his way, and several thousand tons of excellent foodstuffs and miscellaneous goods were sold in London at prices ranging from ten to twenty times those offered in Durban. Butler derived much satisfaction from thus saving the Empire a substantial sum of money—and even more from having outsmarted the contractors.

In Zululand, Wolseley, after a long chase, cornered and captured Cetewayo, and the Zulu war, after having dragged on for eight months, was officially at an end. The Zulu king, guilty of having resisted the invasion of his country, was treated as an outlaw by Wolseley, who first ignored him and then harangued him for an hour on his sins. When Cetewayo was carried off to prison in Cape Town, Wolseley retained possession of the defeated king's necklace of lion's claws. But not for himself. After his return to England he had the necklace broken up and the claws, appropriately mounted and engraved, distributed as charms among the wives of influential politicians.

Before he left Natal, Butler heard that the imprisoned Cetewayo was begging for a few bundles of green rushes from which mats of the kind he had slept on all his life might be made, for he could find no sleep or rest in a prison cot. Butler at once arranged for three large bundles of rushes to be sent from Zululand to Durban, and these he brought with him by ship to Cape Town. From the dock he drove directly with the precious bundles to Cape Town Castle, where Cetewayo was imprisoned. The once-great king wept at sight of the rushes. 'Say to him that he has brought sleep to me,' he told the interpreter. 'Now I can rest at night.' Butler was close to tears too. 'It was the same as putting a bit of green sod into the cage of a lark,' he said.

On the voyage back to England the ship carrying Butler stopped at St. Helena. For two hours only, but the chance was not to be missed. Butler at once went ashore, hired a pony and hurried over the road he had first travelled sixteen years before, and so came to what was already a familiar scene—this time shrouded in a twilight that accorded perfectly with the spirit of the place and the mood of the beholder:

There in the dusk was the silent tomb again, the dark cypress trees, the old Norfolk Island pines, the broken willow, the iron railings, the big white flagstone in the centre of the railed space—all the lonely excompassing lava hills merging into the gathering gloom of night; and only a yellow streak of afterglow, still lying above the western rocks, to make the profound depths of the valley seem more appropriate.[4]

At home Elizabeth Butler had painted *The Defence of Rorke's Drift*, inspired by the heroic resistance of a heroic few, who, outnumbered by the Zulus twenty to one, stood off an all-night assault on the Rorke's Drift mission house and in all probability saved Natal from invasion. Butler's reaction to the painting was unfavourable. 'Once more picture like this'. he said to the distressed artist, 'and you will drive me mad.' A conflict between spears and breech-loading rifles was not, in Butler's opinion, a fit subject of art. Besides, he liked Zulus and didn't appreciate a landscape littered with their bodies. Some of his acquaintances suspected that he liked Zulus better than he did Englishmen.

Butler—a lieutenant-colonel now after more than twenty years' service—arrived back in London to find the Conservative Government of Benjamin Disraeli tottering to its fall. He was delighted when the fall came, early in 1880, for he loathed Disraeli's expansionist policy. For a time it appeared possible that he might go to India as secretary to the newly appointed Viceroy, Lord Ripon, who had himself proposed Butler for the post. But Gladstone would have none of it. A Catholic viceroy was in itself a sufficiently risky experiment without having a Catholic secretary as well. Instead of India, Butler went to Devonport, headquarters of the Western Command, as chief staff officer. He bore Gladstone no ill will for having vetoed the proposed secretaryship. Nor did he hold Gladstone—in his eyes the greatest living Englishman—in any way responsible for the succession of wars that broke out in Afghanistan,

South Africa and Egypt shortly after the Liberals came into power. Gladsone was merely reaping the fruit of the bad seed sown by his predecessor in office, particularly in South Africa, where in 1880, two years after the annexation, the Boers declared the independence of the Transvaal. A series of military disasters for the British followed the Boer declaration, culminating in the Battle of Majuba Hill, 1881, in which General George Colley, the most brilliant member of the Wolseley Ring, died while attempting to rally his disorganized forces in the face of the terrible rifle-fire of the Boers. Butler mourned Colley, and approved Gladstone's recognition of Boer independence. He was probably the only professional soldier in England to do so.

Many years earlier Butler had written 'obedience is . . . the first duty of the soldier'[5], and this view he maintained to the end of his life. But he also maintained that since the soldier fought the wars others resolved upon, he had a right to know what he was fighting for. Or against. He held in utter contempt those who proclaimed, with the Laureate, 'their's not to reason why'. Once the command was given the soldier had no choice but to keep silence and obey. But before—and afterwards if he lived—he should be free to say what he thought and believed. 'The nation that will insist on drawing a broad line of demarcation between the fighting man and the thinking man', Butler wrote, 'is liable to find its fighting done by fools and its thinking by cowards.'

The day was coming when Butler was to be accused of being a 'political' soldier. The truth is that he was always less a politician than a philosopher, who believed more and more strongly as he grew older that the causes of war had little to do with party politics.

The year 1881 saw the publication of Butler's first book since *Akim-foo*—a collection of essays and sketches, several of which had appeared earlier in periodicals, entitled *Far Out: Rovings Re-Told*. The most entertaining of the sketches, the delightful 'A Man And His Dog', is a retelling of the story of Butler's wanderings in north-western Canada—this time with the splendid husky dog, Cerf Volant, the hero of the narrative. The other items in the book include several South African history and travel sketches based on Butler's experiences of 1875 and 1878 and remarkable for their prophetic insights; the highly original and painstakingly documented 'A Plea For the Peasant'; and a lengthy but always readable account of Butler's visit to Cyprus in 1878. Apart from their intrinsic merits (whatever his literary sins Butler is rarely dull), 'A Visit to Cyprus' and 'A Plea for the Peasant' are of unusual interest because they attracted the attention and earned the fulsome praise of John Ruskin.

A book has just been published by a British officer [Ruskin wrote] who, if he had not been otherwise and more actively employed, could not only have written all my books about landscape and picture, but is very singularly of one mind with me (God knows of how few Englishmen I can say so) on matters regarding the Queen's safety and the nation's honour. Of whose book . . . I will content myself with quoting . . . the memorable words which Colonel Butler himself quotes, as spoken to the British Parliament by its last Conservative leader, a British officer who had also served with honour and success.[6]

Ruskin then quotes from 'A Plea for the Peasant' a speech which, so Butler said, was delivered by the Duke of Wellington to the House of Lords in support of the Catholic Emancipation Bill:

It is already well-known to your Lordships that of the troops which our gracious Sovereign did me the honour to entrust to my command at various periods during the war—a war undertaken for the express purpose of securing the happy institutions and independence of the country—at least half were Roman Catholics. My Lords, when I call your recollection to this fact I am sure that all further eulogy is unnecessary. Your Lordships are well aware for what length of period and under what difficult circumstances they maintained the Empire buoyant under the flood which overwhelmed the thrones and wrecked the institutions of every other people:—how they kept alive the only spark of freedom which was left unextinguished in Europe. . . . My Lords, it is mainly to the Irish Catholics that we all owe our proud predominance in our military career, and that personally I am indebted for the laurels with which you have been pleased to decorate my brow. . . . We must confess, my Lords, that without Catholic valour no victory could have been obtained, and the first military talents might have been exerted in vain.

It is pleasant to speculate on the nature of the language the great Duke would really have used had he ever read the purple rhetoric which Butler and Ruskin attributed to him. The 'speech', a favourite test-piece of patriotic amateur elocutionists in the mid-nineteenth century, appears to have been the composition of an Irish writer, Richard Shiel, who represented it as the speech the Duke of Wellington *should* have made in the House of Lords in reply to Lord Langhurst's charge that the Irish were 'aliens'. The speech was published in 1870 in O'Callaghan's *History of the Irish Brigades*, this time with positive attribution to the Duke and no mention of Shiel. O'Callaghan was Butler's source.

The speech was omitted from subsequent editions of *Far Out*.

The second passage from *Far Out* to win Ruskin's praise was Butler's bitter comment on the hostility of the Englishman to alien religions and his indifference to his own:

On an Austrian Lloyd's steamboat in the Levant a traveller from Beyrout will frequently see strange groups of men crowded together on the quarter-deck. In the morning the missal books of the Greek Church will be laid along the bulwarks of the ship, and a couple of Russian priests, coming from Jerusalem, will be busy muttering mass. A yard to the right or left a Turkish pilgrim, returning from Mecca, sits a respectful observer of the scene. It is prayer, and therefore it is holy in his sight. So, too, when evening has come, and the Turk spreads out his strips of carpet for the sunset prayers and obeisance towards Mecca, the Greek looks on in silence, without a trace of scorn on his face, for it is again the worship of the Creator by the created. They are both fulfilling the *first* law of the East—prayer to God; and whether the shrine be Jerusalem, Mecca or Lhassa, the sanctity of worship surrounds the votary and protects the pilgrim.

Into this life comes the Englishman, frequently destitute of one touch of sympathy with the prayers of any people, or the faith of any creed; hence our rule in the East has rested, and will ever rest, upon the bayonet. We have never yet got beyond the stage of conquest, never assimilated a people to our ways, never even civilized a single tribe around the wide dominion of our Empire. It is curious how often a well-meaning Briton will speak of foreign church or temple as though it presented itself to the mind in the same light in which the City of London appeared to Blucher—as something to loot.

The following year, 1882, saw the publication of two more books. *Red Cloud*, or *The Solitary Sioux*, is an exercise in nostalgia, an attempt to recapture through the written word the wonder, delight and melancholy of the great days which Butler had spent long ago on the prairies of the west—the land which still claimed his heart as no other part of earth had been able to do. The hero of the novel is a youthful Butler, and the tragic story unfolded that of the passing of the Indian. *Red Cloud* fully deserves its place on the shelf of better Victorian juveniles. It suggests that Butler, by reason of his lofty if at times quixotic idealism, his flair for the dramatic, and his lifetime of adventure in far away places might well have become, had his interest lain in that direction, a most successful writer of juveniles in the manner of G. A. Henty, although working within a framework of an almost precisely opposite set of prejudices and preconceptions. The superiority of the white man to the native, the Englishman to all other whites, was never a part of Butler's belief.

The second book of Butler's to appear in 1882 is an oddity belonging to the literature of prophecy. Published anonymously (the authorship was almost immediately known and acknowledged), *The Invasion of England*, purportedly written by an old soldier in the year 1890, was intended as a warning to England of the fate in store for her unless she mended her ways, cast down the Golden Calf, restored the peasant to the land and faced squarely the fact that war with Germany was inevitable and for that war she was totally unprepared. In the England of 1882, so Butler wrote, the survival of the fittest had become the survival of the fattest, the richest were nurtured at the expense of the best; and with the eloquence and anger of an Old Testament prophet he denounced the sins of his people, the corruption of body and soul following the industrialization of the nation and the setting-up of false gods:

Our victories had so often been achieved against great odds that we had come to think we were the chosen people of God, and that whatever harm might befall other nations we were safe—a dangerous belief even if it be held in unison with a firm faith in a Supreme Being, but a false hallucination when it is found side by side with a most palpable abandonment of God's teaching, and the open denial of his precepts.[8]

The description of the invasion is brilliantly done. It reveals as does none other of his books Butler's preoccupation with military strategy and tactics, and his conviction that the British soldier was neither trained nor armed to meet the demands of modern warfare as fought by the German military machine. A feint at Wales, a landing in strength on the East Coast, the decisive battle near Chelmsford, the shattering impact of war on a peaceful rural community—all these things are described with impressive and uncharacteristic restraint and a concern for realistic detail which result in an unwilling suspension of disbelief for the moment—the highest kind of tribute that can be paid to a prophecy of doom.

The defeat of the British is attributed to the nation's almost total lack of preparation for a major war, and the outdated training methods of the Army. The soldiers who face the Germans are brave enough, but their equipment is poor, they do not know how to make use of cover, and they still march into battle in the close formation—used since Fontenoy and to be used again in the Boer War—which in the face of modern weapons was no less than suicidal.

One of the most interesting passages in *The Invasion of England* is a remarkably accurate prediction of the actual conditions that prevailed in the early stages of the Boer and World Wars when the only materials of warfare in abundant supply were men.

> The men were coming in fast enough, but the departments of supply had completely broken down under the sudden pressure of the mobilization following the declaration of war. The clothing of the soldiers was utterly unfit for the campaign. Many of the regiments were in very old tunics, the stores were without boots or greatcoats. . . . The different ammunition used by the militia and the regular troops caused great confusion. The supply of tents was insufficient. The pouches and knapsacks carried by the militia were found to be quite unsuited to the requirements of modern warfare, but more deplorable than all was the state of our artillery. . . . Terrible are these moments when a nation realizes the awful fact of the short-comings of the military system when the enemy is at the gate.[9]

But the end, after the superbly trained and equipped German Army has overwhelmed the valiant but badly led, badly trained and ill-equipped defenders of England, is not all bad. The new England that arises after the war is over and the staggering indemnity demanded by the victors paid in full, is humbler, poorer, healthier and infinitely wiser than the old. The bloated city plutocrat has been deflated, the yeoman restored to the land, and the country is governed by responsible hard-working statesmen, rather than 'a vast debating club whose deliberations began when the fox-hunting was closing and ended when the grouse-shooting was beginning'.

The Invasion of England was a curious book for a man who still had much of his way to make in the Army to write. Almost as curious as Swift's *A Tale of a Tub*, that devastating satire on the Christian churches which imperilled Swift's ecclesiastical career and perhaps lost him a bishopric. Butler lacked Swift's genius, but the two men had much in common. Like Swift, Butler was prepared to risk his advancement in the world for the sake of saving mankind from its follies and the pleasure of vexing it.

CHAPTER TWELVE

Tel-el-Kebir

ONE OF THE MOST CURIOUS and seemingly irrational aspects of nineteenth-century British imperialism is the degree to which it stemmed from the operation of forces beyond the control of any government in power at any given time. The complications of foreign policy, the expense of conquest and the administrative problems expansion gave rise to were factors which inhibited the political parties—except the Tories under Disraeli—from openly advocating or even covertly encouraging the extension of Empire. Yet nearly everywhere—in Africa, Asia, North America and the islands of the sea—the story was the same; of the spread of commercial, political and even religious interests to a circumference from which withdrawal was impossible, advance inevitable. Everywhere, it seemed, the red stain was widening, yet hardly ever by deliberate intent of the governments in power.

British involvement in Egypt—which ended disastrously as late as 1956—may be said to have begun when the Khedive Ismail, seeking to consolidate Egyptian suzerainty over the Sudan at a time when his officers were 'distinguished for nothing but their public incapacity and private misbehaviour', introduced the practice of hiring British soldiers to train his army for him and in some instances to govern those parts of the Sudan which for a time fell under Egyptian rule. Ismail's most notable appointees were the explorer Sir Samuel Baker, who at least partially annexed the region of the Upper Nile to Egypt, and Colonel—later General—Charles Gordon, successively Governor of Equatoria and Governor-General of the entire Sudan.

But the real involvement was the consequence not of Ismail's territorial ambitions but his extraordinary financial manipulations. Ismail, who became Viceroy of Egypt in 1863 at a time when Egypt was still nominally under Turkish rule, was a bland and genial individual, plump and bewhiskered, whole enthusiasm for horse-racing commended him to Europeans—and especially Englishmen—as a thoroughly good sort; and whose frequently expressed determination to Westernize Egypt was accepted as evidence of superior intelligence and as security for the loans he needed to carry out his schemes.

There is a kind of oriental splendour about Ismail's borrowings and spendings which must have excited the imagination of all those whom his inability to pay back his borrowings did not touch. Cairo was partially rebuilt; and the new buildings—none of them paid for—included a splendid new palace for Ismail, a modern theatre, and an opera house for which Verdi was commissioned to compose *Aida*. The Civil Service was remodelled and modernized along Western lines, a railway was built across the desert to nowhere in particular; and in 1869 the Suez Canal, financed by French and Turkish money, was declared open to the ships of all nations. To celebrate the opening of the Canal, Ismail provided a four-days entertainment—attended by half the crowned heads of Europe—on a scale of magnificence such as the gorgeous East had never witnessed even in the days of Haroun-el-Raschid or Kubla Khan.

By the mid-seventies the Khedive Ismail could look with some satisfaction on his material achievements. He had extended Egyptian rule over a large part of the Sudan, he had modernized his capital, he had brought Eygpt into the orbit of Western civilization, and he had made his own name familiar throughout Europe.

There were, unfortunately, a few flies in the ointment; in the execution of his projects and the satisfaction of his ambitions Ismail had quadrupled land taxes, increased Egypt's national debt from three million to one hundred million pounds and bankrupted the nation.

He could not, of course, legally declare bankruptcy like a shopkeeper and pay off his creditors with a penny or two on the pound. The creditors included not only small individual investors but corporations, great banking houses and national governments. In 1874 Sir Evelyn Baring, who was to become one of England's greatest civil servants, arrived in Cairo to look after British interests. One year later Disraeli bought Egypt's Suez Canal shares, four tenths of the total, at the bargain basement price of four million pounds; and control of his country's finances, and hence his country, passed out of Ismail's hands. In 1879 Ismail was

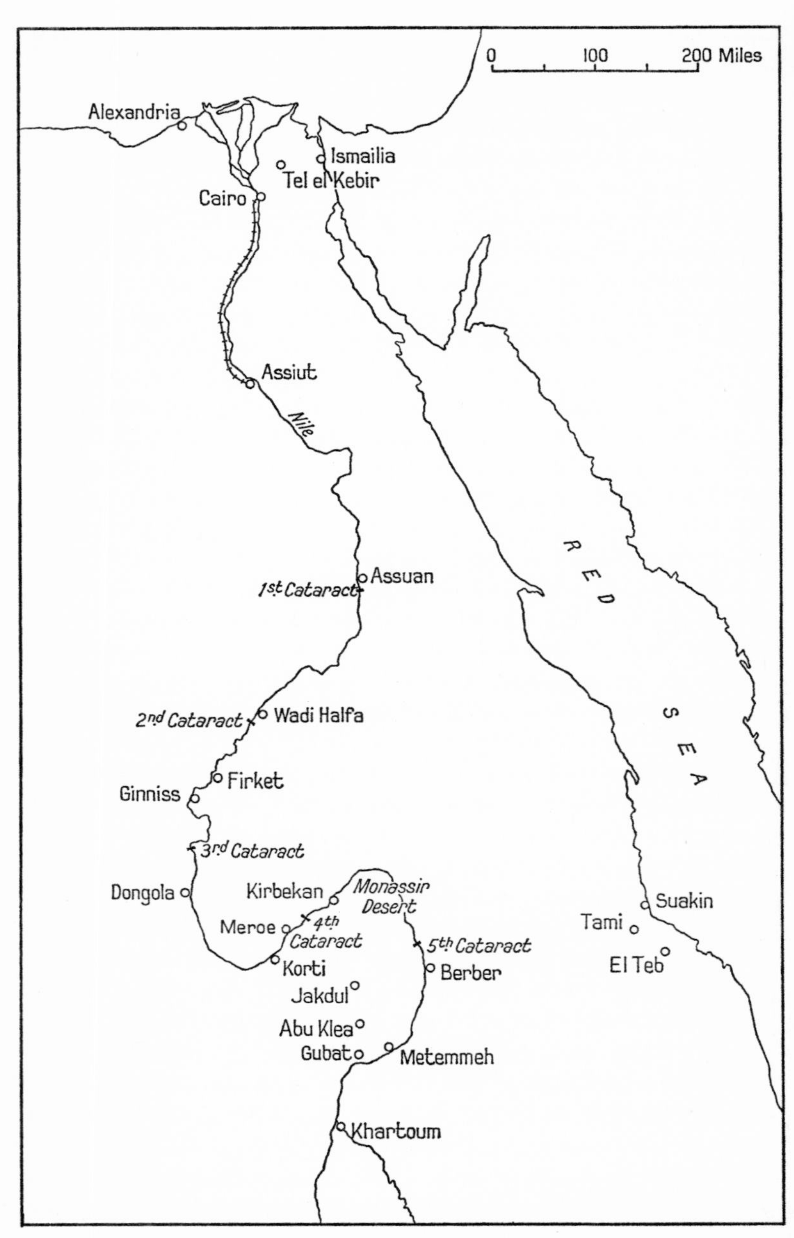

VALLEY OF THE LOWER NILE 1884

quietly got rid of. Baring and the French and Turkish representatives installed in Cairo arranged for his deposition, and Ismail, to the end a flamboyant and not unattractive figure, sailed away from his native land to the Golden Horn in a luxurious yacht, taking with him his favourite women, a vast quantity of jewellery and over £3,000,000 in cash which he had thoughtfully put aside against a rainy day. In Ismail's stead there reigned as Khedive his eldest son Tewfik, a colourless weakling completely subservient to the European representatives who, headed by Baring and the Frenchman de Blignières, were now the real rulers of Egypt.

The Egyptian native is long-suffering, uncomplaining and fatalistic; but the conditions of living in the late 1870s and 1880s under a staggering burden of taxation were such as to incite even the meekest and most complaisant of men to unrest. Foreign officials enjoying diplomatic immunity swarmed everywhere, their purpose to safeguard the interests of the investors they represented no matter what the cost in human misery to the hapless fellaheen. Even Evelyn Baring, a highly civilized, essentially humane man, inevitably set the interests of the country he represented ahead of those of the country he ruled. The sullen hate which nearly every Egyptian felt for the foreigner found a focus at last, not in a European, but in the collaborator Tewfik, the man responsible, so his subjects believed, for their enslavement to the foreign moneylender. Tewfik, they said, must go.

There was a time when the peasant, armed with scythe or pitchfork, could fight the soldier armed with sword and spear on not altogether hopeless terms; but the weapons of modern warfare foredoom any kind of active revolutionary movement unless it enlists army support. In Egypt the soldiers—wretchedly paid, half-starved and often brutally mistreated—were ripe for revolt; thus the people and the Army were united in their hatred of the foreigner and Tewfik, and in 1882 the leader appeared to direct that hatred towards a positive goal. Colonel Ahmed Arabi, born a fellah, by blood and instinct one of the people, was endowed with all the qualities of a successful revolutionary leader except physical courage and skill in battle. The overthrow of Tewfik required neither.

Inevitably the popular rising under Arabi which drove Tewfik out of Cairo and made Arabi dictator of Egypt brought Egypt into direct conflict with Great Britain. Gladstone, the British Prime

Minister, did all in his power to avert the clash. He was a lifelong opponent of imperialist expansion on practical as well as ethical grounds, and he felt that for the British to go openly into Egypt with an army was to invite the bitter resentment of the French. 'My belief is,' he said, 'that the day which witnesses our occupation of Egypt will bid a long farewell to all cordiality of political relations between France and England.' But there was never any real hope of averting armed intervention—the stakes being played for were too high. The moneylenders must be assured of their interest, British subjects in Egypt of their lives; and the Government itself had a huge investment in the Suez Canal, now a lifeline to India that must be kept open at all costs.

The intervention followed an easily predictable pattern. First a naval bombardment of Alexandria which reduced much of the city to ruins and strengthened the will of the people to fight; next the landing in Egypt, in August 1882, of an army of 20,000 men under the command of Sir Garnet Wolseley.

Butler, a lieutenant-colonel now, went to the war as a member of Wolseley's staff. He was delighted to be again on active service. but at the same time a little depressed by the all-too-familiar feeling of being on the wrong side. The outcome of the campaign was inevitable; Wolseley as usual had left nothing to chance and the Egyptians could not hope to stand for long in the way of the force he proposed to throw against them; but what troubled Butler more than the prospect of a one-sided fight was the conviction that he was campaigning not for a worthy cause but for the bankers of Europe.

Compared with most of the old causes of conflict which our fathers knew of [he said], it is decidedly below the average standard of dynastic jealousies, the rivalries of states, the great social or political questions, such as underlay the Civil War in America— even the old loves of men and women. . . . But the soldier of today must be content with what he can get, and the gift war-horse which the Stock Exchange is now able to bestow upon him mustn't be examined too severely in the mouth.[1]

At Wolseley's side were many of the brotherhood of the Ring besides Butler. Herbert Stewart was there and McCalmont, Baker Russell, Redvers Buller and a dozen more—proud, confident men all, and fiercely jealous of their military reputations. General Sir John Adye, on loan from the War Office, was made Chief of Staff. He was Wolseley's senior by fifteen years, but the two got along better than Wolseley had hoped. There were other appointments which could not be justified on the grounds of military necessity. Such officers as Arthur, Duke of Connaught, the Queen's favourite son, and the Duke of Cambridge's undistinguished offspring George, were mere nuisances on a campaign, since they had to be carefully protected from harm; but Wolseley regarded their appointments as necessary social evils and approved them as such.

Wolseley's efficiency was seldom more in evidence than in the Egyptian campaign of 1882, which he afterwards described, with some justification, as the tidiest war in British history. He was appointed to the command on July 20; by mid August 20,000 men had been landed at Alexandria and Wolseley's plan of campaign was complete to the last detail—including the typical Sir Garnet touch of supplying false information to the newspaper men and two of his own generals. The Egyptian Army was based at Tel-el-Kebir, a strongly fortified military encampment on the Sweetwater Canal, some twenty miles west of the Suez and forty north-east of Cairo. Most observers, including Arabi, assumed that Wolseley would follow the Napoleonic route straight up the Nile valley to Cairo. Wolseley was ambitious to follow in the footsteps of Napoleon, but only in a figurative sense. The Nile valley in August with its hundreds of miles of flooded irrigation ditches was no place for complicated military manoeuvres involving the use of cavalry and artillery. There was an easier, neater way of doing things which had not been available to Napoleon, and Wolseley took it. A feint at Aboukir which deceived Egyptians and newspaper men alike, a night passage of the army down the Suez Canal which Arabi had foolishly failed to block—or even guard—and on August 20 Wolseley was in possession of all important points on the canal with his army based at Ismailia, only twenty-five miles east of Tel-el-Kebir.

There followed a period of seeming stagnation during which, however, every desultory inconsequential military action or manoeuvre ended the same way, with the British forces a little deeper in the desert, a little closer to Tel-el-Kebir. The heat was intense, blowing sand prickled tempers as well as skins, and it was not a time during which complete harmony prevailed at Headquarters. Wolseley's army was encumbered with a plethora of generals—one general to every nine hundred men—and there developed among them what Butler euphemistically described as 'domestic differences'. But no matter. By September 12 the army was in position at a place called Kassassin only six miles east of Tel-el-Kebir. And only then were Wolseley's plans revealed to the soldiers who would be called upon to execute them. 'There was to be launched out into the night', so Butler wrote 'a gigantic bolt of flesh, steel and iron shot westward into the darkness.'

No man knew better than Wolseley the risk a night march involved. It was nearly impossible to maintain a precise course in darkness, difficult to preserve an even pace among the units making the advance, and the slightest hitch in the prearranged movements could result in a confused tangle of men and guns. (Several of the worst disasters to befall British soldiers in the Boer War—notably Stormberg, Magersfontein and Nicholson's Nek—followed on night marches into unfamiliar territory.) But the risks involved in a night march on Tel-el-Kabir seemed trifling in comparison with the probable advantages to be gained. The desert terrain offered no obstacles of any kind to such a march; the Egyptians, Wolseley was sure, would be caught completely off guard. And even if by some odd chance he should find them on the alert, he was confident that he had man and gun power enough to overcome the strongest opposition that Arabi's ill-equipped, ill-trained forces could offer. From a night march there was much to gain and almost nothing to lose.

The army, numbering nearly 20,000 men and heavily supported by artillery, moved out on to the desert shortly after midnight on a front a mile deep and four miles wide. The advance was made in extraordinary silence. The accoutrements of war were muffled, the desert gave back no sound of footfalls, and the only soldier who disturbed the uncanny stillness was a Scot, who having filled his bottle with rum instead of water, suddenly reached a degree of intoxication which made life a joke to be laughed at. He was instantly tied up and chloroformed into silence.

Butler rode with Wolseley, his thoughts strangely divided between the present with its anticipations of stirring things to come and the remote past; for the desert, like the prairie, always moved him to melancholy reflection on the transient nature of man and all his works:

Sir Garnet Wolseley had in his possession a very fine repeater watch. . . . By striking the watch he knew the exact moment of the night, and as the minutes between four and five o'clock began to strike longer numbers, they seemed to draw into tighter twist all the strands of our expectations. And yet . . . what did it matter to this old desert and these older stars? Our guides, we thought them. Ours! Had not Moses led his Israelites here three thousand years ago? Had not Napoleon marched the best soldiers known to the world over these sands and under the same stars? Countless Pharaohs had driven their chariots across these brown ridges; and one day did there not come along this route into Egypt a man leading an ass on which a woman rode, bearing in her arms a Babe who was to be a wider conqueror than they all? What did our little night-march matter in that catalogue or context? Perhaps the poor hysterical Scottish soldier, whose weird laugh broke so rudely upon the desert silence an hour before, knew as much about it as the best of us.[2]

The drunken Scot had disturbed the silence early in the march; the second bad moment for Wolseley came much nearer the Egyptian encampment. An order to the Highland Brigade to halt reached the centre of the line without a hitch, but its whispered transmission to the flanks was delayed a minute or two. The centre halted, the flanks continued to march and at the same time retain contact with the centre, with the inevitable result that they turned in to the point where the soldiers of flank and centre were almost face to face with one another. Butler assisted the brigade commander to disentangle the badly confused Highlanders, and the advance was resumed.

Precisely at dawn the thunderbolt struck.

The Egyptians were caught, as Wolseley knew they would be, totally unprepared. But they did not panic. They fought bravely and hopelessly with whatever weapons they could lay their hands on, and died under the bullets and bayonets of the British infantry. The battle of Tel-el-Kebir was over in thirty-five minutes. There followed a period of mopping-up operations—a convenient euphemism for the slaughter of unarmed fugitives—and an hour after the opening shot Wolseley sat down on the parapet of a stone bridge crossing the Sweetwater Canal and wrote the despatch which told the English people of the victory of Tel-el-Kebir.

Two days after the battle Colonel Arabi surrendered his sword to Herbert Stewart, and Egypt's bid for freedom was ended. The next day Wolseley entered Cairo by train and took up residence, together with most of his staff, in the magnificent Abdin Palace that the Khedive Ismail had built for himself in the glittering days of his ascendancy. Shortly afterwards Butler and Herbert Stewart moved to the much older Abbassiyeh Palace, in which the harem of the 'late Pasha of the blood' was still lodged. Moving-in was a protracted operation for, so Butler reported. 'the ladies had to be removed from room to room before we were allowed to enter the apartments, and thus we were playing a sort of hide-and-seek with them through the palace'.

Butler no doubt thoroughly enjoyed the game.

During the remainder of his stay in Cairo Butler's chief concern was for Colonel Arabi, now facing trial on a charge of high treason. That Arabi had headed a genuine national movement (even Baring conceded as much), that he had behind him the overwhelming majority of the Egyptian people, that he and the movement he headed had been ruthlessly crushed by a foreign army would count not for but against him when he faced his accusers. Or so Butler feared. For the court-martial before which Arabi would come to trial was sure to be made up of officers who hated him, men loyal to Tewfik—and behind the officers and demanding the death sentence for Arabi were the foreign representatives, the money-lenders, the whole malodorous crew now swarming into Egypt on the heels of Wolseley's victorious army.

All the passions were now in entire possession of the Egyptian vantage points; the Levantine jackal, the Khedival eunuch, the bloodthirsty Circassian . . . these were now flocking into Egypt in thousands. With them were coming the former advisers of the English foreign office, whose persistently erroneous counsels had . . . produced the crisis which had just been closed by the slaughter at Tel-el-Kebir. Behind these various persons and professions this unfortunate fellah, Arabi, had ranged against him the entire tribe of the Levites and the High Priests of finance, foreign and Egyptian, from the heads of the great Jewish banking-houses in Europe to the humble money-changer at the street corners of Alexandria.[3]

Not only in Egypt was the cry raised for Arabi's head; back home in England, Sir Samuel Baker, the African explorer who in 1872 had served as Ismail's viceroy in the lower Sudan, wrote pontifically to *The Times*: 'The question now arises, what is to become of Arabi and the ringleaders of the rebels? Those who defy the law must suffer the punishment determined by the law, and no exception should be made to this stern exigence of necessity. . . . Nothing could be more fatal to the true interest of Egypt than our advising moderation towards the vanquished.'

Moderation towards the vanquished was precisely what Butler

sought. He did not hesitate to nail his colours to the mast, let it be known he was on Arabi's side. When Arabi was moved for greater security from Abbassiyeh Palace to the Abdin a large group of British officers gathered at the Abdin to see the arrival of the vanquished leader. Arabi alighted from the carriage, drew himself up and saluted the British officers. Two officers returned the salute. One was General Drury Lowe, who had commanded Wolseley's cavalry. The other was Butler.

The salute might charitably be interpreted as no more than misdirected courtesy; but when *The Times* correspondent in Cairo reported that 'the Khedive, Sherif and Riaz Pashas all insist strongly on the absolute necessity of the capital punishment of the prime offenders, an opinion from which there are few, if any dissentients', Butler, to save Arabi, took positive action which in the eyes of the orthodox must have seemed that of a man bent on his own destruction. General Sir John Adye, Wolseley's Chief of Staff and a close friend of Gladstone's, was about to return to England. Butler sat up the entire night before Sir John's departure writing a letter which he delivered to Sir John on the station platform the next morning with the terse comment, 'Not about myself, sir.' The letter, written in absolute disregard of military protocol, is probably one of the most remarkable documents ever handed a chief of staff by a subordinate. It read in part:

Nothing but a very strong belief in the necessity of doing what I can to avert what I believe would be a national crime makes me now write to you upon a subject far removed from the sphere of military duty which has hitherto given me a claim as an officer of your staff to communicate with you. I write to urge you to telegraph from Alexandria to England to stop the execution of Arabi Pasha (should the court which is sitting, or about to sit, condemn him to death) until you have arrived in England and are in a position to place before the Government a full view of the Egyptian question as it then will have taken its place in your mind, in just and true proportion.

After a review of the evil effects, in the light of history, of executions carried out to satisfy the lust for vengeance rather than the ends of justice—'the wounds inflicted in war, no matter how deep they may be, soon heal compared to those which are left in the memory of a people by the work of the scaffold'—the letter concludes with a vehement declaration of British responsibility for Arabi's fate:

In what light will history regard the execution of Arabi? It will be written that we, a great and powerful Empire, vanquished this man and then surrendered our prisoner to the vengeance of the weak, and therefore cruel, rulers. The voice of the civilised world will be against us. . . . It will be useless to say that the act was not ours, we cannot get rid of our responsibility that way: the world will not accept the transfer.[4]

It is unlikely that the letter had any influence on Arabi's fate (Arabi's death sentence was commuted to exile to Ceylon); but no doubt Butler slept better after writing it, even though he must have known that his action was to his personal disadvantage. Sir Evelyn Wood, in his review of Butler's *Autobiography*, probably expressed the view of most army men who knew about the letter:

(Butler) relates an incident more creditable to his heart than to his sense of subordination which occurred during the Egyptian expedition of 1882 after our troops had reinstated the Khedive in his capital. The Egyptian ministers intended to execute Arabi and his companions. Butler, who felt it would be an everlasting disgrace to England, did not do the natural thing, that is, approach his General and warm personal friend, Sir Garnet Wolseley, but sat up all the night previous to the departure of Sir John Adye, who had just relinquished the position of Chief of Staff, writing a powerful protest. Next morning at the Cairo station, when Sir John was leaving for London, Butler gave him his memorandum urging him to telegraph from Alexandria to his friend Mr. Gladstone to intervene and prevent Arabi's execution. All this was unnecessary . . .[5]

Sir Evelyn, who never violated protocol in his life and rose to the rank of field-marshal, would doubtless have disapproved of what Butler had done even had he known what Butler knew—that Wolseley favoured Arabi's execution.

Life in Cairo was not all work and worry for Butler and his fellow officers. One of their happiest experiences was a picnic expedition to the pyramids, arranged by Wolseley and dominated by the extraordinary figure and personality of Colonel Valentine Baker Pasha, the brother of the explorer, Sir Samuel Baker. Valentine Baker had enjoyed a brilliant career in the British cavalry until, at the age of forty-seven, he was found guilty of indecently assaulting a girl in a railway carriage compartment and sent to prison for a year. On his release he found employment with the Egyptian Army. He arrived at the picnic wearing striped trousers, frock coat and silk hat. At the end of a long hot afternoon of tunnel-exploring, pyramid-climbing and donkey-riding a good deal of the gloss had been taken off Baker's costume—coat split up the back, trouser-legs bunched below his knees, and silk hat collapsed like a concertina.

Butler was a conscientious sightseer; but relics of ancient greatness, tombs of kings who were dust 3,000 years ago, excited him less than the life that teemed around him:

More interesting to me than the tomb or temple of the dead past in the desert was the endless picture of the life of the fellah in the soft green level of his homeland; his fields of grain in their many stages between seed and stubble, his plots of onions, sweet-smelling beans, deep green clover, cotton, and flowering flax; the brown canal banks where the cattle, goats, donkeys and camels stood in the shade of the acacia-trees in the hot hours, munching the stalks of sugar-cane or nibbling the golden 'tibbin'; the big blue buffaloes, with their horns and noses just showing above the yellow water; and the date palms rustling in the cool north wind round some old marabout's tomb, whose little dome shows very white over the green fields; and under the glorious sunshine the great flocks of white pigeons skimming over villages, the strange 'paddy' birds standing in the inundated fields; above all, man, woman, and child at work everywhere, sowing, reaping, weeding, working the water wheel in winter, and in summer, when the Nile is pouring down its flooded waters, opening the little water courses from one field to another with their feet to let the saving flood flow on its way.[6]

Not ancient ruins but living people brought history to life, established contact with the past. Looking at the fellaheen opening the watercourses with their feet made Butler remember his Bible: 'The land whither thou goest in to possess it, is not as the land of Egypt from whence ye came out, where thou sowedst the seed, and wateredst it with thy foot . . . !'

Butler left Egypt in October with reluctance, never dreaming that he would be back in two years to fight the hardest campaign of his life.

Meanwhile Elizabeth Butler was busy on a picture for the 1883 Academy showing. It was called *After the Battle*, and showed Sir Garnet Wolseley, flanked by Sir John Adye, Redvers Buller and Butler, receiving the cheers of the Highlanders on the stone bridge over the Sweetwater Canal just after the battle of Tel-el-Kebir. *After the Battle* was one of Elizabeth Butler's most dramatically effective pictures, painted with her characteristic technical skill and regard for realistic detail, and Butler hated it. Tel-el-Kebir was not a battle at all, it was a slaughter of the ignorant and innocent, a mismatching of a superbly equipped modern army with a rabble of peasants, and as such a subject unfit for art—at least as Elizabeth had treated it. 'To beat those poor fellaheen soldiers was not a matter for exultation,' he told her—and added that the capture of Arabi's earthworks had been 'like going through brown paper'.

Elizabeth Butler, as strong-willed upon occasion as her husband, none the less submitted the picture to the Academy, and it enjoyed great critical acclaim and popular success. But after her husband's death, perhaps to secure peace to what she feared might be his still-angry shade, she cut the picture to pieces. The central portions, including Wolseley's head, survive in the Butler family archives.

It was typical of Butler that in addition to protesting the unworthiness of the battle of Tel-el-Kebir as a subject of art, he alone among the scores who wrote of the Campaign of 1882 saluted, in one of his most moving passages, the men forgotten in life and death—the humble fellaheen of the Egyptian Army:

> There is one thing I should like to put on record regarding this battle of Tel-el-Kebir. Complete surprise though it was to the Egyptian soldiers behind their entrenchments, they nevertheless fought with the greatest determination and gallantry against overwhelming odds. Not a moment was given them to awake, form up, prepare, or move into position. The assault fell upon them as a thunderbolt might fall upon a man asleep. The leaders in whom they could trust were, like themselves, fellaheen; few among them knew anything of war, its acts, manoeuvres, or necessities; they were betrayed on every side, yet they fought stoutly whenever ten or twenty or fifty of them could get together in the angles of the lines, and in the open desert between the lines. The heaps of dead lying with and across their rifles facing the upcoming sun bore eloquent testimony to that final resolve. . . . Peace be to them, lying under these big mounds on the lone desert—ten thousand it is said. No word should soldier utter against them; let that be left to the money-changers. They died the good death. Dust to dust. They did not desert the desert, and Egypt will not forget them.[7]

CHAPTER THIRTEEN

The Campaign of the Cataracts

IN NOVEMBER of the year 1883 an Egyptian army made up of 10,000 men, 5,000 camels and an uncounted mob of camp-followers straggled across the burning desert south-west of the city of Khartoum towards a miserable end. The European officers commanding the army did not know where they were; the soldiers—many of them survivors of Arabi's army who had been sent to the Sudan in chains—were half-dead from thirst and exhaustion; and between them and their objective, a besieged Egyptian outpost on the western fringe of the desert, a force of 40,000 Arab warriors had gathered for the kill. The death agony of the Egyptian Army lasted three days; on the first day of fighting most of the camp-followers perished; on the second the main body of the army, struggling to advance in cumbersome squares, the officers distracted and the men without will to fight, was systematically cut to pieces by the Arab warriors, who, knowing that victory was certain, fought with discretion and killed without haste. On the third day the Arabs took some prisoners for slaves—a few hundred of the original force of ten thousand—and saluted the courage of the dead leader of the dead army by giving him honourable burial on the field where he had fallen instead of leaving his body to the jackals.

The leader thus honoured was Colonel Hicks Pasha, an English officer formerly of the Indian Army, who had been appointed by the Khedive Tewfik to subdue an Arab revolt in the Sudan which had reached serious proportions. The death of Hicks and the destruction of the Egyptian army meant the triumph of the rebels; except for a few outposts the entire Sudan above Khartoum was now in Arab hands, and in the minds and hearts of those who had long suffered the tyranny of Egyptian rule, the man who had led them to freedom, a priest named Mohammed Ahmed, was in truth the Mahdi whom he claimed to be—the second Prophet chosen to lead the faithful nearer God and purge Islam of the infidel.

From the beginning of the nineteenth century Egypt had ruled over the Sudan, that vast and primitive region of desert, grazing-land, lush river valley and jungle stretching from the Egyptian frontier south to the Equator. Her rule was at best desultory, at worst brutal; her policy consistent only in its degree of exploitation. Every Sudanese official, from the Governor-General at Khartoum to the pettiest tax-collector in the remotest outpost, lived only to extort from the miserable natives as much as possible of their money and goods. 'The government of the Egyptians . . . is nothing else but brigandage of the very worst description,' Colonel Charles Gordon said, after having himself served for two years as Governor of Equatoria, the southernmost part of the Sudan. Most of the black aboriginal population accepted with passivity the tyranny of their rulers; but the people called Arabs, in the main a mixed race of Arab stock crossed with the black aboriginal, were less acquiescent. The Arabs were desert nomads, fierce predatory tribesmen, who, loving freedom, lived by enslaving others. In Winston Churchill's words,

> Some of the Arabs were camel breeders; some were goat-herds; some were Baggaras or cow-herds. But all, without exception, were hunters of men. To the great slave-market at Jedda a continual stream of negro captives had flowed for hundreds of years. Thus the situation in the Soudan for several centuries may be summed up as follows: the dominant race of Arab invaders was unceasingly spreading its blood, religion, customs and language among the black aboriginal population and at the same time it harried and enslaved them.[1]

By the Egyptian conquest of the Sudan the Arabs were in turn enslaved; and they hated their Egyptian oppressors only one degree less than they did the European infidel who in the employment of Egypt was beginning to infiltrate the Sudan.

The uprising against Egypt began as a holy war in response to the Mahdi's summons to the Arabs of the Sudan to fight for a purified religion, freedom of the soil, and God's holy Prophet—himself. At first his followers numbered only a handful; they were armed mostly with sticks and stones, but they were inspired by the fanaticism born of passionate religious conviction and by the recklessness born of sufferings so great as to make life a small thing to lose. They found the Egyptians, who had grown fat and soft and careless, surprisingly easy to kill; and by the midsummer of 1883 most of the Egyptian garrisons beyond Khartoum had been overwhelmed, the rest were under siege, and the collapse of Egyptian power in the entire Sudan seemed imminent.

Mohammed Ahmed, born a nobody, left fatherless in early childhood, without money or influential friends to help him, made his way in the world with the aid of an exemplary piety, a high level of intelligence, and an unshakeable faith in his own high destiny. His piety attracted the attention of devout believers ever on the look-out for the Mahdi, the second Prophet whose coming would make them free men again; his intelligence told him when to refrain from striking and when to strike; his faith in himself, being absolute, readily communicated itself to others, so that hope became certainty and simple shepherds and herdsmen followed him, as simple peasants had followed Joan of Arc, because they believed he was God-inspired.

God-inspired or not, Mohammed Ahmed was too much for the Egyptians; and the British, more firmly entrenched than ever in Cairo, were faced, as they had been faced in 1882, with the prospect of having to intervene openly in the affairs of a country they reluctantly—and in the main covertly—ruled. Gladstone at once made the position of his Liberal Government clear—Great Britain had no interest whatsoever in the desert wastes of the Sudan. The Egyptians were therefore advised to withdraw their garrisons and civil servants as quickly as possible and abandon their empire to the Arabs. The Egyptians protested so loudly that, as Churchill dryly commented, 'they provoked Lord Granville to explain the meaning of the word "advice" '. The policy of evacuation was therefore adopted and it was agreed by both British and Egyptian authorities that the Egyptian soldiers and civilians scattered in large numbers throughout the Sudan should be removed with all speed and the land left to Mohammed Ahmed and the Arabs to rule.

The policy was easy to devise, impossible to execute. Most of the garrisons which had not already fallen to the Mahdi were under siege and could be relieved only by a substantial military expedition; and at Khartoum a curious lethargy had settled on Egyptian soldiers and civilians alike. They seemed reluctant, despite the obvious threat of encirclement, to make any sort of move to save themselves, and there was no strong man among them to lead them out of the land they could no longer rule. To even the most obtuse official in Cairo or London it soon became clear that without British or other European intervention the entire foreign population of the Sudan would be condemned to slavery or death.

In England, pressure on the Government to do something rapidly mounted. It was exerted by the humanitarian organizations which flourished almost without number in the Victorian Age, by business and financial corporations whose interests were not confined within the bounds of Egypt proper, by the Press, and by a general public feeling that the Hicks disaster had hurt British prestige—the Egyptian army had been led by British officers. National pride demanded that the Mahdi be given a proper dusting by a proper British army.

The compromise plan accepted by the Government satisfied, on paper, Gladstone's desire to avoid any serious involvement in the Sudan, but not the demand of the voters that some action be taken immediately to save the garrisons and chastise the Mahdi. No military expedition would be sent up the Nile or across the desert from the Red Sea, nor would a strong man be sent to Khartoum 'to assume absolute control of the territory, to relieve the garrisons, and do what can be done to save what can be saved from the wreck of the Soudan', as W. T. Stead, the editor of the enormously influential *Pall Mall Gazette*, demanded. A British representative would indeed be sent to Khartoum, but not one invested with extraordinary powers. Rather, it would be his duty to investigate, report, and perhaps, if circumstances seemed propitious, try to make some sort of peace treaty with the Mahdi. The presence of such a representative in Khartoum would, it was felt, assure the public of Government concern without committing the Government to any course of action whatever.

The choice of General Gordon for representative was the most popular with the British public that the Government could possibly have made, and the most disastrous for the Government. At the age of fifty, Gordon, perhaps the supreme original of the era, was already a legend. He had fought bravely in the Crimea; he had led the Ever-Victorious Army of the Imperial Government of China to a series of astonishing victories over the Taiping rebels; he had served with extraordinary distinction as the Khedive Ismail's Governor of Equatoria and later as Governor-General of the entire Sudan. He was a devout Christian and Bible student who belonged to no church and did not believe in hell; and in the eyes of the Victorian middle class his contempt for the rewards of this life—he rejected the Khedive Ismail's offer of a Governor's salary of £10,000 a year, saying £2,000 was plenty—seemed to place him outside the operations of natural law and invest him with the attributes of divinity.

But Gordon was not the man to send to the Sudan to play an observer's role. He was no man's servant, and Sir Evelyn Baring knew it. Baring opposed the appointment with all the strength of his will and authority, and in vain. The public would not be denied its drama nor the Government its economical face-saving. Gordon himself was eager to go to Khartoum. He had intended resigning from the British Army in order to assist in the administration of the Belgian Congo under H. M. Stanley; but when approached by the British Government he at once accepted what he felt was the greater and more urgent mission.

At this point agreement between Gordon and the British Government ended. From the moment of his arrival in Khartoum, Gordon recognized the impossibility of peacefully evacuating the Sudan; the revolt of the Mahdists was a national uprising whose object was the extermination of the detested foreigner, Egyptian and European; and Gordon, with only a weak force of Egyptian and Sudanese soldiers under his command, could no more hold back the Arabs than he could compel a desert whirlwind to stillness. Immediately, in response to what he called a 'mystic' inspiration, he took the one action that might have saved the people of the Sudan who so far had escaped the vengeance of the Mahdi—he asked for the appointment of Zobeir Pasha, the most notorious slave-trader in the whole of Africa, as his special aide and prospective successor in the governorship of the Sudan. What Gordon knew was that Zobeir—whom he had once prosecuted—and Zobeir alone still held enough authority among the Arabs of the Sudan to provide a counter-balance to the Mahdi and prevent the spread of Mahdist influence north to Khartoum and beyond. Give him Zobeir, he said, and he would do the job he was sent to do.

Sir Evelyn Baring and the Egyptian Government approved Gordon's request, but the home Government and the people of England rejected it out of hand—they would have no truck with slavers. They were, it seemed, prepared to sacrifice the Egyptians rather than their principles. But in actual fact, as Winston Churchill points out, 'the refusal to permit Zobeir's employment was tantamount to an admission that affairs in the Soudan involved the honour of England as well as the honour of Egypt; when the British people—for this was not merely the act of the Government—adopted a high moral attitude with regard to Zobeir, they bound themselves to rescue the garrisons, peacably if possible, forcibly if necessary'.[2]

The policy of intervention adopted by the British Government was marked from the beginning by indecision and vacillation. An expedition mounted by the Egyptian Government to rescue two hard-pressed garrisons near the Red Sea coast was approved, and a force of 3,500 Egyptian soldiers under the command of Valentine Baker Pasha dispatched to the area. The Arabs butchered the Egyptians at the wells of Teb; Baker and a handful of fellow officers almost alone cutting their way through the Arab hordes to safety. Both the isolated garrisons were shortly thereafter overwhelmed. When there was no one left in the area to rescue, the British Government mounted its own full-scale Red Sea expedition. The Arabs were soundly defeated at Teb and Tamai and the first step taken towards establishing a secure route to Khartoum from Suakim on the Red Sea coast by way of Berber, 250 miles inland on the Nile and 200 miles below Khartoum. But nothing more was done. The Arabs had been taught a lesson, the victorious British army recalled, the Arabs repossessed the desert between the Red Sea coast and Berber; and only a few weeks after the British victories at Teb and Tamai the forces of the Mahdi occupied Berber and closed the trap on Khartoum. Gordon was cut off—'not surrounded, merely hemmed in', as Gladstone explained in one of the most curious and unconvincing word-juggling acts in the history of the House of Commons. And thereafter, for a period of nearly four months, nothing at all was done about Khartoum.

The defence of the city must rank as one of the great triumphs of human personality. One lone man possessed of extraordinary courage, magnetism, and unshakeable faith in God—as well as an unusual measure of ingenuity and common sense—raised and sustained the spirit of the city's people and garrison to a point which enabled them for nearly a year to hold off the Mahdists, fighting not only the enemy outside the walls but the deadlier enemies within—disease, hunger, and the terrible heart-sickness

HAULING WHALE-BOATS THROUGH BAB-EL-KEBIR, THE GREAT GATE OF THE SECOND CATARACT
From 'The Illustrated London News' November 29th, 1884

DEPARTURE OF THE DESERT COLUMN FROM KORTI. *An illustration from 'The Campaign of The Cataracts: A Personal Narrative of the Great Nile Expedition of 1884-5'*

born of hope endlessly deferred. The world looked on in admiration and suspense and did nothing else until too late.

The decision of the British Government to send a strong military expedition to Khartoum was forced upon a reluctant Prime Minister by pressure of public opinion, the demands of prominent members of his own party, and General Gordon's flat refusal to come away from Khartoum by himself—which he could easily have done by any one of the river steamers under his command—and leave the city and such garrisons as were still holding out at isolated points to the mercy of the Mahdi. Gladstone, who from the first had been reluctant to commit Great Britain to involvement in the Sudan, felt with some reason that he was being made the victim of a kind of moral blackmail, and for a long time ignored the popular clamour; but when two members of his Cabinet threatened to resign unless an attempt was made to save Gordon he capitulated. In August of 1884, six months after Gordon had gone to Khartoum, the Government announced that a military expedition was being sent up the Nile at once to relieve Khartoum and rescue Gordon. Sir Garnet Wolseley was appointed to command the expedition.

Wolseley, always alert to anticipate contingencies, had laid his plans for the campaign much earlier. He had evolved them in discussions with Butler, Buller, Herbert Stewart, Brackenbury and a dozen other trusted subordinates of the Ring; and among these men there was almost unanimous agreement that the only practicable way of reaching Khartoum was by river-boat up the Nile, rather than by the overland route from Suakim on the Red Sea coast across the waterless desert to Berber. The problems of supply on the desert route would, so Wolseley believed, be insurmountable—4,000 camels would be needed to transport water alone, and the supply line stretching across the desert would be vulnerable to attack. The Nile route eliminated entirely the problem of water supply, and Wolseley was confident that boats carrying soldiers and food supplies could, if properly handled, surmount the five great cataracts of the river and bring the force within striking distance of Khartoum in time to save Gordon. Wolseley's problem was to sell his plan—bitterly opposed in some high places—to the War Office and the Government. As usual he had his way. Early in August Butler and Colonel Alleyne of the Royal Engineers were commissioned to 'proceed at once to find four hundred boats similar to those used in the Red River Expedition'. The idea of a flotilla of Canadian river boats on the Nile excited Butler's imagination; and he rarely undertook a commission with greater enthusiasm or showed more resourcefulness in its execution. The design of the Nile 'whaler', as the boat used by the Expedition was popularly called, very closely resembled that of a Hudson's Bay Company York boat; and it was determined upon only after Butler and Alleyne had carried out the most painstaking experiments with various types of craft in Portsmouth Harbour. No fewer than forty-seven boat-building companies all round England stood ready to begin construction the moment the project was officially approved, and so well had Butler and Alleyne looked after the preliminaries that within a month of the order being given the 400 boats had been built and shipped to Egypt. (An additional 400 were put into use later.) Diehard supporters of a conventional overland drive from Suakim to Berber looked on appalled. Said the voice of orthodoxy, *The Army and Navy Gazette:*

A more wicked waste of money has never been perpetrated, a more silly quackery was never devised by any public department than that which Lord Hartington, and the Duke of Cambridge, representing the War Office and the Horse Guards, have really and truly been guilty of in ordering that monstrous armada of boats, that unfloatable flotilla for the Nile! Burn them for firewood! Send them to Jericho, to ply in the Palestine canal of the future! Make matches of them, do anything with them. Put men in them and try to send them up the Nile cataracts—never, we beg of you!

Wolseley's preparations for the campaign were marked by his usual meticulous attention to detail and his concern for flexibility. If one plan failed, or threatened to fail, he intended to be in a position to try another. The main infantry force was to be transported upriver by boat; but should the movement fall far behind schedule in the passing of the cataracts between Wady Halfa, the point of departure, and the end of rough water 300 miles below Khartoum, Wolseley planned to have on hand a Camel Corps of 2,000 men, recruited mostly from the crack Guards regiments, which would, if circumstances demanded, make a dash across the neck of the great bend in the Nile between Korti and Metemmeh. Such a movement would by-pass the rough water running through the terrible Monassir Desert region, shorten the distance to Khartoum by several hundred miles, and, so Wolseley hoped, place a strong enough relief force inside the city to enable it to hold out until the arrival by boat of the main body of the Expedition.

Butler had no doubt whatever that the boats would reach their objective in time. He seldom had doubts about the success of any undertaking he took charge of, and this time his confidence was strengthened when Wolseley, acting on the advice of his Red River officers, asked that a special civilian corps of Canadian boatmen be recruited to take the whalers up the Nile.

The corps of voyageurs was the most extraordinary feature of an extraordinary campaign. The men were enlisted—as civilian workers, not as soldiers—mainly through the offices of Lord Melgund, Military Secretary to the Governor-General of Canada (and later, as the Earl of Minto, himself Governor-General), and the required number reached within a few days. True, the recruits did not greatly resemble the corps of voyageurs Butler and Wolseley had dreamed of; most of the men were recruited not from the rivers of the west but the Ottawa lumber-camps, and some of them knew nothing about boats. From Winnipeg came a large group of young business and professional men, eight of them lawyers, engaged by the colonel of a militia regiment in which most of the men served. They were eager for adventure, reluctant to work, useless as voyageurs and ultimately an acute embarrassment to their officers.

The voyageurs sailed from Montreal aboard the *Ocean King* under the command of Lieutenant-Colonel Dennison, a militia officer from Toronto. They were drunk before they sailed, they were drunk aboard ship, and they stayed drunk until their smuggled liquor ran out. After that their behaviour was exemplary until they reached Gibraltar, where the two Ayotte brothers from Montreal defeated half the waterfront police in a pitched battle and had to be subdued by their own comrades. From Alexandria the voyageurs travelled up the Nile by rail to Assiout and thence by Thomas Cook and Sons' steamers to Wady Halfa. Butler was working round the clock on details of transport, but he found time to welcome many of the voyageurs in person, and in particular one trusted companion of the old Red River days:

One day . . . I was engaged in the daily work of the dockyards, when across the river a strange object caught my sight. . . . A small American birch-bark canoe, driven by those quick down-strokes that seem to be the birthright of the Indian *voyageur* alone, was moving up the further shore. When this strange craft had got well abreast of our dockyard, it steered across the swift river and was soon underneath my tent. Out of the canoe, with all the slow gravity of his race, stepped a well-remembered figure—William Prince, Chief of the Swampy Indians from Lake Winnipeg in North America. . . . Fourteen years earlier this same William Prince had been the best Indian in my canoe when we forced our way up the rapids of the Winnipeg to meet the advance of the Red River Expedition through the wilderness of the North-West. And here today, on the Nile, stood William Prince, now chief of his tribe, grown more massive of frame and less agile of gait, but still keen of eye and steady of hand as when I last saw him standing bowman in a bark canoe among the whirling waters whose echoes were lost in the endless pine-woods of the Great Lone Land.[3]

For the boats in his charge Butler had already developed an immense sympathy and affection—the sight of one mishandled caused him an almost physical pain. From first to last he looked upon the boat transport scheme as his own; and it was to be his shortcoming—or perhaps his strength—that he was intolerant of any other. All his energies, hopes and loves were for the time concentrated on the boats, and any interference with their progress roused in him a passion which he expressed in language more picturesque than diplomatic.

At Wady Halfa, where Wolseley had established the Expedition base, Butler was in fine fettle, his confidence as yet unshaken and his hopes undimmed. In spite of the tensions which his work inevitably gave rise to, he enjoyed unusual peace of mind because for the first time in his military career he was fighting a war he believed in. The others—in West Africa, Zululand, Egypt—he dismissed contemptuously as 'sutlers' wars', fought to humble the deserving and line the pockets of the unworthy. But the campaign to save Gordon, the most splendid man of the age, was on the highest level of chivalric enterprise; it was, he told Elizabeth, 'the very first war in the Victorian era in which the object was entirely worthy'.

And indeed there was some justification for what he said. It is true that no war was ever fought for purely disinterested or philanthropic ends, but from the viewpoint of the practical realist—or the sutler—the Nile Expedition must have seemed the ultimate manifestation of human fatuity—Red Indians from the Saskatchewan, black croomen from West Africa, 10,000 British soldiers,

6,000 camels, 800 Nile whalers and the steamers of Thomas Cook and Sons launched on a strenuous and costly campaign to save a single man who did not want to be saved.

It is possible now, being wise long after the event, to see at a thousand points errors of judgement, flaws of character, obstructions no human foresight could anticipate, which impeded the progress of the campaign to the point where what might have been a magnificent success ended in tragic failure. But it must never be lost sight of that the Nile campaign was unique in the experience of those directing it in that its success did not hinge solely on victory over the enemy but on achieving an objective within a time limit the length of which no man could specify. What can be said with certainty is that the failure of the campaign was not due to the errors of any one man. Perhaps the most significant factor in that failure was nothing more obvious than a barely perceptible slowing-down of mental and physical drive on the part of the members of the Wolseley Ring. They were no longer young men; many of them had won their spurs long since or were no longer ambitious and they were losing their hard bright edge. Buller in particular, to whom Wolseley unwisely had entrusted the vital duties of Chief of Staff, had grown stout and sluggish and too fond of the flesh-pots—forty camels were required to carry his personal goods and comforts. And Colonel Dennison of the voyageur corps raised an eyebrow when he saw his men transporting the supplies which Sir Evelyn Wood considered essential to survival in the desert. 'General Wood's baggage passed through here today', he wrote to his brother from a point near Dongola. 'Besides tents, camp furniture, etc., he has 96 cases with stores, about 40 being wines of different sorts. He evidently intends being comfortable.'

Whatever Butler's sins, self-indulgence was not one of them. In his *Life* of Napier he quoted with approval words spoken by Napier before going on a campaign: 'What does an officer want in the field? His bed, tent, a blanket, a second pair of shoes, half a dozen shirts, a second flannel waistcoat, a couple of towels and a piece of soap. All beyond is mere luxury and not fit for a campaign.' Butler himself ate stewed bully beef and ship's biscuit, drank Nile water and slept much of the time in the open, using his saddle-bags for pillow. He worked with prodigious energy from break of day until darkness, and frequently stayed up most of the night writing the letters, communiqués and lengthy telegrams with which he bombarded superiors and colleagues, all urging upon their recipients the need of greater exertion, greater haste. The campaign of the cataracts, to use Butler's own descriptive phrase, was in every way a remarkable one; and the fact that it almost achieved its objective in the face of the most disheartening obstacles is due mainly to Butler's heroic exertions.

Soldiers rowed the boats, the voyageurs—one in the stern, one in the bow—guided them. It was the business of the voyageurs to choose the water which to their experienced eyes seemed the most readily navigable and nurse the boats through. In exceptionally rough water or a powerful current the soldiers went ashore, leaving only the bowman and rudder man aboard, and tracked the boats upstream with ropes drawn over their shoulders. Early in the campaign Butler hit on the idea of stationing teams of voyageurs at fixed points on the river, thus giving them a chance to become thoroughly acquainted—in the way of an old-fashioned river-boat pilot—with all the shifts and vagaries of a particular stretch of water. On the whole, men and boats behaved admirably, and casualties were few. Only three boats out of 800 were wrecked on the entire 500-mile stretch of river from Wady Halfa to El Kab, the farthest point of advance; and of the twelve voyageurs who died during the campaign only five were victims of the river.

Ian Hamilton, that gallant, gossipy and luckless soldier who took part in nearly every British military disaster from Majuba to Gallipoli, served during the Nile Expedition with a detachment of the Gordons; and his account of the advance of the River Column is rather less enthusiastic than Butler's:

My Company took their seats in eleven small row-boats to struggle hundreds of miles up the Nile in order to save Gordon; a vague and typically British adventure—just like a fairy tale. . . . Our feelings were as nearly as possible those of a party of Boy Scouts dressed up like Red Indians and let loose in a flotilla of canoes. Each boat of eight rowers, a poleman and a coxswain was—and had to be—a self-supporting, independent unit. At the best, the company got together about once in ten days. . . . The tale has the ring of glorious adventure, and so it was, only, at the time, it was incessant toil, much of it waist-deep in water; bad food, broken nights, the lack of any drink but sand and water; the resultant scurvy; all those wore health and nerves to fiddle-strings.[4]

But whatever the inconveniences of rowing up the Nile, Ian Hamilton agreed with Butler that the flotilla represented the only hope of saving Gordon. When Wolseley decided to create a second striking force, the Desert Column, thus dividing the interest of his men and doubling the labour of supply, he sealed Gordon's fate:

The whole campaign would have been a fiasco had it not been for the River Column sideshow. . . . Our River Column was made up of four battalions of British Infantry plus a handful of Egyptian Auxiliaries; Cavalry and Camelry with pop-guns. For the Desert Column was to be 'the go' as they called it then; into *that* the cream of the British Army had been poured with no niggardly hand. Far from the nursemaids of Hyde Park, mounted now on magnificent, groaning camels, the Household Cavalry and the Guards performed the most wonderful evolutions. . . . Wolseley was in advance of his time. Dissect this stunt of his, you will diagnose the incipient boom-or-bust disease very easily. . . . The Desert Column was a brain freak of his. No one but Wolseley, in the days of railways, as leading soldier of the greatest industrial nation of the nineteenth century, could by his creating fancy have persuaded bovine Hartingtons and serious Gladstones to re-embark upon the methods of the ninth century. Had he stuck to his boats those river men, the other poor common soldiers, the outsiders, would have saved him; they would have enabled him to rescue Charles Gordon (which he was by no means mad keen about) and to wipe the floor with Roberts's march to Kandahar (on which he was absolutely set). But the pressure of the Ring; the urge to do something for his pals; the picturesqueness of the idea of putting London society on camels and marching them over a desert; these were too much for him. . . . The scheme was semi-social, semi-political. Charles Gordon was doomed when Wolseley hatched out the Desert Column. But the River Column though weak was homogeneous. Four battalions of 'Contemptibles'. There was nothing in the Sudan which could prevent them from getting to Berber, thence with reinforcements to fight an earlier Omdurman; to save millions of lives; to save Gladstone's soul; to save Wolseley's prestige from the knock from which it never recovered.[5]

Butler's vexations began early. Hardly had the movement of the boats from Cairo to the Nile by rail begun when it was suspended to permit passage of food supplies to units of the Egyptian army stationed at various upriver points. Butler sent telegrams of protest in all directions, including one to Buller, the Chief of Staff, at Wady Halfa: 'Three days lost through action of Egyptian Army officials. Wouldn't it be better to send the Egyptian army back to the beans and lentils, than to send the beans and lentils forward to the

Egyptian army?' The telegram helped to relieve Butler's feelings, but not to improve Anglo-Egyptian relations.

Soon, however, the first hold-up seemed a triviality by comparison with the later troubles that beset the flotilla. Demands for various priorities from ambitious British officers commanding Egyptian army units were among the commonest crosses Butler had to bear, but much more distressing was the refusal of Headquarters to accept with whole heart and mind the soundness of the river-transport plan:

Instead of being taken at once as the sole means of reaching in time, and with sufficient force, the destination for which we were bound, our boats had been grudgingly accepted by the various chiefs of staffs and departments, as things which had to prove their fitness for the task before anyone would believe in them. Hence there had grown up the thousand queries and the querulousness which, in an enterprise such as this we were engaged upon, meant a lot of lost power in every day's work and in most men's individual efforts.[6]

Worse than queries and querulousness was what Butler regarded as deliberate violation of orders given to those loading the boats at Wady Halfa. Butler and Colonel Alleyne had calculated with a fine precision the weight of cargo each boat should carry for maximum efficiency; but to his dismay Butler found that many of the cargoes weighed a ton or more above the authorized limit with near-disastrous consequences for several of the boats and a general slowing-down of transport.

But the heaviest blow of all to Butler was Wolseley's refusal to back him to the limit and insist on greater concentration of effort—particularly from Buller, who despised the boats—on moving the flotilla up the Nile with all speed. Indeed, Wolseley, fearful that Butler's uninhibited criticisms of his lethargic colleagues might create even worse dissensions than those already existing among the members of his staff—prima donnas almost to a man—took the extraordinary step of forbidding Butler to go upriver beyond the Third Cataract at Abu Fatmeh. From the Third Cataract to whatever destination the boats arrived at, others were to command.

The letter which Butler wrote to Wolseley on receipt of the order is characteristic of the writer in its vigour of expression and tactlessness. It ran to many pages, but a paragraph or two are sufficient to suggest its tenor:

Was it not through your letting me work this boat idea from the beginning on my own that you have at the present moment six hundred boats ready above the Second Cataract, that I have one above the Third Cataract, and that there might have been fifty more today had the old order of time and despatch been adhered to? And that all this had been done, please remember, within the limit of time which the highest naval authorities in England had declared would be required for only building the boats in England. I go back over the past and speak of the present work now only because your words and actions today have forced these recollections from me. . . . Not that I shall not use every effort, sparing myself in no way to effect the more rapid movement up river; but my words will not be heard in the noise of the slap in the face I have been given today, the sound of which will be grateful to many of whom I am distasteful because I have been identified with this expedition by ceaselessly furthering its interest.[7]

Wolseley, greatly upset, sent the letter to Louisa. Her observations were reassuring. 'Now about your unruly subordinate', she wrote. 'I can quite understand your annoyance, and you were right to pull him up and make him feel he must obey, but I think his chief offence is trop de zele, and the manner of his offence is due to his being, well, a very *imperfect* gentleman, if you can call him one at all. *I can't*.'[8]

Just why Louisa thought Butler an imperfect gentleman—or none at all—she never says. Perhaps it was enough that he had scolded her husband.

The judgements of his officers which Wolseley passes in his letters to Louisa are often at variance with what he says in his autobiography, where all is good fellowship and praise. It is clear he had early made up his mind that Butler was too much an individualist to be a good team man. 'I do hope nothing will prevent him (Baker Russell) from obtaining his regiment,' he wrote in December 1878, from Cyprus. 'It will be hard on him if it be given to that fellow Butler, who is no use as a commanding officer.' Butler's behaviour on the Nile Expedition confirmed Wolseley's view. As the race tightened, as tension mounted and tempers shortened Butler became more and more outspoken in criticism of his colleagues, particularly Redvers Buller, whose inability to keep supplies moving smoothly to Wady Halfa was a handicap to the entire expedition. 'Butler is becoming an impossible man for me,' Wolseley wrote to Louisa. 'He has great natural ability, but no business habits—wants to be the whole machine himself—I like him but I shall have to drop him from my list except for a big war where I could make him a Brigadier-General and see what he would be worth in that position.'[9]

But the war against the Mahdi was a small war and it was Herbert Stewart and not Butler who was made Brigadier-General. 'Butler is furious that Stewart has been made a Brigadier-General,' Wolseley reported. 'Butler is not the man for Stewart's place and in my selection of officers I choose those whom I think best for the work and I have no idea of being dictated to as to my selection by Butler or by anyone else. . . . I shall send Mr. B. a few lines giving him to understand that he may go to the devil as soon as he likes.'

The trouble was, Wolseley concluded, that brilliant men are rarely team men. When the members of the Ring were young with their ways to make they obeyed orders without question; now each man thought he should be a law unto himself. He poured out his troubles to Louisa in one of the most querulous of the many querulous letters he wrote to her:

Old Wellington was perhaps right in never having able men about him. Nearly all his generals were duffers and he made no secret of the fact, and most of his staff were selected for social reasons, a few outsiders with no family influence or position to give them power or influence . . . being kept in the background to do all the real work under his own direct guidance . . . I have always gone on the principle of getting hold of all the really able men I can find, but as soon as they feel they have an assured footing and can do really good staff service they torture themselves with jealousy one of the other and sometimes even in their dealings with me are inclined to kick over the traces. . . . It is often a sort of Chinese puzzle to fit them into the square they should make when put together, for their [sic] are some of such curious shapes, like Col. Butler for instance—who will fit in with no one and who think they should form a square by itself.[10]

While the Expedition dragged its slow length along, the man it had come so far to rescue was passing into history. General Charles Gordon's defence of Khartoum must rank among the greatest of man's heroic endeavours in all times and places, but not even Gordon could hold out for ever against disease and starvation and the fears which stalked the city and towards the end destroyed the will to fight in all except the strongest. Few men were less dependent on others for companionship and support than Gordon, whose Bible was his constant staff, but now loneliness closed in—

the loneliness born not of solitude but isolation, the severing of all contact with humanity beyond the ring of the Mahdi's armies. Help was on the way, he knew, but he had no great hope that it would reach Khartoum in time. And if it did, what then? The relief force could not evacuate the inhabitants or the garrison and Gordon was resolved never to abandon the people who trusted him. He would never run away, and what he might be ordered to do did not matter to one who, 'inattentive to the clamour of men, enquires what is acceptable to God'.[11] What was acceptable to God, he decided, was his life. The last lines of the *Journals*, that marvellous record of Gordon's days and thoughts and the supreme illustration of the man's indestructible spirit, make clear his recognition and acceptance of the sacrificial role he would be called upon to play: 'Now mark this, if the Expeditionary Force does not come within ten days *the town may fall;* and I have done my best for the honour of my country. Goodbye.'

At the time the words were written the advance units of the Nile Expedition were grouping at Korti, 400 miles downriver from Khartoum. Time was fast running out and Wolseley, against all his inclinations and his better judgement as a soldier, had decided to send the specially trained Camel Corps across the desert from Korti to Metemmeh, thereby shortening the distance to Khartoum by more than 200 miles. Four of Gordon's steamers lay at anchor off Metemmeh, and from Metemmeh the Corps would fight their way by land and steamer into Khartoum, there to strengthen the garrison and await the arrival of the main force by the roundabout river route.

Since camels were in short supply the advance from Korti to Metemmeh, begun on January 1, 1885, had to be made in two stages. Sir Herbert Stewart, whom Wolseley had appointed to lead the Camel Corps (popularly called the Desert Column as distinct from the main or River Column) first established a supply base at the Jakdul Wells, 100 miles in the desert, then returned to Korti to bring up further supplies and the main body of 1,600 men. The shuttling back and forth was costly in terms of time, and it was not until mid-January that the Desert Column was able to advance in full strength on Metemmeh, where Stewart hoped to place a token relief force aboard Gordon's steamers.

Fifty miles beyond Jakdul, at the Wells of Abu Klea, a force of 10,000 Arabs gave battle to the Desert Column. They charged the

British square with typical ferocity, strong in the hope of victory or paradise, and for a minute or two victory seemed certain, for they penetrated the square. But the soldiers did not panic, they closed the gap and in ten minutes or less the Battle of Abu Klea was over. In those ten minutes the British losses, in killed and wounded, totalled nearly 200 men, more than 10 per cent of the full strength of the force. Among the dead was the most spectacular figure of the British Army, Burnaby of the Guards—balloonist, big-game hunter, explorer, author of the immensely popular *A Ride to Khiva*, and true-blue Englishman who believed in and loudly proclaimed 'the supremacy of the Anglo-Saxon race'. Burnaby had fought heroically with Valentine Baker at El Teb; and now at Abu Klea he took an Arab spear in the throat and choked his life out. The British buried their dead, gave the wounded what shelter and care they could, and plodded on towards the great river now only a few miles away.

The Arabs had re-formed and lay in strength between the weary thirst-bedevilled soldiers and the river. On the afternoon of January 19, three days after Abu Klea, the opposing forces again joined battle. The British square jerked awkwardly forward over stony ground under a scorching sun; the Arabs, armed mostly with spears, rose up on three sides from the scrub, and led by mounted Emirs hurried across the rough ground to the attack. This time they did not reach the square. The soldiers, after Abu Klea, knew what to do. They aimed low and fired fast; they were the pick of the British Army and they did not miss. The Arab attack faltered and died, the Arabs fled away into the scrub and the way was open to the river and Khartoum. But the men who had fought two savage battles in three days were exhausted, their commander, Sir Herbert Stewart, was dying of a bullet wound, and Burnaby, whom Wolseley had named second in command, was dead at Abu Klea. The leadership of the Desert Column now devolved on Sir Charles Wilson, an executive officer with no experience in the field prior to Abu Klea.

Into the concluding act of the drama played on the vast desert stage are crowded the elements of a deliberately conceived and constructed tragedy—the upswing of fortune and the upsurge of hope, the fatal delay of three days before Sir Charles Wilson dispatched a handful of soldiers by steamer to Khartoum and started upstream with the main force of 1,500 men; the agonizing hour of suspense aboard the steamers following the first glimpse of Khartoum, when men crowded the decks heedless of Arab gunfire from the river banks and looked with passionate intensity for the sign of victory—Gordon's flag flying from the Palace flagstaff. But the flag was not there; it had come down two days before and Gordon was dead.

Sir Charles Wilson is in some respects the most tragic figure in the drama of the Nile campaign, for, after having been thrust into a position for which he had neither inclination or training, he was made the scapegoat for the sins of the entire High Command. The countless days wasted because of the reluctance of men to recognize the pressures of time, the weeks cast away through blunder and miscalculation, all earlier hesitations and delays and stupidities were in the common mind concentrated into the three days at the very end which Sir Charles Wilson spent on the banks of the Nile repairing the steamers and resting his men. If only he had advanced upon Khartoum at once the expedition would have ended in triumph rather than tragedy, and the night of Mafeking anticipated by fifteen years. Such was inevitably the popular view, which the longer view of the historian has done much to correct. For even had the men on the steamers arrived before the fall of Khartoum they would probably have done so only to share Gordon's fate. The popular belief that the Mahdi, discouraged by his losses at Abu Klea and Metemmeh, would have fled with his 30,000 men at the sight of a few red coats is founded on nothing more reliable than wishful thinking and the dubious evidence of Father Joseph Ohrwalder, a prisoner of the Mahdi for many years. Winston Churchill, one of the earliest writers on the Nile Expedition, has said what is surely the last word on Wilson's failure to reach Khartoum two days earlier than he did:

The fact that the two steamers arrived only two days after the capture of the town has given colour to the belief that, but for the three days' delay at Metemmeh the catastrophe might have been averted. This view appears incorrect. The Arabs had long held Khartoum at their mercy. They hoped, indeed, to compel its surrender by famine and to avoid an assault . . . they knew must cost them dear. Gordon has stated in his *Journals* that the town became defenceless by the middle of December. The arrival of twenty British soldiers and a few officers could not have materially affected the situation—could only, in fact, have increased the loss. Yet nearly everyone who reads the tale will wish—in spite of reason

—that some help, however little, had reached the lonely man; that before the darkness fell he had grasped one English hand, and learned that his countrymen had not abandoned him, had not forgotten, would never forget.[12]

Butler did not learn of the tragedy at Khartoum until three weeks after Gordon's death. When he had assured Wolseley, in the letter protesting the order prohibiting his going upriver, that in spite of his disappointment and chagrin he would spare himself in no way 'to effect the more rapid movement up-river' he spoke only the truth; the extraordinary drive and enthusiasm he continued to display communicated themselves to the men immediately under his command with such satisfactory results that late in December he was summoned upriver to Korti, the jumping-off place of the Desert Column, and instructed to proceed with the advance boats of the River Column which, it was hoped, would eventually relieve the Desert Column in Khartoum itself. At Korti Butler observed with apprehension the inadequate supply of camel transport assembled for the desert crossing—'every camel doing, or trying to do, the work of three animals'—and received congratulations on the success of his precious boats. 'Truly had these wonderful little whalers brought their own revenges with them', he noted with immense satisfaction and more than a little complacency.

Here, in the face of guardsmen and journalists, and officers and men of twenty different regimental corps was written large in the vast verity of victuals—the only truth that appeals to all classes and creeds—the fact that by means of these long-derided and abused boats, and by them alone, had this concentration of men, horses and camels been possible at this Bayuda village fourteen hundred miles from Alexandria—all done within four and a half months from the date on which the long delayed permission to build and equip these same boats had been grudgingly given to me in London.[13]

The River Column, under the command of General Earle, whom Butler had known in Canada, moved rapidly upstream with Butler riding on patrol duty well in advance of the boats. On a ridge called Kirbekan in the strange and terrible Monassir Desert, 'a tossed and tumbled region of black and lighter coloured rocks', a strong force of Arabs opposed the advance of the River Column. General Earle and most of his staff favoured a frontal attack on the Arab position, but Butler, who had scouted the ground held by the Arabs, recommended a flank attack which would eventually enable the

British to take the Arabs in the rear. His plan was adopted and executed with skill and success. At Kirbekan the River Column won a swift and easy victory, for which Butler undoubtedly deserved most of the credit.

A day later came certain news of the death of General Gordon. Butler was deeply moved; but he was artist enough to recognize that Gordon's death at Khartoum was the only fitting end to a life such as his: 'Too often the soldier's end is unworthy of his knightly life,' he wrote, 'but with Gordon the harmony of life and death was complete, and the closing scenes seem to move to their fulfilment in solemn hush, as though an unseen power watched over the sequence of their sorrow.'

Nor could he share the common regret that Gordon's body was denied Christian burial in a Christian land—better that he should be for ever a part of the desert waste which had been his dwelling-place in the time of his greatness:

> The dust of Gordon is not laid in English earth. . . . Somewhere, far out in the immense desert, whose sands so often gave him rest in life, or by the shores of the river which was the scene of so much of his labours, his ashes now add their wind-swept atoms to the mighty waste of the Soudan. But if England, still true to her long line of martyrs to duty, keep his memory precious in her heart—making of him no false idol of praise or brazen image of glory, but holding him as he was, the mirror and measure of true knighthood—then better than in effigy or epitaph will his life be written, and his nameless tomb become a citadel to the nation.[14]

Gordon's death and the fall of Khartoum deprived the Nile Expedition of an objective. For a time there was talk in England of an extended campaign to destroy the Mahdi, and plans were laid for running a railway from Suakim on the Red Sea to Berber, which Wolseley, with the forces already at his disposal, would in the meantime take from the Arabs. But the Nile Expedition had shot its bolt. True, the River Column had passed the last of the rough water and could now make smooth and swift progress upriver, but the Desert Column was exhausted and demoralized. Buller had hurried out from Korti to take over command from Sir Charles Wilson, but instead of advancing on Berber as Wolseley had ordered him to, he was compelled to retreat with all speed back to Korti with 40,000 Arabs at his heels. Since it was soon apparent that only a vastly augmented force could hope to defeat the Mahdi, plans for the railway were quietly dropped and the order came to Wolseley to destroy supplies and withdraw from the Sudan.

With the execution of the order the evacuation of the Sudan was, ironically, completed. No garrisons or foreigners were left behind except those who were dead.

Butler received the order to turn back without bitterness or regret. Gordon was dead and all virtue had gone out of the Expedition. To 'smash the Mahdi' would be an act of senseless vengeance and Butler wanted no part of it. His mood, as he prepared to obey the order, was one of melancholy occasioned less by a sense of frustration than the knowledge that the noblest adventure of the Victorian age had drawn to a decisive and tragic close. From a high point above the river he looked for the last time up the gleaming stretch of water from which the River Column must now retreat:

> The Nile lay a blue belt amid the waste of yellow drift, far stretching to the east, with a rugged outline of purple mountain in remotest distance. A few red and black hills rose in the bare level of the middle distance, and one lofty rock, shaped like a gigantic sphinx, stood looking at us from across the river.
>
> It was noon. The sun burned fiercely overhead. Around lay a vast silence, broken only by the north wind rustling low in the dry leaves of the dom-palms, as we turned back over the desert.
>
> The Campaign of the Cataracts was over.[15]

At Meroe, a mud village on the Nile close to Metemmeh, Butler unexpectedly found himself in command of a force under orders to hold the place till autumn. There he spent a busy two months, from the beginning of April to the end of May, building mud huts, biscuit-box lean-to's and palm-leaf shelters, and strengthening the defences of the little mud fort in his charge. From time to time he cast a longing eye across the river at the ruins of Gebel Barkel, once the capital of Queen Candace's kingdom and 'a mine of Egyptian art and antiquities as yet untouched'. But the chance to explore the ruins never came; at the end of two months Butler was ordered to blow up the fort and shelters and withdraw downriver 200 miles to Dongola, picking up at half a dozen stations along the way the horses, camels and heavy equipment of the retreating Desert Column that could not be transported downstream by boat. Nearly all the animals thus collected were in the last stages of starvation and died on the way to Dongola. On the other hand, the

COMMANDER-IN-CHIEF OF THE BRITISH FORCES IN SOUTH AFRICA
From a sketch by Lady Butler, made at the Cape in 1899

'A RADICAL GENERAL'
Cartoon by 'Spy' from 'Vanity Fair'

camels in Butler's charge at Meroe over a period of two months reached Dongola in excellent condition. Butler had been ordered to burn his grain supplies at Meroe, but had fed them to the camels instead, thereby precipitating the most ludicrous squabble of his stormy career. His temporary commander, 'an excellent but choleric little man', found out that Butler had failed to burn the grain as ordered and demanded an explanation. Butler somehow found time to provide the explanation—at length and in his purplest prose:

I replied that, although I had departed from the letter, I had still observed the spirit of the order, inasmuch as I had used the grain as extra fuel to keep the ebbing fire of life in my unfortunate camels, and while expressing regret at even the seeming departure from the letter of the regulation, I added that my penitential feelings were somewhat mitigated and consoled by the reflection that while the camels of the censorious commander had lost some eighty percent of their members on the short march, mine on the longer route had not lost above two percent.

The choleric commander, like most of his superiors to whom Butler addressed facetious communications on serious subjects, was not amused; however, Butler's certain knowledge that he had done himself no good at Headquarters was more than compensated for by the account he received from a staff officer of the commander's reception of the letter:

As the thermometer was that day about one hundred and twenty degrees Fahrenheit in the shade, he was able to relieve his overburdened feelings while perusing my letter, written on a sakeyeh wheel at Debbah in the middle of the night and left at his hut when I passed it at daybreak three hours later, only by making several short leaps in the air as he ejaculated, 'Consoled! – Consoled! – Mitigated! – Mitigated! – D—! – D—!'[16]

Butler's contempt of red tape and the colourless jargon of official communiqués may have annoyed a few of his superiors, but the efficiency with which he played his part in the withdrawal down the Nile restored him fully to Wolseley's favour. Before returning to England, Wolseley offered Butler command of the new Egyptian frontier, to be fixed at Wady Halfa. The position, which Butler assumed at the beginning of September 1885, with the temporary rank of Brigadier-General, was a good deal less impressive than it sounded, since Butler at first had under his command only a single battalion of British troops and at no time did his force exceed four battalions. The Arabs were no longer led by the Mahdi, who had died shortly after taking Khartoum, but their territorial ambitions were in no way diminished; and by the time Butler assumed his command they had occupied Dongola 500 miles below Khartoum and were threatening the railway line running from Wady Halfa to Akasha, a distance of ninety miles.

For four months Butler with his handful of troops defended the railway line and the outposts he had established at strategic points against the hit-and-run raids of the Arabs. Gradually reinforcements were moved up from Cairo, and by the end of the year a force of 4,000 men was concentrated at a point called Firket, half-way between Wady Halfa and Dongola. General Sir Frederick Stevenson, Commander-in-Chief of the British army in Egypt, came up from Cairo to take command of the troops and force a showdown with the Arabs who were concentrated in large numbers at Ginniss, a point on a river bend a few miles south-west of Firket. Butler, who had been on the frontier since September and knew every inch of the ground, offered a plan of attack which General Stevenson wisely approved. Butler was himself to command one of the two brigades making up the British force, and it was hardly a surprise to Sir Frederick that the plan called for Butler's brigade to take the lead in the action.

It is impossible to estimate how effective a leader Butler might have been of a large army fighting a full-scale war; but his skill in the conduct of small-scale manoeuvres is beyond question. He himself would doubtless have said that Napoleon and Wolseley were his military instructors (from his study of Napoleon's campaigns he learnt the value of swift troop movement, from service with Wolseley the necessity of detailed planning and precise timing), but it is possible that he owed most of his success in the field to Fenimore Cooper. In his plans for the action at Ginniss he borrowed a leaf from Wolseley's book and staked the success of the venture on a night march timed to reach a high ridge dominating the Arab encampment precisely at daybreak; but in determining the line of march and the means to maintain it in the dark he leaned heavily on the plainscraft of Leatherstocking. He slipped quietly into the desert by himself and lined up a series of stones bearing on a mountain whose top, at night a darker outline against the dark sky, was discernible over the centre of the Ginniss ridge. An hour and a half before daybreak he 'dressed' his brigade squarely upon the stones, and keeping his eyes fixed on the mountain-top showing dimly above the ridge, led his men into the desert.

The advance was conducted without a single hitch or wasted movement; and within a minute or two of the time set by Butler the troops were scrambling up the ridge commanding the Arab encampment. Day was breaking; Arab sentries gave the alarm and Arab warriors swarmed out of their tents and raced towards the summit of the ridge. It was a close thing, but the Arabs lost by a few hundred yards. The British and Egyptian soldiers held the ridge; the second brigade, which had not been ready to move out of camp on time and for which Butler had flatly refused to wait, was now closing up fast; and the Arabs, driven back from the ridge with heavy loss, abandoned their camp and fled towards Dongola. They carried their wounded and their supplies upriver in sailboats commonly called Nuggers; and it was Butler who organized the cavalry pursuit which resulted in the capture of nine of the Nuggers.

After the fighting and the pursuit were over Butler gathered up the captured Arab standards and sent them to Headquarters loaded on two donkeys. It is not likely that this typical Butler touch amused Sir Frederick Stevenson as much as it did Butler; but the Commander-in-Chief formally acknowledged the excellence of the work his brigade commander had done in the field:

The Lieutenant General desires to express to Br.-General Butler the satisfaction with which he has read the report of his proceeding since the action of the 30th ulto., and of his activity and energy in following up the enemy which has resulted in the important capture of nine laden Nuggers, which it is believed are the remainder of the enemy's river transport north of Keiber.

The Arabs were routed and the short campaign was over. Sir Frederick Stevenson and his large staff returned to Cairo and Butler was left with four battalions of infantry to police the border. He had already lived through one hot season in the desert and knew what the coming months would bring. From his headquarters in Wady Halfa he sent to Cairo and London a constant stream of warnings of impending sickness, and requests for medical supplies, hospital beds, sun helmets, kettles for boiling the river water—the simplest necessities essential to maintain health in a desert station when the thermometer reaches 120 degrees in the shade.

Sunstroke and typhoid were not the only dangers threatening the soldiers. Butler did not hesitate to call to the attention of the home authorities the serious consequences of the sense of isolation afflicting many of the men, who regarded themselves as being 'almost beyond the outside edge of Empire. They look in vain for any reference to them in the home newspapers, and the very existence of this distant frontier appears to be lost sight of at home'.

As time passed Butler had more and more reason to feel that he was the forgotten commander of a forgotten brigade. His men sickened as he had known they would, and some of them died; but few of the supplies he had begged for reached him—only demands that he 'show cause' for his requests—and the language of his communiqués became progressively less diplomatic and more violent. Suddenly word came that the British troops were to be withdrawn from Wady Halfa downriver as far as Assouan; and by June Butler was almost alone at Wady Halfa, in the hottest time of year. He wrote to Elizabeth:

> In face of the intense heat now prevailing, you must only expect short letters from me. The last two nights have been nearly as bad as the days, and last night sleep was not possible. It was the hottest night I ever remember. One gasped and struggled for breath. I could not lie down. I got at last into the dinghy . . . and dipping a sponge into the Nile, kept pouring water at intervals over my head and body. . . . Nevertheless I am keeping well, thank God, but our poor officers and men are suffering terribly at Assouan. In the twenty-four hours ending at 3 p.m. yesterday, eleven officers and men died there. More than three months ago I told the authorities what they might expect, but I wasn't listened to. Not a word about this mortality goes to England, and yet we have not had in this generation such a rate of mortality as this among British soldiers. More than a hundred and thirty have died in two months, and six hundred sick men have been sent away. . . . The temperature yesterday was one hundred and seventeen degrees in the shade.[17]

Butler's habit of bluntly telling the authorities 'what they might expect', instead of diplomatically leading them to adopt his conclusions under the impression that they were their own, almost certainly did him and the causes he sought to advance more harm than good. Sir Evelyn Wood, whose mediocre talents in no wise hindered his rise to the rank of field-marshal, said with truth of Butler, that the fact 'that he was generally right in his conclusions does not indicate that he always went the right way to attain them'.

Whatever gifts the gods may have bestowed on Butler, tact was not one of them.

Of all the operations which Butler conducted at Wady Halfa, after the withdrawal of the British soldiers, none pleased him more than his disposal of a slave convoy brought in to the station by a party of Arab slavers. Theoretically the slave-trade was forbidden in Egyptian territory, but the slavers in this instance were friendly to the Egyptians and it was deemed wise to keep them so. With the approval of Cairo, Butler bought the entire convoy of slaves, some eighty in number, of whom sixty were women. The males he at once declared free, then hired as labourers, but the disposal of the women, whom freedom would leave unprotected and helpless, posed a serious problem. Butler solved it by proposing that each woman be invited to choose a husband from among the soldiers of a Sudanese battalion stationed near by. The soldiers were agreeable, the women delighted. The proceedings, directed by Butler, were carried out with pomp and circumstance and in strict observance of civil and religious law. In the presence of an assembly of civil, religious and military officers of the district each woman chose from a group of three soldiers the one of her choice, to whom she was married on the spot. The women conducted themselves with a poise and assurance not shared by the men and made their choices 'easily and without restraint'. The multiple ceremonies lasted over three hours, and the joy they occasioned the chief participants did a good deal to lift Butler's depressed spirits. 'Never in the long sad history of African slavery,' he said, 'had there been a happier ending to a slave convoy.'

A fashion parade followed the marriage ceremonies.

All the married men vied with each other in decking their brides in the best European finery which the Bazaar in Wady Halfa could furnish, and within an hour or two of the conclusion of the marriage contracts the sable brides were resplendent in the brightest-coloured muslins and calicoes, many of them in high-heeled boots, and nearly all displaying, as they strutted about the Bazaar, parasols, scarves, and feathered hats in great variety. The process of civilization in its most modern and advanced form had taken about two hours. . . . Who knows ? Perhaps the French fashion-plate in the halfpenny papers is destined to do more for African civilization than all the humanizing effects of minister, soldier, sailor, marine, and ordinary European trader in the past five hundred years. . . .[18]

In July 1886 Butler, worn out by constant hard work, heat and frustration, was invalided home. He found that the letters he had written from Wady Halfa to the War Office had caused great offence—so much that instead of having his temporary rank of Brigadier-General confirmed, as he had confidently expected, he was notified that on the expiry of his sick leave he would be placed on half-pay—'less than two hundred pounds a year after close upon thirty years' service, hot and cold, in all parts of the Empire'.

Butler gathered up his books and his young family and went off to Brittany, where living was cheap. There he was to remain eighteen months, reading, writing and regaining health in the tranquil French countryside. Happily, once he was out of England more judicious counsels prevailed at the War Office and in November 1886 Butler was gazetted Brigadier-General—still on half-pay—and given a K.C.B.

His run of good fortune did not last long. In the same month he was named a co-respondent in what was to prove the most sensational divorce case of the century.

CHAPTER FOURTEEN

Man of Honour

IN THE COMMON VIEW the marriage between Miss Gertrude Blood and Lord Colin Campbell seemed as likely to succeed as most alliances uniting beauty with a title. Miss Blood was indeed beautiful—and talented as well. She played the piano, sang regularly at charity concerts, contributed to the *Saturday Review* and wrote a children's book which went through several printings. Lord Colin Campbell, a younger son of the Duke of Argyll, had few talents, little money and a querulous disposition. The Campbells were unpopular in London society because 'they were queer-looking and haughty', and Lord Colin had even fewer friends than most of his clan. The small number diminished when, in 1883, just two years after her marriage, Lady Colin obtained a judicial separation from her husband on the ground of legal cruelty.

Thereafter, so Lady Colin's counsel in the divorce suit affirmed, Lord Colin, who had bitterly opposed the suit for separation, lived only for revenge. His detectives followed Lady Colin with 'bloodhound pertinacity', particularly when she was travelling on the Continent 'in the care of her venerable father and mother'. In Paris, Lord Colin attempted to have her arrested as a common prostitute; and at home he was assiduous in gathering statements from servants and persuading them to tell all they knew or imagined about Lady Colin's indiscretions. 'It was difficult to believe that there existed a man capable of so degrading the wife who had leaned on his bosom,' Lady Colin's counsel declared, 'but Lord Colin Campbell's pride had been so lowered to the dust, and he seemed to be so influenced with a desire for revenge as to think that there was nothing so low that he might not stoop to it in order to gratify that desire.'

Among Lord Colin's few close friends was a certain Lady Miles, a second cousin to Lady Colin—a bustling, aggressive, essentially good-hearted woman, who made everybody's business, and particularly Lord Colin's, her own. She was shocked to learn from Lord Colin's own lips that he was gathering evidence to divorce his wife, and told him bluntly that unless he abandoned his absurd and heartless plan—clearly intended to humiliate Lady Colin publicly—she would tell Lady Colin—and if need be a jury—what she knew about Lord Colin's carryings-on with a pretty housemaid named Mary Watson. Lord Colin, in reply to Lady Miles, affirmed both his innocence and his determination to sue his wife for divorce. Lady Miles at once hurried to Lady Colin, warned her of Lord Colin's intentions and told her what she knew of Lord Colin's indiscretions with the housemaid. Whereupon Lady Colin's lawyer, acting with remarkable speed and foresight, filed petition for divorce against Lord Colin on the grounds of his immoral relations with Mary Watson. The petition anticipated that of Lord Colin against his wife by a few hours. It was filed, Lord Colin's counsel told the jury, so that Lady Colin 'would appear to have brought the case into court, when in actual fact she herself was being dragged there'.

A charge against a husband of immoral relations with a housemaid was hardly likely to raise more than a ripple of amusement in the London society of 1886. Lord Colin, it was felt, had served the public interest rather better in drawing up his list of the men with whom he accused Lady Colin of having had adulterous relations. The men so named were Captain Shaw, the Fire Chief of London; Dr. Bird, a prominent Mayfair physician; the Duke of Marlborough; and General Sir William Butler.

Some surprise was expressed in Mayfair that no representative of the Church was included in Lord Colin's otherwise comprehensive list.

The appearance of the Duke of Marlborough's name among those of the co-respondents surprised no one. The Duke, who had only lately succeeded to the title, was a divorcé of notorious reputation; his charms were considerable, his mistresses numerous. But the other names occasioned a succession of shocks. Captain Shaw was a man in his mid-fifties, a model of respectability and father of a large brood of grown-up daughters, one of whom had been a bridesmaid at Lady Colin's wedding. Dr. Bird was a popular physician of admirable bedside manner, and, so far as was generally known, equally admirable morals; and General Butler, whatever his idiosyncrasies, was held to be in the broadest sense of the term an honourable gentleman.

The hearing of the consolidated suit was held before Mr. Justice Butt from November 27 to December 21, 1886; it was conducted by the most impressive and expensive batteries of counsel ever assembled to contest a divorce case (their fees were said to total roughly £1,000 a day); it was the longest case of its kind in English judicial history; and it was publicized by the most extensive newspaper coverage ever given a divorce suit. (*The Times*, while bitterly regretting the necessity of having to expose its readers to an account of the 'nauseous proceedings', did so to the extent of more than 100,000 words.)

The opening remarks of Sir Charles Russell, Lady Colin's counsel and the most celebrated and expensive advocate of the day, quickly removed the case from the realm of the merely titillating to the sordid. Lord Colin had asked for Miss Blood's hand the day after his first meeting with her at a deer-shoot in Argyllshire; but the proposed marriage between them was many times postponed, and even after the actual ceremony had been performed was not consummated for several months. This on the order of Lord Colin's physicians, because, so Sir Charles revealed to a genuinely horrified jury, Lord Colin was suffering from venereal disease. When the marriage was at length consummated Lord Colin had infected his young wife. Lady Colin had thereupon informed Lord Colin 'that she desired to continue to be his friend, companion and nurse', but no more than that. Lord Colin, however, had insisted on his conjugal rights so long as Lady Colin remained under his roof—hence Lady Colin's successful suit for separation; and the determination of Lord Colin, whose illness made him 'sensitive, morbid, suspicious', to avenge himself on the woman who refused to be more than his wife in name only.

It was shortly evident that Lady Colin's case against her husband would not stand up. Lady Miles made an excellent witness; she was a crowd-pleaser with a great deal of poise and a strong sense of drama. She gave her testimony with remarkable forthrightness and provided most of the few moments of comedy which lightened the trial. Her suspicions about Lord Colin and the housemaid, Mary Watson, had been aroused on an occasion when, while she was visiting Lord Colin, the housemaid had been impertinent and Lord Colin had taken the housemaid's part. Shortly afterwards Lord

Colin, complaining of a pain, had gone upstairs to bed. The housemaid followed him with a poultice. Lady Miles then pretended to leave the house. In actual fact she had slammed the dining-room door, and after a short interval slipped upstairs to observe Lord Colin and the housemaid in a compromising position. She could—and did—name the precise date of the episode, because, as she explained to an amazed cross-examining counsel, 'I read the Psalms every morning and I put a line under the Psalm for the 17th of June for the purpose of marking the date of the Mary Watson episode.' Lady Miles's methods of fixing the date no doubt served its purpose admirably, but it also provided Lord Colin's counsel—Mr. Finlay, Q.C., a hard-headed Scot—with a unique opportunity to inquire about the mental state of a woman who could make a memorandum of such an occurrence in a prayer-book. 'Could there be conceived,' he cried, 'a more revolting compound of devotion and depravity?'

Lady Miles's answer to a question put to her by Mr. Finlay to determine why she had written a certain letter in a certain way—'Well, Mr. Finlay, it was because I wrote the letter and not you'—won her a round of applause from not only the spectators but the Junior Bar; but the case against Lord Colin, shaky enough to begin with, since Lady Miles could testify only that she had seen the housemaid sitting on Lord Colin's knee, collapsed completely when two Harley Street physicians testified that they had examined Mary Watson and found her to be *virgo intacta*.

From the beginning of the trial the courtroom had been crowded; now extra police were called in to control the throngs seeking to gain admittance; for with the case against Lord Colin—'ridiculously weak from the start', as *The Times* correctly observed—out of the way, the real drama might be expected to begin with the roles of the protagonists reversed—Lord Colin now the accuser and Lady Colin the accused.

A careful reading of the evidence today suggests the probability, amounting almost to certainty, of a liaison between Lady Colin and the Duke of Marlborough—or Lord Blandford as he was when their association was at its most intimate. In the opinion of Mayfair such a liaison seemed logical—indeed inevitable—once the two had established a relationship of any kind. Lady Colin was one of the most beautiful women of her time; she was young, perhaps passionate, and if so frustrated, for she was married to an ill-mannered brooding outlander with whom cohabitation was not only repulsive but dangerous. Lord Blandford bore a great name, he was a highly-polished gentleman; and around him there clung that aura of scandal which many women find infinitely alluring. But no clear case was established in court against the Duke; it broke down under sheer weight of evidence intended to establish it, but which in fact confused the jurors and sometimes the judge and gave Sir Charles Russell innumerable opportunities to reveal contradictions in testimony that suggested at best mistaken, and at worst perjured, evidence.

It was in truth a sorry procession of witnesses who followed one another into the box to report what they knew or suspected or had dreamed of Lady Colin's infidelities—which if proven would have rightly established her in the public mind as not only a fallen woman but a nymphomaniac as well. The witnesses included a footman who described what he had seen through a keyhole; a personal maid who reported that Lady Colin had had her dress off during an evening out with Lord Blandford (when she returned the hooks were done up differently from the way the maid had done them); a nurse who expressed certainty on no reliable evidence that Lady Colin had had a miscarriage; private detectives who had trailed Lady Colin over half Europe; cabmen, doormen, hotel waiters and chambermaids—all these and a dozen more had their little hour in the witness-box, and all, or nearly all, were impartially torn to pieces by Sir Charles Russell. But there was one formidable witness whom for a time not even Sir Charles was able to break down. This was Rose Baer, a woman of strong character and some education—she spoke three languages fluently—who for several months had served Lady Colin as personal maid. In her testimony she spoke of many notes and books exchanged—often covertly—between Lady Colin and Lord Blandford, of assignations and lover-like partings, of adjoining bedrooms occupied by the two at Leigh Court, the country residence of Sir Philip and Lady Miles, and of unmistakable signs that another person had shared Lady Colin's bed. All this and much else besides. Sir Charles Russell's cross-examination revealed that the notes exchanged were nearly all concerned with social engagements, that the books exchanged included Green's *History of the English People*, Lecky's *History of Rationalism*, and Motley's *Rise of the Dutch Republic* (the latter in six volumes), that in talking of a house party at which, she swore, Lord Blandford had slept every night with Lady Colin, Rose Baer had confused Christmas with Easter, and that among fellow servants she had the reputation of being a vicious scandalmonger. But in some of her most damning testimony she could not be shaken until Sir Charles asked her, seemingly as an afterthought, if when at Lord Colin's request she had agreed to appear in the witness-box she had known what evidence she would be asked to give. Rose Baer said she hadn't known. 'And you agreed to give evidence for Lord Colin Campbell without knowing what the evidence was to be about?' Sir Charles thundered. The jury did not miss the point. A witness who had agreed to give evidence without knowing what it was to be about would obviously swear to anything.

'Perjury, gentlemen, is stalking abroad,' cried Mr. Murphy, Q.C., Butler's counsel. He was right. In the witness-box Lady Colin's enemies lied to convict her, her friends lied to save her, and at the end to sift the few grains of truth from the mountains of falsehood was perhaps beyond the skill of any man. But if no simple truth was uncovered, no satisfactory verdict arrived at, society had its sport and its victims. The show, most people agreed, was an excellent one, equally rich in dramatic incident and human interest. 'There were several really amusing incidents,' one alert observer reported.

One was when Mr. Finlay, in opening Lord Colin's case, grew excited as he denounced the 'vile conspiracy' imputed by him to Lady Miles and Lady Colin, and suddenly thumped the desk before him like a second Spurgeon. The poor old Duke of Argyll, who was sitting just in front of him, jumped as though he had been shot; and though all who saw the incident felt sorry for the Duke, none could help a smile at the tragic expression with which he turned round upon the all-unconscious orator. . . . Again, when Sir Charles Russell, who is dreadfully given to mixing up names, abused Lord *Walter* Campbell for the fifth time in the latter's hearing, the plaintive cry of disclaimer, 'Lord Colin!' from paternal lips, was bound to provoke a smile. And Mrs. Neptune Blood's evidence, given saucily, in a strong American accent, was quite a relief to the dreary monotony of indecency which had so long been pouring from the witness-box, from her first 'Yes!' to her last answer, 'That's a lie!' Counsels' wrangling, too, was occasionally amusing, and even the Foreman of the Jury made a pun, though nobody noticed it. . . .

Lady Colin looked very handsome throughout the trial. . . . Her Ladyship dresses well, and looks well in all her dresses. She wore at least five during the trial, varying from a costume of purple velvet to a tailor-made garment of blue serge. Lady Miles was resplendent daily. She was Lady Colin's *fidus Achates*, never failing her for a moment. . . . Together they plied their fans and together they sniffed their smelling-salts—this last no less often than Sir Charles 'snuffed'. Mrs. Blood, Senior, looked wretched for the most part, but brightened up in the witness-box, whence she gave some extraordinary evidence as to the fitness of certain males as intimates of 'beautiful young married women'. Her husband, a fine-looking old man, broke down before the trial was over, and disappeared from the scene. Mrs. Neptune Blood looked charming, her husband truculent, more especially when the Foreman of the Jury was publishing the worthlessness of his mis-statements. The various Campbell brothers sat about like so many stolid Scots, stonily staring around them. Their father was pale, and gave the idea of burly wretchedness. Everyone felt sorry for his Grace until he left the witness-box and London for Inverary. Dr. Bird behaved as though he were in church, Captain Shaw looked martially healthy throughout, and the Duke of Marlborough was uniformly and cynically amused throughout.[1]

In this sordid welter of charge and counter-charge, of occasional truths and innumerable lies, of transient loves and enduring hates, the person who in the end attracted and held the attention of the public more powerfully than any other, who provoked the harshest newspaper comment and drew from judge and jury strong public rebukes for his behaviour, was the co-respondent against whom there was the slightest evidence—General Sir William Butler. Indeed, in the light of that evidence it is difficult to understand why Lord Colin's lawyers permitted Lord Colin to name him at all, for to do so seemed at first mere irresponsible mischief-making. Sir William and Lady Butler had known Lady Colin and her family for years; Butler had met Lord and Lady Colin on the occasion of the presentation of the Freedom of the City of London to Lord Wolseley in 1883, the year after Tel-el-Kebir, and Lady Colin, in the presence of her husband, asked Butler to call. He did so a day or two later. Lord Colin charged that on that occasion he had been alone with Lady Colin for five hours; Rose Baer testified that he called frequently thereafter, and that on one occasion after he left Lady Colin looked flushed. (Subsequent testimony reduced the length of the first call to an hour and a half and the total number to two, with a third person present at least part of the time on each occasion.)

Mr. Murphy, Q.C., urged that the evidence against Butler was so frivolous that the learned judge 'might feel it his duty to say that, as regarded General Butler and Lady Colin Campbell, there was no evidence for the jury's consideration'. The charge against them, he said, 'was founded on an ordinary visit paid by a gentleman to a lady of whose family he had been a friend for many years'.

With this statement Mr. Finlay, Lord Colin's counsel, had already tacitly agreed; thus far in the trial he has said only—and with some evidence of embarrassment—that the citation of General Butler as co-respondent stemmed from a call he had made on Lady Colin in 1883, during which he had been alone with her in her drawing-room for 'some hours'.

Mr. Murphy, for Butler, added that even if the case against his client was an undefended one he was sure that his Lordship would rule that it was not made out. However, he would not ask his Lordship so to rule, for General Butler would, of course, come forward in person to deny the accusation.

Three days later Mr. Murphy informed judge and jury that he did not propose to call General Butler and asked his Lordship to instruct the jury that there was no evidence against his client.

This Mr. Justice Butt, obviously flustered and therefore annoyed, refused to do. There was, he said, *some* evidence against General Butler; and added that 'one would expect a gentleman in General Butler's position to go out of his way to be present if he were really an innocent man'.

Mr. Murphy—red-faced, hideously embarrassed—struggled to account to the jury for the absence of his client, who, he had earlier assured the court, would come forward to deny the accusation against him. His client's absence, he said, would doubtless be explained on the ground that General Butler was a guilty man, but an honourable man, who would not deny the charge against him and tell an untruth. (Here Mr. Murphy was anticipating Mr. Finlay.) Mr. Murphy would, however, remind those who said that this was the only possible inference to be drawn from his client's absence that 'there were some men who held that all divorce proceedings were contrary to God's laws, and that an accusation of this kind made against a man of honour was sure to fail because of its own inherent weakness'.

Of all the many sensations which the trial provided, Butler's failure to appear in the witness-box was beyond question the greatest. Up to this point not even the most lascivious-minded of those who had followed the case in court or the newspapers had taken the charge against Butler seriously. He had no reputation for licentiousness, the evidence against him was trivial, and although his behaviour was sometimes unorthodox to the point of eccentricity he was in all things, so far as was known, a man of honour. Now all was changed, and at once a thousand reasons suggested themselves to those eager to find them why Lady Colin should be attracted to Butler and he to Lady Colin. True, he was middle-aged, but Lady Colin liked mature men; he was strikingly handsome, he was very brave, he had adventured in far-off places, and he had written many excellent books. Like called to like. Lady Colin was beautiful, she was unconventional, and she, too, wrote books. So the tide of gossip flowed, reinforced and reinvigorated from an unexpected source, and the Campbell case overnight achieved a new notoriety.

Mr. Finlay, Lord Colin's counsel, had up to this point no really damning evidence against Lady Colin to present to the jury—now he moved in for the kill. All in the courtroom, he said, had been held spellbound listening to the impassioned tones in which his learned friend Mr. Murphy had denounced the discreditable conduct of Lord Colin Campbell in bringing a charge of adultery against his gallant client. His learned friend had left no doubt in the mind of anyone that General Butler would go into the witness-box to answer the charges against him. Now they learned to their astonishment 'that all that heavy artillery of my learned friend was only meant to cover the retreat of the gallant general'. In a dexterous double-edged thrust Mr. Finlay, while acknowledging that everyone knew that General Butler was an honourable and gallant soldier, pointed out that he might indeed be an honourable and gallant soldier without being a Joseph. The Victorians knew their Bible, and it is unlikely that any juror missed the implication which cast Lady Colin in the role of Potiphar's wife.

Mr. Finlay's final charge was a telling one; the absence of General Butler, he declared, was sure proof that he knew he would be committing perjury if he swore that he had had no immoral relations with Lady Colin Campbell. General Butler was in truth an honourable gentleman who refused to add the sin of perjury to that of adultery.

Mr. Justice Butt, who was accused by the newspapers of a wide variety of judicial sins (bias, misdirection of the jury, childish insistence on little jokes—'he should remember that what is sport to him may be shocking pain to many a woman publicly charged with adultery before him'),[2] was clearly taken aback by Butler's failure to present himself for examination and worried lest the jury attach too much significance to its implications. In his summing-up he reminded the jurors that he had earlier rejected an application from General Butler's counsel to dismiss the case against Butler out of hand; he had said at the time that there was 'some evidence' against the gallant soldier. That evidence was, however, such that if he were trying the case without a jury he would dismiss the petition against General Butler. Nor could he agree with Mr. Finlay's contention that the only reason why Butler refused to appear was his unwillingness to add the sin of perjury to that of adultery. It might be, the judge suggested, that General Butler simply refused to submit himself to general cross-examination. Having thus in effect told the jury to dismiss the charge against Butler and Lady Colin, Mr. Justice Butt, in a clumsy attempt at fence-sitting, hastened to add that he did not wish to go a hair's breadth out of the way to shield the gallant soldier, but rather wished to emphasize the point that absence from the courtroom was not to be confused with admission of guilt.

The jury retired at 6.45. Two and one-half hours later they returned to the courtroom, where the foreman announced that while the jurors were agreed on Lady Colin Campbell's petition they had found it impossible to agree on Lord Colin's counter-petition. Mr. Justice Butt, obviously perturbed, told the jury to make a further effort to reach a verdict, and the jurymen again retired. In the courtroom tension mounted. Lady Colin in particular showed signs of the agonizing strain: 'As the absence of the retired Jury extended into hours she grew paler and paler until at last, in spite of her pluck, she looked a miserable woman.'[3]

At 10.30 the jury returned to the courtroom for the second time and the foreman informed the judge that they had reached agreement. The verdict of the jury was that Lord Colin Campbell had not committed adultery with Mary Watson and that Lady Colin Campbell had not committed adultery with any of the co-respondents named in the suit.

The foreman, having reported the verdict, added that the jury desired to express the opinion 'that in not coming forward in the interests of justice General Butler's conduct was unworthy of a gentleman and an English officer and was the cause of the difficulty which the jury had experienced in coming to a decision'.

Most of the London newspapers and popular periodicals seem to have turned thumbs-down on Lady Colin, and feeling cheated by a verdict which denied them the kill, commented on the verdict, the judge's conduct of the trial, and the behaviour and characters of the witnesses with a freedom and maliciousness which today would almost certainly have resulted in charges of contempt of court and criminal libel. *The Times*, after recording with a profound sense of relief the termination of the 'nauseous proceedings', accepted the verdict of the jury without enthusiasm, hinted at bias in Mr. Justice Butt's summing-up, pointed out with grim satisfaction that Lord and Lady Colin were still married to one another—'for both the marriage tie has become a galling chain, but when all that is doubtful on one side or the other is discarded enough remains to convince every impartial person that neither is too severely punished by that infliction'—and speaking of General Butler acknowledged with some indignation that 'it is extremely difficult to find any theory consistent with the consciousness of innocence that can account for his conduct. . . . Every motive that can be supposed to weigh with a gentleman dictated a frank and positive denial of the charge if denial was possible, yet General Butler did not appear.'[4]

Vanity Fair, the most sophisticated society periodical of the time, was a good deal more forthright and libellous:

The general opinion throughout society—with the sole exception of that select Ring which believes in the sacred right of the married woman to misconduct herself with the proper people—is that the verdict in the Campbell case was a wrong and unjust one. With that opinion we concur. The most eloquent of all the many witnesses in the trial was one who did not appear to give evidence; and his absence was, we hold, in his case conclusive proof that he could not deny the charges formally laid against him.[5]

The writer of the commentary then went on to applaud Butler's conduct in a most ingenious sophistry which cast Butler in the role of the guilty man of honour:

We say that General Butler's conduct leads irresistibly to the conclusion that he was conscious of his inability to deny the charge; and that, under such circumstances, it would have been far less worthy of an English officer and a gentleman to come forward to admit it than to remain away and say nothing; while it would have been distinctly contrary to the interests of justice for him to come forward falsely to deny it. On the assumption of his guilt, his conduct in refraining from giving true evidence in the box was the conduct of a gentleman, since true evidence would have sacrificed Lady Colin; his conduct in refraining from giving false evidence was not at variance, but in accordance with the interest of justice, his conduct in refraining from giving any evidence at all, true or false, was apparently the course by which he reconciled his duty as a gentleman with his duty as a citizen; and it by no means deserves censure, for it was prompted at once by regard for truth and by consideration for Lady Colin.[6]

Vanity Fair offered no explanation of Butler's conduct on the assumption of his innocence.

Yet the assumption of innocence is more logical than the assumption of guilt. To say that Butler was unwilling to add the sin of perjury to that of adultery is to ignore the fact that through his counsel he had denied the charge against him; and to Butler the distinction between a lie and perjury was a legal and not a moral one. If he were willing to lie through his counsel, it is logical to assume that he would have been equally ready to lie in person under oath.

Wilfred Meynell, Lady Butler's brother-in-law, is said to have reported that Butler refused to appear in the witness-box because, although innocent himself, he was afraid that truthful testimony under cross-examination might implicate others and convict Lady Colin. In order, therefore, to protect Lady Colin's reputation he gallantly risked his own, and in so doing nearly destroyed both. Such behaviour would not be inconsistent with Butler's chivalrous temperament, but the explanation seems a little too facile, too obviously shaped by materials drawn from a romantic imagination rather than life, to be readily acceptable.

It should not be forgotten that in the year 1886 Butler was a sick and disillusioned man, suffering not only the pangs of physical illness but of unrequited merit, and a good deal fed up with the human race and particularly that part of it represented by the Colin Campbells and their circle. It may be, therefore, that his refusal to appear in the witness-box was, in fact, a refusal to lend himself to the making of a Mayfair circus; and that he was untouched by the charge of having washed his hands because he knew he had not soiled them.

As for Lady Colin, there was almost unanimous agreement that not only was she guilty of adultery but that in failing to conceal her indiscretions from the public eye she had failed shockingly in her duty to her class. An editorial in the *Standard*, a morning newspaper which had published a special evening edition during the progress of the trial, thus summarized the popular view:

The cumulative effect of repeated departures from commonplace rules, of continuous defiance of the restrictions of ordinary existence, is dangerous, especially to those who belong to what are called the higher classes. . . . The aristocracy, as a body, are not more vicious than men and women in a lower social order, but their follies are more curiously scrutinized and more severely condemned. Had Lady Colin Campbell shown a better sense of duty to her Order, she would have been spared much of the sorrow and humiliation which have befallen her and her household.[7]

In the light of this condemnation of Lady Colin's failure to behave as a lady should, it is of interest to note that an *Etiquette of Good Society*, which Lady Colin revised and edited shortly after the trial, sold more than one hundred thousand copies.

CHAPTER FIFTEEN

The Years of Peace

'FAILURE AT FIFTY is terrible. The sand in the hour-glass of life is crumbling very fast away; the old friends of childhood are gone; a younger generation press us from behind; the next turn of the road may bring us in sight of the end.'[1]

Butler knew whereof he wrote. He was fifty years of age in 1888; for two and a half years he had been an unemployed half-pay Brigadier, he was out of favour at the War Office, there were no wars going on anywhere in the Empire, and it seemed that in his professional life he could look forward to nothing more than a few years of stagnation, an inadequate pension, and on retirement perhaps the compensating sop of promotion to the rank of major-general. In 1888 he was almost, but not quite, prepared to acknowledge that whatever the future held of interest for him must lie outside the profession of arms.

After eighteen months' residence in France he moved with his growing family to Ireland and settled in Delgany, a beautiful little village lying between the sea and the Wicklow Mountains—blossom-banked, deep-shaded lanes radiating in all directions from the village, wild mauve-tinted moorland only an hour's ride away. In Delgany, Butler kept bees (he was frequently stung, but never discouraged), argued endlessly with a near neighbour, Major MacFarlane of the Indian Cavalry, on the relative importance of 'balance' and 'grip' in horseback-riding, shot snipe with a more distant neighbour, Charles Stewart Parnell, wrote a great deal and brooded upon blasted hopes and thwarted ambitions. Most of the members of the Ring who were still alive had long since passed him by—men who, he felt, did not possess half his talent or energy (Buller and Wood were obvious examples)—and he was haunted by forebodings of a life dragged out in stagnant backwaters, of a name forgotten and ambitions unfulfilled.

Though the years from 1886 to 1888 were bitter, they were far from wasted. The Nile Expedition provided Butler with material for two books which rank among the best he wrote—*The Campaign of the Cataracts*, and a *Life* of General Charles Gordon. *The Campaign of the Cataracts* opens with a passage which reflects Butler's love of the dramatic, the sensational:

It is the 20th March, 1885. I am writing these lines at a spot named Merawi, on the left shore of the Nile, in Nubia or the Soudan, as map-makers determine, but in any case a place about midway in the great river's length, and nearly 1500 miles from the Mediterranean.

All around us lies the desert . . . the great, lonely, waterless sea, terrible in the noonglare of day, beautiful in the moonlight of night, wonderful at flush of dawn and hush of eve; but ever a waste where desolation has cut deep into the face of earth—always a wilderness where the breast of the Great Mother is dead, and dry and withered; where clay has burned to ashes and rock has calcined into cinder; where sight aches with distance, and sound finds utterance in winds moaning over endless space; where earliest man has left his name in sand-swept pyramid and buried temple—a vast, dead withered world, with its unburied skeleton left bleaching under heaven—in whose depths the stars at night alone seem to have life.

The opening statement is quite literally true—much of the book was written while Butler was playing his part in the withdrawal from the Sudan or sweating out his command at various points on the vaguely defined Egyptian frontier; but despite the discouraging conditions under which its author worked, and the fact that like *Akim-Foo* it is the story of a failure, *The Campaign of the Cataracts* is a buoyant book. Butler loved the great river; and the desert, despite its insentient cruelty, reminded him in many of its aspects of the Great Lone Land. There was thus a kind of exhilaration, which he had not experienced when writing *Akim-Foo*, in re-creating the feel of an environment which moved him profoundly. Further, in writing *The Campaign of the Cataracts* Butler was not obsessed, as he had been in *Akim-Foo*, with a sense of personal failure. The Nile Expedition had failed to achieve its objective, but the fault was not Butler's; few men could look upon the part they had played in the Expedition with greater pride.

The Campaign of the Cataracts is neither apologia nor recrimination; it is primarily a stirring adventure story, with, however, more emphasis on local colour and character than is common to the conventional literature of adventure. It won immediate favour with public and critics, and later high praise from Winston Churchill. Elizabeth Butler's admirable sketches, full of movement and vitality, no doubt contributed a good deal to the success of the book.

The *Life* of Gordon, published in 1887, is in some ways Butler's most interesting work. There is on Butler's part a feeling of personal identification with his subject which invests the book with a sense of life and a passion so powerful, so convincing, that in spite of factual error, prejudice and a dozen other venial sins it communicates the personality of Gordon as does no other book of the time, with the obvious exception of Gordon's own *Journals*.

The most original aspect of the biography is Butler's absolute refusal to accept the common view of Gordon as an eccentric genius. Genius, yes, eccentric, no. His charity work with down-and-outs—and particularly with boys—during the years when he was living in obscurity at Gravesend, was not the kind of activity commonly indulged in by officers of Her Majesty's Army, and inevitably drew sniggering comment from those to whom the dispensing of charity was woman's work, and association of any kind with boys evidence of homosexual tendencies. Butler's explanation of Gordon's interest in the poor of Gravesend and the downtrodden everywhere has at least the merit of simplicity; and it is expressed with a vigour bordering on belligerence. What set Gordon apart from his fellow men, made him appear in their distorted view a freak, was the simple fact that with him there was no 'separation of the sense of God' from the everyday work to which he put his hand.

> His life at Gravesend was that of a sound, common-sense Christian man, intent upon doing that best he could to better the misery that lay around him. . . . It mattered not on what the light of his charity was to fall; old and young, the rough sailor boy in the fishing smack, the street Arab, the sick in hospital, the old paralytic wearing out the worn thread of life, the urchin of the Ragged School, or the hag in the garret—they were each entitled to their share. . . . True, this light was only a rush-light in the night of the island's misery, but that did not matter; his work was to do what he could to lift the load that lay near his hand.[2]

The old could be helped to die; the young must be helped to live. In nothing, so Butler argued, was Gordon's solid common sense more evident than in his resolution to provide for the future as well as immediate needs of the boys whom he took in charge:

He was not content to teach the ragged boys of Gravesend or to give them only a day's food or a night's lodging. He was too thorough a worker to be satisfied with patchwork benevolence. He began at the beginning and he did not leave off until the boy he had rescued from the gutter had found his billet on board ship, or in a situation. . . . Wherever I have been able to watch and weigh the life and acts of Charles Gordon, I find him always even, practical, earnest, unemotional in his charity, full of sound common sense.

In a world of professing Christians Gordon almost alone lived up to his profession; if, therefore, Butler concluded, Gordon was guilty of foolishness, it was 'the foolishness of the Cross'.

In one of the most controversial and startling passages of a highly original book, Butler, seeking to account for the delay in the dispatch of the Nile Expedition and its subsequent failure to save Gordon, draws a clear distinction between what he calls the temporary and permanent governments of England: the temporary is the one elected by the people, the permanent the one always in office which in reality controls government policy.

The meaning of the term 'permanent government' in England may appear strange; but there is a Government of England, and a very powerful one too, which is always in office—a Government that has no more relation to the will of the majority of the people of England than it has to the wishes of the people of Van Dieman's Land. In every public office, in the army and navy, in the countless departments of the state, this permanent Conservative Government is entrenched.[3]

Butler's 'permanent Government'—which greatly resembles today's Establishment—was the body which through powerful family alliances, the control of important offices and the highest positions in the Services, in reality governed England, instituting and executing policies which frequently contradicted the wishes of the people and their elected representatives.

Elsewhere Butler identifies this permanent Government with what he calls the 'educated opinion' of England, meaning thereby the products of the best-known public schools and the two great universities; and in a passage of extraordinary bitterness assails that educated opinion as the reactionary champion of privilege and the enemy of the people:

Since this century began, there is hardly a question of foreign or domestic politics upon which what is called the educated opinion of

England has not been chiefly on the wrong side. It opposed religious freedom, parliamentary reform, Free Trade, Free Education, the right of the labourer to his rest. Abroad it was on the side of the slave-owner, supported the Turk, protected the opium-seller, threw all its energies into the cause of the Southern slave states. It would be curious to take from the division lists of the last ninety years the votes of the representatives of the two great English Universities, and to see on what side of the beam that weighs right and wrong in the world these votes were cast. . . . Has the educated opinion of England ever supported the people, save when they or a section of them, misled for a moment, happened to be on the side of Feudality, Despotism, or Injustice? The educated opinion of England regarded Mr. Cobden and Mr. Bright as traitors worthy of the gallows until the grave had taken the one and old age benumbed the faculties of the other. Today the same opinion detests our greatest statesman because he is on the side of the people. If he would side with ignorance, restricted franchise, intolerance, privilege . . . the educated opinion of England would grovel before Mr. Gladstone tomorrow.[4]

Like her husband, Lady Butler made good use of the years of semi-retirement. While living in Delgany she painted several of her best-known pictures, including *An Eviction*, now hanging in the Municipal Gallery in Dublin, and the *Camel Corps*. Butler was on intimate terms with the local peasantry, and on one occasion invited several village ancients to view his wife's pictures. One old man glanced at the *Camel Corps* and hastily averted his eyes. As he hobbled away from the house, convulsed between pity and laughter, he was heard to cry out—'Glory be to God—them harses!'

Lady Butler loved Ireland, but her view of the Irish people was a good deal more realistic than that of her husband. 'Ireland's beauty was an inexhaustible source of joy to her,' her daughter Eileen said. 'but her English common sense was often irritated by the Irishman's habit of blaming present-day ineptitude on bygone injustice. "I suppose this is all Oliver Cromwell's fault," I heard my mother mutter, as she entered a filthy Dublin cab whose harness was held together with string and whose floor was carpeted with straw.'[5]

Towards the end of 1888 Butler's long run of misfortune and unemployment came to an end. He was appointed to conduct an inquiry into the administration, organization and personnel of the Army Ordnance Department. Ever since his experiences in South Africa Butler had held strong views on ordnance and he undertook the inquiry with enormous enthusiasm and a complete disregard of the verbal obliquities normally employed in reporting the shortcomings of government departments. Unfortunately it is not possible to examine the report which Butler submitted. His condemnation of Ordnance and all its works was so severe and uninhibited, his recommendations for more efficient administration so revolutionary that a shocked Secretary of State ordered all printed copies of the report destroyed. Butler acknowledged spending 'a very uncomfortable Christmas'. He was in disgrace with the civil side of the War Office and again unemployed.

Not for long. His next job was one in which he could do little harm—that of agent for the War Office in the purchase of suitable sites for the building of a ring of fortifications to guard London's southern and eastern approaches. Butler regarded the entire defence project as an antiquated absurdity—it was, in fact, soon abandoned—but he enjoyed his work while it lasted. It gave him an excuse to travel widely through the English countryside—even an Irishman must concede beauty to Surrey and Sussex and Kent—and it brought him after several years' separation into close association with some of the men he had worked with in far-off places of the earth—Wolseley and Buller and half a dozen other veterans of the Ring. Butler was, after all, a professional soldier; bee-keeping in the Wicklow hills was a poor substitute for going to the wars, and with the men of the Ring he could at least relive battles fought long ago.

This renewed intimacy with old comrades shortly proved of great value to Butler. Wolseley, although a conservative in all things else, held radical views on army reform; he had the professional soldier's contempt for the War Office civilian and he fully approved the recommendations which Butler had made in his ill-fated report. His earlier misgivings about his 'paddy-whack' subordinate had been overcome to such a degree that in 1890 he offered Butler a choice between the overseas commands of Singapore and Egypt. Butler hated the jungle, loved the desert. Without hesitation he chose Egypt.

Butler was to look back on the three years, 1890–3, which he spent in Alexandria as among the best of his life. His physical energy was undiminished and he was at the peak of his intellectual powers. He studied history, both ancient and modern, several hours a day; explored on foot and by donkey the lakes—remnants of old Nile mouths—lying inland from Alexandria; observed the prolific bird life of the delta with the enthusiasm of the dedicated bird-watcher, but returning always to his first interest and first love in all the lands he had explored—the people who tilled the earth and lived by its fruits. The continuity of human life was more apparent in Egypt than in any other country, with the exception of India, that Butler had previously known, and like Thomas Hardy he derived a peculiar satisfaction from the knowledge that the humble earth-worker endures while dynasties pass: 'Here, in this brown-skinned mud-puddler, in that pitcher-carrying wife of his, and in these naked pot-bellied children, old Egypt and middle Egypt and young Egypt live, move and have one continuous being.'[6]

There was much besides the past and immediate life of Egypt to attract and hold Butler's interest. He was becoming more and more deeply absorbed in his study of Napoleon, and Alexandria was rich in Napoleonic associations. He was delighted to learn that an aged Arab living in a palm grove on the shore of Aboukir Bay remembered the great naval battle of Aboukir fought ninety years before, and hastened to meet him. The Arab looked wizened enough to have lived a century or more, but once again Butler found that the memories of the very old tend to concentrate on what the eager historian regards as trivia. Yes, the old Arab remembered the battle, because while it was being fought a boat loaded with oranges capsized in Aboukir Bay.

During the time of his Egyptian command Butler made a long-planned and many times deferred visit to the Holy Land. He and Lady Butler sailed from Alexandria to Port Said, a city which to Butler was the very essence of evil—'brutality boiled down, ugliness smoked and hung up to dry in the sun'—and from Port Said to Jaffa aboard a vessel crowded with 'grim pilgrims' travelling under the aegis of Thomas Cook and Sons—'man-eyed English and Scottish women in helmets and great puggarees, with husbands of a more feminine type; clergymen of many persuasions, hopeless-nosed men'. From Jaffa the Butlers travelled overland to Jerusalem in the springtime, when the earth-smells of the East are at their freshest and the plain of Sharon 'beautiful as the mind of God'. In Jerusalem Butler busied himself gathering evidence to verify the authenticity of the holy sites (he did so to his own satisfaction) but the Holy City did not move him as profoundly as the Plain of Esdraelon, which he viewed one golden morning from a high point encompassing a view of many miles. In one of the most curious passages of the *Autobiography* Butler reconstructs, as he saw it in the mind's eye, the 'glorious sight' that must have been spread upon the plain that day in 1798 when Napoleon, with the dazzling Murat playing a leading role, crushed and combined Turkish and Arab armies and littered Esdraelon with the bodies of the slain; then passes, with no awareness of incongruity, to contemplate glories of a different and opposite kind, remembering it was here

that the Master prepared to manifest all that infinite knowledge of soul and sense, the pale reflection of which, as it is found in the Evangelists, has come as a moonbeam over the troubled river of the lives of men, silvering the turbid stream, lightening the gloomy headlands, and shedding its benign rays far out upon the endless ocean in which the fevered flood is at last to rest.[7]

There were other visits to other lands, nearly all intended to combine the pleasures of sightseeing with the more substantial satisfactions of research. The great work on Napoleon was rapidly taking shape, and the pilgrimage which Butler had made in his subaltern days to the battlefields of Belgium he now extended, with equal thoroughness and enthusiasm and energy, to cover nearly every battlefield Napoleon had fought over, including Arcola, Marengo, Austerlitz, Aspern, and Wagram. Significantly he did not follow his hero to Moscow. The invasion of Russia and its consequences were a part of the Napoleonic epic about which Butler maintained an almost complete silence.

During his stay in Alexandria Butler enjoyed even the official entertaining which his position demanded of him—he was, in fact, a most sociable man so long as he was not denied the occasional periods of solitude essential to one of his temper. And it is typical of the man that he delighted in the visit of the Duke of Cambridge in 1891, even though he considered the Duke a woolly-headed reactionary unfit to command a corporal's platoon let alone the British Army. But the Duke was a warm-hearted old bumbler whom Butler liked as a human being; and he was, besides, a 'character' whose quaint mannerisms charmed his host and hostess. 'We had the Duke of Cambridge to luncheon,' Lady Butler noted in her diary.

He arrived on board the *Surprise* from Malta, and Will, of course, received him officially but not royally, as he is travelling incog, and he came here to tea. Today we had a large party to meet him, and a very genial luncheon it was, not to say rollicking. . . . H.R.H. seemed to me rather feeble but in the best of humours, a wonderful old man to come to Egypt for the first time at 72, braving the burning sun with such a high colour to begin with! One felt as though one was talking to George III, to hear the 'What, what, what? Who, who, who? Why, why, why?' . . . I was gratified to hear his praise of our cook—very loud praise, literally as he is not only rather deaf himself but speaks to people as though they also were a little hard of hearing! 'Very good cook, my dear.' (to me). 'Very good cook, Butler.' (Across the table to Will). 'Very good cook, eh, Sykes?' (Very loud, to Christopher Sykes, further off). 'You are a gourmet, you know better about these things than I do, eh?' C.S. 'I ought to have learned something about it at Gloucester House, sir.' H.R.H. (to me): 'Your health, my dear.' 'Butler, your very good health.' Aside to me: 'What's the consul's name?' I: 'Sir Charles Cookson.' 'Sir Charles, your health.' When I hand the salt to H.R.H. he stops my hand. 'I wouldn't quarrel with her for the world, Butler.' . . . He started at four for Cairo, leaving a most kindly impression on my memory. The last of the old Georgian type! 'Your mutton was very good, my dear. Not at all *goaty*,' were his valedictory words.[8]

In 1893 Butler returned to England to take up a home command at Aldershot, where, so he observed in his autobiography, 'the British Army was preparing for the disasters of the South African war'. Nothing had changed, it seemed, since he had first drilled at Fermoy thirty-four years earlier—'the march past was still the supreme test of tactical fitness for war'; and the inspecting officers were all too often 'terrible old dotterers' whose great age, reactionary views on all things military, and all-round obtuseness were their only qualifications for the job. Sir Evelyn Wood, who had lately relinquished the command at Aldershot, considered a good seat in an officer more important than a good head; and his frequent justifications of fox-hunting as an essential part of an officer's training must rank among the most entertaining of the *non sequiturs* with which his writing abounds. As late as 1917 he wrote, in answer to a newspaper article hostile to fox-hunting,

While I do not assert that Sir David Beatty and Sir John Jellicoe won the battle of Heligoland and the Jutland Bank, by their practise of fox-hunting, which certainly braces the nerves, it may interest the . . . objector to fox-hunting, whose arguments I am answering, and who is a well-known journalist and writer on naval affairs, to learn that the Vice-Admiral is said to ride brilliantly to hounds, and that as late as the season 1913–14 I saw the Admiral riding well in front of the Essex pack.[9]

In an even more remarkable passage Wood was able—being protected at all points by the armour of insensitivity against the weapon of irony—to enlist the support of Gladstone, not usually considered sympathetic to the chase, on the side of the huntsman:

In the seventies I was staying with Mr. Glyn, later Lord Wolverton, who had a pack of black St. Hubert stag-hounds, and he mentioned that in order to entertain me he had given himself another holiday from his duties as Chief Liberal Whip in Parliament, where some contested question was coming forward for decision. Next day, on my expressing regret that I had inadvertently been the cause of his absenting himself from his voluntary duties, he showed me a letter which he had received that morning from the Prime Minister, written in the kindest strain, and saying how glad he was to think of him riding for health and amusement instead of being in the House of Commons all night.[10]

In spite of the feeling that he had slipped back nearly half a century, Butler liked Aldershot. He drilled his own brigade according to his fancy and enjoyed, as a counter-balance to the luxuries of Alexandria, a taste of Spartan living. He occupied one of the last of the old army huts, and perhaps the chill winds whistling past ill-fitting window frames and under shrunken doors recalled the environment of the Canadian West, still his most haunting memory. And near by, at Farnborough Hill, lived the last significant relic of the House of Napoleon—the Empress Eugénie. The Empress, Lady Butler observed, possessed 'the remnants of a certain masculine power', but she was still woman enough to appreciate a handsome figure in uniform and grateful to Butler for his kindness to her son, the Prince Imperial, dead long ago in South Africa.

She became very fond of talking politics with Sir William [Lady Butler reported], and she used to sit in that confidential way foreign politicians have, expressive of the divulgence of tremendous secrets and of occult plots and plans. . . . She talked incessantly to him but was a bad listener; and if a subject came up in conversation which did not interest her a sharp snap or two of her fan would soon bring things to a stop.[11]

There were other remote connections with his hero's shade. Prince Louis Napoleon visited Farnborough and Butler invited him to witness a sham fight in the Fox Hills. When the fight was over Butler asked Prince Louis to take the salute of the Guards. The Prince protested that he was not in uniform. Butler's reply is so apt as to sound studied, although he must have spoken spontaneously: 'One of your name, sir, is always in uniform.' And once three Frenchmen bearing three great names, Murat, Ney, Massena, sat together at the Butler luncheon table. The hero-worshipper no doubt gloried in the associations the names evoked, and flinched at the mockery of their investment in petty princelings who had no place in their own land.

From Aldershot, Butler went in 1896 to Dover, a Major-General now and Commander of the South-Eastern District. His advancement since 1888 had been unspectacular but consistent, and his radical theories of military training now found favour at the War Office, where Field-Marshal Lord Wolseley had been installed as Chief of Staff. The improvement in Butler's fortunes was neatly epitomized in his change of residence, from Aldershot hut to Dover Castle, the two almost equally draughty but otherwise as unlike as the cottage and the palace. From his study window, where he worked long hours putting the finishing touches on his account of Napoleon's last years, Butler was able to look across the Channel and see lights flashing on the French coast where ninety years earlier the great Emperor had massed his forces for the assault on England which never came. Lady Butler, too, was pleased with the move, since she was able to exchange an Aldershot hut for a well-lighted spacious studio; and in Dover Castle the Butlers lived with their growing family in the greatest happiness and peace of mind they had known in their nearly twenty years of marriage.

Except, perhaps, during those periods when Butler, strong in the conviction that any institution could be run most efficiently on military lines under the supervision of a military man, invaded the domain normally in charge of Lady Butler. His youngest daughter, Eileen, has left an amusing and sympathetic portrait of a man who, whatever his achievements in other fields, was something less than a success as head of a household:

My father would assert that unless *he* saw to the running of the house nothing was properly done. On days such as Bank Holidays when he did not go to his office in the morning the whole household was upheaved. He would stride from department to department leaving consternation in his wake; and then during the unpunctual and indifferent lunch that followed, express satisfaction at his successful handling of his difficult task—so much more difficult, he would declare, than the running of the entire district.[12]

In the role of parent he was hardly more successful. Between himself and his children lay a gulf neither he nor they ever crossed; and between them anything approaching companionship was impossible.

What is surprising [Eileen Butler wrote] is that one who, in public life, invariably championed the under-dog, should in his own home have been a complete autocrat. No one there ever dared dispute my father's will—least of all my mother, in whom loyalty was an outstanding quality, who detested rows, and who, fortunately for herself, had her studio into which to retreat. . . .

To me, as a child, he was an idol; but an idol to be worshipped from afar. My love for him was one of the strongest emotions of my life; but I was too shy of him ever to be able to demonstrate it to him. All I could do was—unknown to him—to half-kill myself with work at school, so as to please him by bringing home all the prizes possible. Once when, with nervously thumping heart, I brought him the pile of books and he beamed down at me, quoting:

And still he gazed and still the wonder grew
That one small head could carry all (she) knew—

I longed for him to know that the one small head had worked itself almost into a brain fever to achieve this result, and that it was the wish to give *him* pleasure that had been the driving force. But I could no more have told him that than I could have jumped over the moon.

With my brothers my father was overstrict. He would summon them to his study to receive what they called a 'jaw' for the most minor misdemeanours, and the atmosphere of the meals which followed was nerve-racking.[13]

In time of illness Butler knew better than any doctor the cause of the ailment, and the remedy. He diagnosed (an outbreak of boils was caused by eating unripe gooseberries); he prescribed (usually a large dose of castor oil), and it speaks well for the constitutions of the five Butler children that they all grew to adulthood suffering no marked ill effects from their father's ministrations.

During his time at Aldershot and Dover Butler's literary reputation was steadily growing. After nearly twenty years *The Great Lone Land* was still a best-selling travel book; the *Life* of Gordon had proved a great popular success, and the *Life* of Sir Charles Napier, published in 1891, commanded nearly as large a reading public—

surprising since Napier, unlike Gordon, was neither a contemporary hero nor a martyr. But like Gordon the conqueror of Scind was a subject admirably suited to Butler's talents and sympathies. He was an Irishman, a passionate individualist contemptuous of brass hats and red tape who infuriated his superiors, charmed his subordinates, and won his laurels late in life when it seemed that fame had long since passed him by. Indeed, there are times when Butler's justifications of Napier's wildly erratic behaviour reads like an *apologia pro vita sua:*

There are those who, writing and speaking of him (Napier) since his death, have regretted his 'utterances of passion', his 'want of serenity'. 'They (Charles Napier and his brother William) lived in storm instead of above the clouds' wrote one of their greatest admirers when both brothers had passed away; and if this has been said since they left us, a hundredfold stronger was the censure of the world when they still moved among their fellow-men. But the passion and the vehemence of the Napiers was only the ocean wave of their hatred of oppression thundering against the bulwarks of tyranny. They should have dwelt above the clouds, foresooth, made less noise, toned down the vehemence of their denunciations. How easy all this is after the battle is over, and when we are sitting in a cushioned chair with our feet to the fire. But find me anything overthrown without noise . . . any citadel of human wrong captured, any battle ever won by the above-the-cloud method—and I'll say you are right about the Napiers.[14]

A reviewer writing in the *Spectator* observed with considerable acumen that 'Sir William Butler was certainly the right man to have written this short life of Sir Charles Napier. The impassioned pages in which he has recorded the story of the great soldier, great administrator, and great lover of people, suit the subject in a way that no calmer or even juster record could have suited it.'

Surprisingly, however, the best appraisal of the book was made not by a professional critic but by Lord Wolseley, whose observations, prompted by the irritation felt by one prejudiced individual towards another harbouring equal and opposite prejudices, are seldom wide of the mark: '(Napier) is good and it is bad,' Wolseley wrote to Louisa.

Some parts very good, but it aggravates me occasionally, when he magnifies France to depreciate England. Anything that will tell against what I prize most—namely, the honour and reputation of our Empire—he loves to dwell upon; anything that can be twisted into a glorification of the Celtic race is made to perform on his stage and lauded by a magniloquent chorus. He writes very well, and often most touchingly and sympathetically, but there is always too much straining after word-effect, too great a consciousness of superior skill.[15]

It was during the time of his Dover command that Butler completed what he believed to be his most significant work—the account of Napoleon's last years entitled *Napoleon on St. Helena.* Whether he ever submitted the manuscript to a publisher is not known; it is possible that he kept it by him to the end of his life, polishing and refining. After Butler's death Lady Butler, discouraged by a publisher's comment that the book would add nothing to her husband's reputation, presumably destroyed the manuscript. The existing version is an earlier draft, painstakingly revised and corrected, and almost certainly the copy from which the final draft was typed.

The publisher's comment was just. As an objective historical study *Napoleon on St. Helena* does not deserve serious consideration. Butler's regard for Napoleon amounted to an obsession; he could not bear to read a criticism of his hero, however far removed from his immediate subject, without replying to it; thus his attempt to refute the charge that Napoleon abandoned his army in Egypt and left it to perish, while in itself of considerable interest is, within the framework of the overall design, an irrelevancy. In Butler's pages Napoleon emerges as the spotless knight, the champion of the oppressed, the enemy of the privileged, the Christian hero hounded to martyrdom by evil men. No one can deny Butler's enormous industry; he read everything relating to his subject, examined and sifted evidence with scrupulous care—and discarded as irrelevant anything that did not square with his preconceptions. He hints at a vague possibility favourable to Napoleon and damning to his enemies. The possibility, without any further evidence having been advanced to support it, soon becomes a probability and shortly thereafter a fact. Thus Butler suggests that Sir Hudson Lowe, Napoleon's persecutor on St. Helena, might have had something to do with the execution of Murat, Prince of Naples, in 1815, solely on the evidence that Lowe was somewhere in the Mediterranean at the time of Murat's death. A chapter later and Lowe is described, without qualification, as one of Murat's murderers.

None the less, for all its dubious documentation and obsessive hero-worship, the MS. is well worth reading for its revelation of

Butler himself, and for its occasional passages of excellent prose. Never were Butler's powers of invective more in evidence than when he wrote of Fouché—'to the ex-priest, ex-republican, ex-imperialist and ex-royalist still remained the one role to which not even he could prove false—that of Judas'. Or of Sir Hudson Lowe and the men who hired him:

The basis of Sir Hudson Lowe's character was fear; the highest motive power of his nature was hate; but no man, no matter how he watched him, could define where one ended or the other began. His frenzy of suspicion never ceased. His fury of hatred never slumbered. In his meanness he could stoop to any depth of indignity. He could examine servants as to gossip they had heard at key-holes, or order his staff-officers to pry into a basket of dirty linen. . . . He could deny freedom to a slave who had been basely entrapped, simply because Napoleon asked the boon as a favour. . . . He could act the bully and the tyrant to the subordinate officers in his power and cringe and toady with almost ridiculous subservience before the least suspicion of authority. . . . He knew the exact value of every doubtful piece in the coinage of words, and could frame a despatch or dictate a letter the real object of which was as cleverly concealed as was its false purport strenuously and diplomatically elaborated. All these things and more, he could and did do during the term of his Governorship of St. Helena, but . . . neither in fear, falsehood, persecution nor merciless hatred did he reach, still less surpass, the vengeance of the men who selected him for the office and kept him in it five long years. The essence of the great crime of St. Helena was not Sir Hudson Lowe's. Far as his shadow will project itself into the future (and it will be found when the sunlight which never sets upon English dominion will go down on the disrupted fragments of Empire) the crime of the men who selected him to represent them on the exile rock will stretch further, and loom darker. For, to them, there was not even the excuse which the murderers of Tudor times might advance in their defence. There was neither policy, expediency, self-aggrandisement or necessity in it. It was pure, gratuitous cruelty.

What might indeed have been Butler's most significant work fails because it is not history but special pleading, not biography but apotheosis:

And since his enemies have come to proclaim him the greatest of all great men—even while the ashes of the conflict still glow under every breeze that ruffles the world of existing politics—nothing can be better assured than that when these ashes have lost their spark and grown cold in the winters of Time, the voice of impartial History will declare that, given the attitude which Europe assumed towards the French revolution, and the position into which France had been forced as a consequence of that attitude; given, in fact, the world as Napoleon found it at the close of the 18th century, his policy, his action, the entire plan, purpose and effort of his life were not alone explicable, reasonable and coherent, but that they followed the only channel possible to them. When Destiny builds a human machine of superlative genius and grandeur of mind, she shapes, if she does not level, the track over which it is to roll.

Unfortunately godhood has little in common with humanity. To make a god of Napoleon, Butler had to kill the man.

In 1887 Butler had written: 'Fate, it is said, knocks once at every man's door, but sometimes it is when the shadows are gathering and the fire is beginning to burn slow.'[16] The words were prophetic. The knock on his own door came in 1898 when he was sixty years of age. In that year he was appointed Commander-in-Chief of the British forces in South Africa, and, in the absence of Sir Alfred Milner, acting High Commissioner of South Africa and Natal.

CHAPTER SIXTEEN

According to His Lights

Radix malorum est cupiditas. Men fought not for justice, not for love of country, not for loyalties or causes however worthy or however misguided; the armies of the world, so Butler was coming more and more strongly to believe, were set in motion by human greed concentrated in the forms of vast corporations, international banking houses, war supplies contractors, armaments manufacturers—forms which by virtue of the protective camouflage of impersonality remained invisible to the eye of the common man, who all too often gave up his life to further the ends of corporation greed under the illusion that he was dying for his country.

The history of South Africa seemed to support in every respect Butler's view. Until gold was discovered in the Transvaal in the 1880s the Boer led a peaceful pastoral life which, in the eyes of those who were able to overlook his treatment of the native, bordered on the idyllic, and it is probably true that the individual Boer, to whom land and cattle represented the only wealth worth while, wanted no part of the precious bane. But the outside world could not thereafter leave him in peace; and in the long run the Boer was compelled to fight to maintain his independence not only against a foreign political power but against huge industrial and mining corporations and the banking houses of Europe. And it was not possible for Butler to share the view, propounded with sincerity and passion by such dedicated Empire-builders as Rhodes and Joseph Chamberlain and Sir Alfred Milner, that British Imperialism, whatever its accompanying transient evils, represented the one best hope of the world, and that in the long run the Boer would benefit immeasurably from the overlordship of Great Britain. When William Ernest Henley saluted England as 'chosen daughter of the Lord' he spoke what was for most Englishmen of the late Victorian age, including Rhodes and Chamberlain and Milner, the sober truth.

But not for an Irishman who remembered the evictions and the Great Hunger.

From the Imperialist point of view nowhere, in those golden days of the late Victorian age, did prospects for the expansion and consolidation of Empire glow more brightly than in South Africa—the last continent where large-scale territorial acquisition was still possible; and nowhere was opposition to the Imperialist policy potentially more dangerous. For the Boer, too, had a political goal to strive for; the enormous wealth of the Transvaal goldfields had placed the Transvaal at the head of the South African states and given substance to the Boer vision of a united South Africa which would include not only the independent Boer states but the British colonies as well. In the eyes of all Britishers, therefore, to whom Imperialism was a source of profit or a faith or both, the issue created by the situation in the Transvaal involved nothing less than the fate of the British Empire. In the words of Milner's most perceptive biographer, 'In their eyes the difficulty with the Boers was a test, and on its outcome depended the fate and future course of Great Britain. If they failed, in this case, the Imperial movement would be discredited, not only in South Africa and the Dominions, but also at home.'[1]

In 1897 Sir Alfred Milner, Britain's ablest civil servant with the possible exception of Sir Evelyn Baring—whom in temperament he greatly resembled—was appointed High Commissioner of South Africa and Governor of the Cape Colony. Behind Milner stood the greatest of Britain's colonial secretaries, Joseph Chamberlain. It is difficult to imagine a more formidable combination for the execution of an expansionist Empire policy, for both Milner and Chamberlain were men of brilliant intellect (to which Chamberlain added an abundance of shrewd political sense), and both were convinced Imperialists.

Such dreams of a greater Britain hardly touched the ordinary citizen; for him the issue in South Africa had resolved itself, by 1897, into a bitter clash between Britisher and Boer over the position of the Uitlander (or foreigner)—in most instances an Englishman—in the Transvaal. He was denied citizenship in the Boer state; he was subject to taxation not applicable to the Boer, and he was, so he believed, denied equal justice with the Boer in the law courts of the Transvaal. It was in part Sir Alfred Milner's job to apply pressure on the Boer Government for juster treatment of the

Uitlander, secure in the knowledge that Paul Kruger, the dour old President of the Transvaal who hated Englishmen, would never yield to such pressure. It is clear that almost from the beginning of his tenure of office Milner was convinced that the Transvaal issue could be resolved only by war—and most certainly from February 1898, when Kruger was returned to power by an overwhelming majority over his moderate opponents. Milner wrote to Chamberlain, immediately following Kruger's re-election, 'There is no way out of the political troubles of South Africa except reform in the Transvaal or war. And at present chances of reform . . . are worse than ever.'

Milner has been described by one who knew him intimately as a Roman of the Augustan Age whose 'absorbing passion was the British Empire. . . . He saw in the preservation and development of its administrative ideals the principal hope for the progress of mankind.'[2] Such a man was not likely to be concerned about or tolerant of public opinion when he himself saw the best way clearly. Milner was, in fact, a high-minded autocrat, utterly contemptuous of the democratic process and a firm believer in the rule of the intellectual aristocracy. An admirable man—and a little inhuman. There is something chilling about his decision, reached early in life and maintained to the age of seventy, not to marry lest marriage interfere with his career.

When in 1898 General Goodenough, the Commander-in-Chief of the British Forces in South Africa, died suddenly, Sir Alfred urged that his successor be a man 'of energy and resource and of some political sense, rather than some worn-out Lieutenant-General'. By a man of political sense Sir Alfred meant, of course, one who would be entirely sympathetic to his own views on the appropriate policy for South Africa; but by one of those ironies of history which must wake the laughter of the gods the man appointed to the post of Commander-in-Chief, almost certainly on the recommendation of Lord Wolseley, was Sir William Butler.

Butler accepted the post of Commander-in-Chief, and with it, during Milner's three months' absence on leave in England, that of High Commissioner, with the utmost reluctance. He enjoyed the Dover Command; and he knew that trouble, of which he wanted no part, was brewing in South Africa. But he had always made it a rule of his professional life to go where he was asked and he did not hesitate now. An interview with Joseph Chamberlain intensified the vague apprehension he felt about what lay ahead, for he carried away from the meeting no directives of any kind, no inkling of any Government policy he might be expected to encourage—nothing except a vivid impression of the 'eager, white, sharp anxious face which was leaning towards me over the office table'.

In truth Butler's appointment was the worst that could possibly have been made, and particularly for Butler himself. 'The appointment was a grievous wrong to the officer whose career was frustrated by promotion,' J. L. Garvin wrote in his definitive life of Joseph Chamberlain.

> Tall, handsome, very military and very courteous in bearing, Butler was every inch a soldier and something of a Quixote. Married to the painter of *The Roll Call*, his own descriptive books of travel and adventure delighted boys, while fastidious critics ranked him one of the purest stylists of his day. He had lately refreshed his old military knowledge of South Africa by writing the life of Colley, his comrade who fell at Majuba.
>
> So far he might seem the very man. But he was disqualified for this one post by the ardour of his political sympathies. As an impassioned Irish nationalist his heart was altogether with the Boers and Afrikanders. By comparison he saw Johannesburg as the chosen city of Beelzebub and regarded Rhodes and confederate magnates as evil beings.[3]

Since he arrived in South Africa uninstructed about British Government plans—the Colonial Office almost certainly assumed that the temporary Commissioner would merely keep Sir Alfred Milner's seat warm for him and say nothing—Butler at once proceeded with the implementation of his own policy—peace for South Africa. On December 17, 1898, only two weeks after his arrival in South Africa, he gave a speech in Grahamstown in which, with unstatesmanlike bluntness, he made his position crystal clear: 'South Africa . . . does not need a surgical operation,' he said. 'She needs peace, progress, and the development which is only possible through the union of many hearts and the labour of many hands.' The affirmation was enthusiastically hailed by the Boers, and by William Schreiner, Prime Minister of the Cape Colony, who recognized in Butler a Commissioner whose sympathies were unequivocably on the side of peace. It was roundly denounced by the Uitlanders and their powerful organization for political action, the South African League. In Butler they saw a man to fear, and presently to hate.

Before the year was out Butler gave further evidence of his hostility to the Uitlanders and his disapproval of their tactics. He refused to forward on their behalf a petition to the Queen protesting the release of a Boer policeman who had shot down, apparently in cold blood, an unarmed Englishman named Edgar on the grounds that he resisted arrest. The Edgar case, in its day a *cause celebre*, was interpreted by the Uitlanders as a glaring example of the arrogance and injustice of the Boer attitude towards foreigners; by Butler (so his terse summary of the case indicates) as a crude attempt on the part of the South African League to make propaganda out of the fate of a dissolute brawler:

A man of British nationality had been shot by a policeman in a midnight brawl in a low corner of Johannesburg. The man's name was Edgar . . . Edgar had already knocked another Englishman to pieces, maltreating him to such an extent that he soon after died of his wounds. Had this drunken brawl occurred in any other city in the world out of the Transvaal it would have occasioned no excitement outside of the people immediately concerned in it. The time, after midnight; a drunken brawl; a man left dead, or mortally hurt, in the street; his assailant is a fugitive in a house; the police are called for; the fugitive shows fight; a shot is fired; the man is killed. . . . On this foundation the South African League seized with avidity, and built upon it a huge international question. Indignation meetings were immediately organized; a petition to the Queen was prepared; all the wires were pulled at once. Telegrams, cablegrams, letters and despatches flew like leaves in a November storm. All the newspapers in Mr. Rhodes' interest in South Africa double-leaded their types. So well had the organization been arranged that the so-called petition to the Queen had already appeared in sensational type . . . and the London journals were in receipt of sensational cablegrams from South Africa before the meeting had even been held which was to denounce the slaying of an unoffending citizen.[4]

Butler refused to forward the Uitlander petition to the Queen; instead he devoted himself during the remainder of his *locum tenens* to bombarding high officials at home with what he regarded as evidence of the machinations of the South African League, with censuring junior officials under his authority for using intemperate language when speaking of the Boers, and with discouraging any attempt on the part of the Uitlanders to enlist his support—particularly the Johannesburg Uitlanders, whom he described as 'probably the most corrupt, immoral and untruthful assemblage of beings at present in the world'. From the moment of his arrival in South Africa Butler set his face resolutely against war; leave South Africa alone and in the long run, so he firmly believed, fusion of the white races through intermarriage was inevitable; precipitate war between them, impose the will of the stronger upon the weaker, and a second Ireland would be created to plague the English to all eternity—and serve them right.

He had, however, little hope that common sense and compromise would prevail. Even the phenomena of nature, such as the eclipse he observed from his headquarters at Rondebosch, to his poet's imagination foreshadowed deeds of blood:

That evening there was a remarkable eclipse of the moon. We stood outside on the verandah . . . watching the shadow slowly creeping over the great disc of the moon until the eclipse became total. There were two or three officers with me, and we all agreed that never before had we witnessed such an extraordinary colour as that which suffused the moon at the moment of totality, or the equally strange, shadowy and spectral light which fell upon the earth at the same moment. The face of the moon seemed to have been washed over with blood-stained cloth, and the old garden . . . with its lofty cypress trees, looked in the sombre light like a nocturnal graveyard.[5]

In February 1899 Sir Alfred Milner returned to South Africa to resume his duties as High Commissioner. The first meeting between Milner and Butler was a chilly one. Milner read Butler's lengthy memorandum on the Edgar case with 'undisguised impatience' and equally obvious disapproval. Butler, bitterly disappointed in the High Commissioner's reception of his exhaustively documented report, said stiffly to Sir Alfred, 'I envy you only the books in your library', and took his leave.

In the sordid and tragic history of the period immediately preceding the Boer War the relationship between the High Commissioner and the Commander-in-Chief provides some moments of comic relief. It has been said of Milner that, although touched by greatness, 'his genius was of the autocratic kind, and in his heart he never recognized with much good humour the right of the opposition. . . . He believed too ardently that he perceived the truth and that others who could not agree with him did not.'[6] The words hold almost equally true of Butler. From the beginning the two men, old Roman and Irish liberal, one born too late in time the other too early, held diametrically opposite positions. To Milner, Butler was 'that brilliant but impossible Irishman'; to Butler, Milner was a man condemned by an Eton and Balliol education to be always on the wrong side.

At first the relationship between the two, while never amicable, was at least tolerable. 'Do not think that Butler is a bad fellow', Milner wrote to Sir Walter Hely-Hutchinson shortly after his return to South Africa. 'He is hasty and rhetorical, fearfully deficient in judgement. But he is well-meaning enough and a most agreeable companion.' As time went on Milner came to recognize more positive qualities in Butler. He wrote to Lord Selborne:

(Butler) *has behaved perfectly well towards me on my return.* He does not meddle in political affairs in any way. On the other hand, he keeps me absolutely at arm's length over military matters. I do not mean that he refuses to answer questions or to give effect to any wishes I express. He answers what I absolutely and point-blank ask and he does what I absolutely request. But there is no freedom of communication between him and me. This is due to two reasons, one his strong feeling, with which I largely sympathize, that everything in the way of military plans and preparations should be a dead secret from everybody, and the other the fact that he does not and cannot sympathize with my policy. I am, for good and all, convinced that to let the S.A.R. go on as it is going is a danger to S.A. He is equally convinced that there is more danger in interfering than in letting things take their course. At the same time he will, of course, loyally do his duty, and he is an able man.[7]

Milner, for all his admirable intellectual resources, was a lonely man who felt isolated in South Africa. What he wanted and needed in his Commander-in-Chief was a confidant eager to co-operate in preparations for the clash between Englishman and Boer which Milner believed inevitable. Instead he found himself saddled with a man implacably opposed to his policy for the resolution of the South African question—ready always to obey orders, but unwilling to exercise initiative.

In his relations with the home Government Butler was equally correct and equally unresponsive to the other side's intent. On instructions from the War Office he carried out an examination of the defences of the British colonies in South Africa and prepared a plan to be acted on in the event of a sudden outbreak of hostilities. But he did so without heart, because apart from all other considerations his instructions were in his view absurd. The communication from the War Office urged that if hostilities broke out Butler should at once push his weak forces into Boer territory—a sure invitation, so he believed, to almost immediate capture or annihilation:

There were to be no supports behind these troops, which were thus, as it were, shot into hostile space, having behind them military voids many hundreds of miles in length, peopled by a strong and active population of Dutch farmers. . . . Here then, had suddenly come upon me, from the point least expected, by far the most formidable force I had yet met in South Africa. The party of the Raid, the intrigues of the South African League, the Boer enemy—these I could all reckon and cope with in my plan of defence. But the War Office friend, the latest staff college strategist, fed to his eyebrows in false military history, with his plan of campaign cut and dried, signed, sealed and delivered in that terrible congeries of confused opinion and congested clerkship which I had so long known in Pall Mall—that was something totally unexpected.[8]

Butler conducted a thorough inspection of the frontiers of the British Colonies and prepared his report on the appropriate disposition of the troops under his command, but showed his contempt for the War Office strategists by withholding the report until it was peremptorily demanded of him. It recommended a strictly defensive policy, even to the point of falling back if necessary on Cape Town itself. Butler had lately published a biography of General George Colley, the brilliant and ill-fated member of the Ring who had died at Majuba (Butler's least successful biography, since temperamentally he and Colley had little in common), and it seemed to him that the War Office plan—penetration into Boer territory with inadequate forces, ill-trained troops and no supports —meant only a repetition of the disasters of 1881 and he wanted no part of it. With the forces under his command he could, he told Milner, do no more than hold certain positions in Cape Colony and Natal. To bring pressure on the Boer Republics would, he added, 'require forty thousand men'.

On May 3, 1899, there opened in Bloemfontein the conference in which Sir Alfred Milner, representing Great Britain, and Paul Kruger, President of the Transvaal, met to determine the immediate fate of South Africa. The franchise for Uitlanders was the issue on which Milner determined to force a showdown. He asked that the Uitlanders be given the right to vote after five years' residence in the Transvaal—on the surface no more than a request for the granting of citizenship on the terms commonly acceptable in the Western world. From Kruger's point of view agreement to such a request was tantamount to a surrender of Boer sovereignty; either the British would pour into the Transvaal in such numbers as shortly to constitute a voting majority or else, if immigration were drastically restricted, rebellion within the colony be fomented with assurance of support from the outside. Alternatively, rejection of Milner's demands meant war. 'It is our country you want—it is our country you want,' Kruger cried out, with tears running down his leathery old face. Crocodile tears those hostile to him said; but to Butler they were real. His summary of the conference proceedings reveals the depth of his pro-Boer—or anti-British—feelings. 'The Conference met on five days. The franchise question had been selected by the Colonial Office as the test subject. If the franchise were refused to the Uitlanders war would have followed at once; if, on the other hand, the franchise was given to the extent demanded . . . then the destruction of the Boer Republic would only be a question of a few years, or perhaps a few months, with the South African League always present to manipulate the scheme and to agitate for rebellion. But, of the two courses, that of the out-and-out refusal of the franchise was the one most desired by the Raiders. That course would leave the road open for the much-desired ultimatum; troops would then be on the sea, and the resort to force could no longer be delayed.[9]

Kruger refused to grant the franchise, but the British Government still hesitated. As late as June 1899, only four months before the outbreak of war, Butler received a communication from the War Office which asserted that, 'Without entering into any close consideration of the political situation, we cannot shut our eyes to the fact that the possibility of war in South Africa has not yet been eliminated.' This equivocal statement was precisely the sort of thing to strengthen Butler's hand in his undeclared war with Sir Alfred Milner. In fairness to Butler it should be pointed out that his efforts to avert conflict between Boer and Englishman, even at the risk of his own reputation, were founded not only on his sympathy for the Boers and his growing hatred of all wars but on the recognition, shared by no other British military men of the time, of the magnitude of the struggle that would ensue if war were declared. He suffered no illusions about the fighting quality of the Boer or the extent of his preparations for war; and he knew the absurdity of contemplating the conquest of the Transvaal with the handful of troops at his disposal. It is a tribute to Sir Alfred Milner's magnanimity that he acknowledged that Butler, although in most things a sore vexation to him, understood better than anyone else the military situation in South Africa. 'His merit was,' Sir Alfred said, 'that he knew the size of the job.'

Butler's relations with the War Office, as with Sir Alfred, were conducted with a nice regard for protocol and in strict accord with his rule that a soldier must obey orders no matter how stupid they might be. He answered questions correctly; did what he was asked to do and carefully avoided exercising any initiative whatever. He was strongly opposed to the sending of more troops from England on the grounds that to do so would be to convince the Boers of Britain's warlike intentions and thus destroy the last faint hope of peace; and since the War Office did not invite him to express an opinion on the number of troops required in case of war he found no occasion to mention the figure of 40,000 he had named in conversation with Sir Alfred Milner. Had he done so he would almost certainly have been laughed at.

There were, of course, many things he wanted to say about the South African position and could not—until an incautiously worded communiqué from the War Office played into his hands. The communiqué directed Butler to authorize the purchase of a considerable number of transport mules for the forces in South Africa, asked several questions about army supplies, and concluded by inquiring if Butler had 'any observations' which he wished to offer.

Butler had. 'You ask my observations. They might fill many pages, but they could be summarized thus: I believe that war between the white races coming as a sequel to the Jameson raid and the subsequent events of the last three years, *would be the greatest calamity that ever occurred in South Africa*'.

The fat was in the fire. A shocked Secretary of State telegraphed Butler:

Concluding paragraph of your telegram of 23rd June. You have evidently misunderstood my telegram of 21st June.

You were invited to offer observations as to suitability of War Office proposals for securing object in view, viz. increased efficiency in existing forces, not as to general merits of policy adopted by H.M. Government.

You cannot understand too clearly that, whatever your private opinions, it is your duty to be guided in all questions of policy by those who are fully aware of our views, and whom you will, of course, loyally support.

Milner understandably was furious when Butler gave him a copy of his reply to the request from the War Office for observations, and his anger was in no way modified when Butler, with obvious sincerity, assured him that he had made his observations in what he believed to be 'the highest interests of the British Empire and for the honour of Her Majesty's Army'.

But no incident reveals more clearly the irreconcilibility of the views of the High Commissioner with those of his Commander-in-Chief than the one involving a certain Wools-Sampson, a trigger-happy Britisher eager to raise a volunteer force of irregular horse to help police the borders of Cape Colony and Natal and if necessary raid into the Transvaal. Milner, after pointing out that Wools-Sampson had been travelling widely in the Transvaal, 'feeling the temper of things', asked Butler to see him and listen to certain proposals he might have to make. Milner, according to Butler, talked vaguely of forming a ring of troops and irregulars around the Boer republics. Butler replied that he had received no instructions from the War Office to take positive action of any sort; he did not know the War Office mind or the Government mind, but so far he had no reason to think that their intentions were warlike. Butler's reply was correct, and no doubt to Sir Alfred, desperately anxious for sympathy and support from his Commander-in-Chief, absolutely exasperating. Butler did, however, agree to see Wools-Sampson.

As might have been expected, the interview failed to produce any positive results except an intensification of Uitlander distrust and hatred of Butler. Ever since his experiences in Natal Butler despised irregular troops; they were, he believed, almost invariably undisciplined scum and he shared whole-heartedly the views of a certain Major Scott Turner of the 42nd Highlanders. 'There is always in South Africa', Turner had written, 'a floating population of loafers, mostly men who have made Europe too hot for them, who are ready to join any corps raised for any service.' Butler considered Sampson—he contemptuously refused to give him the benefit of his full name—as a 'bounder' on the look-out for sensation, booty, freedom from any kind of restraint or discipline—the sort of adventurer who stank in the nostrils of the intelligent professional soldier and corrupted the honourable profession of arms.

He had fought against the Boers in 1881, had done his best to fight them in 1895, and was now very desirous of fighting them again. He knew the Transvaal from end to end; he could serve without pay. He ended with a question whether I could do anything to assist him in his desire of fighting the Boers. I replied that it was impossible I could do anything of the kind: I knew only what I read in the newspapers. I had received no instructions to raise troops or reinforce garrisons. I had no doubt that, if the Government were compelled to resort to active measures, his former services would not be forgotten.[9]

Butler's dispassionate account of his cold-shouldering of Wools-Sampson—and indirectly of Milner—hardly squares with that of an eyewitness who reported furious outbursts of temper on both sides. 'Traitor!' Wools-Sampson shouted. 'Lunatic!' Butler shouted back and all but threw Wools-Sampson out of his office.

Whatever the degree of ruffled tempers and unrestrained language one point is clear—Wools-Sampson was turned away empty handed and the breach between Butler and Sir Alfred Milner perceptibly widened. 'It can never be said, Sir William Butler, that *you* precipitated a conflict with the Dutch,' Sir Alfred remarked wryly, at the conclusion of an even more unsatisfactory interview than usual with his Commander-in-Chief.

For Milner the position was rapidly becoming impossible. There could be no retreat without loss of face and loss of honour (two things so widely different and yet so often indistinguishable), and to go on meant war. Therefore it was imperative that the British forces in South Africa be immediately strengthened, that full use be made of such volunteer units as might be raised on the spot, that a plan be prepared for aggressive rather than defensive action, and that the forces be directed by a man dedicated to the British cause. A man other than Butler. At no time—and in this he showed a measure of understanding shared by few of his countrymen—did Milner question Butler's loyalty. But he rightly questioned his enthusiasm for his job. Butler's view of the South African situation was to the end unshaken. War was the sum of human wrong-doing; war in South Africa would be a crime against humanity committed by 'occult influences . . . backed by enormous means and quite without conscience'. Give South Africa a much-needed rest, discourage the activities of the South African League, thereby winning the confidence and goodwill of the Dutch (Kruger would not live for ever), and in the long run a union of peoples would be effected in peace as it never could be in war. It was a view which a champion of the Imperial ideal could only laugh at. On June 14, shortly after the Bloemfontein Conference, when it was evident that war could no longer be avoided, Milner wrote to Chamberlain:

. . . One word in conclusion. The General. He is too awful. He has, I believe, made his military preparations all right, but I cannot get him to make the least move or take the slightest interest. There are a hundred things outside his absolute duty which he ought to be thinking of, especially the rapid raising of volunteers (there is plenty of good material about) in case of emergency. He simply declines to go into it. He will just wait for his W.O. orders, but till he has commands to mobilize, he will not budge an inch or take the slightest interest. His sympathy is wholly with the other side. *At the same time there is nothing to lay hold of*. He never interferes with my business and is perfectly polite. But he is absolutely no use, unless we mean to knuckle down, in which case he had better be made High Commissioner.[10]

Two weeks later, following Butler's telegram to the War Office asserting that war would be the greatest calamity that ever befell South Africa, Milner expressed himself in even stronger terms.

I am sorry to say that in my opinion the strength of the General's political opinions impairs his efficiency, whatever his military capacity. Anything like cordial co-operation between him and me is impossible. . . . I do not believe any hint given him from home can alter his attitude. I believe he simply can't help it. Under these circumstances I ought to have here a G.O.C. who is a support, and not a weakness to me. I have long shrunk from this conclusion, but I feel it my duty to face the situation now.[11]

On the same day he wrote in his diary: 'Butler or I will have to go.'

Shortly thereafter Butler was seriously disturbed by a private letter from London (he never revealed its authorship) which spoke of growing hostility to him in the War Office and the London Press and hinting that if certain statements about his attitude to the South African situation were true he should resign. He at once called on Sir Alfred Milner and bluntly put to him the question, 'Have I, in my official capacity, been a hindrance or embarrassment to you in the prosecution of your designs?' Milner replied with equal bluntness that indeed he had; and listed several instances—including Butler's telegram in reply to the War Office request for 'any observations', and his refusal to assist Wools-Sampson in raising and equipping a force of volunteers.

On July 4, 1899, Butler wrote a letter to the War Office tendering his resignation as Commander-in-Chief of the British forces in

South Africa. Whatever one's view may be of his behaviour during his period of command one must acknowledge an element of grandeur in the deliberate throwing-away of the opportunity, ardently coveted for forty years and now never to be realized, of leading an independent command in the field of battle. How successful he might have been can only be guessed at, but it seems reasonably certain that he would have avoided the major blunders —underestimating the military strength of the enemy, fighting at the outset an offensive war, attacking an entrenched enemy across open ground in outmoded formation—which led to a succession of appalling disasters in the early weeks of the war and destroyed a score of hitherto distinguished military reputations.

At the War and Colonial Offices there were hesitations and doubts. Acceptance of Butler's resignation would be regarded by the Boers as tantamount to an unofficial declaration of war; refusal would place Milner in an impossible position and negate the British forward policy in South Africa. Milner was absolutely right when he said that Butler or himself must go. And when the showdown came it was inevitable that Butler should be the loser.

On August 9, 1899, Butler was informed by cable that 'Her Majesty's Government has come to the conclusion that Imperial interests would suffer if the situation described by you were to be prolonged. Your resignation is, therefore, accepted, and you should come home as soon as possible.'

Milner not unnaturally rejoiced.

General Butler leaves today [he wrote to Chamberlain]. . . . I have no doubt that the impression in England will be that the cause of his departure was his political difference with me. As a matter of fact I have totally ignored his action in my absence. . . . The last thing which ever occurred to me was that he would allow his political sympathies to affect him in the discharge of his professional duties. However, as the incubus is removed it is perhaps just as well that the true nature of my difficulties should not be generally known. It has been an awful experience.

No doubts assailed Milner about the rightness of his action in urging Butler's recall; and Butler was equally sure that he himself had pursued the only honourable course. He was not opposed to British policy in South Africa or anywhere else because he was an Irishman and a Catholic, but because he was an impulsive humanitarian hostile to the men of any nation who oppressed and exploited their fellows. The Irish peasant dead of starvation in a ditch, the

Egyptian fellah dead in the breaches of Tel-el-Kebir, the Boer farmer dead in his burnt-out home and the English soldier dead at Majuba were victims of a conspiracy all the more terrible because those who manipulated events did so in the names of justice and freedom for all men when, in fact, the only goals striven for were wealth and power for the few. War in South Africa, he was convinced, would result in much human suffering and waste and resolve nothing; therefore a man had no choice but to do all in his power to avert it.

To William Schreiner, Prime Minister of the Cape Colony, he wrote: 'Try to remember me as one who did his best, according to his lights, for South Africa and her peoples.'

Schreiner sent the note to his sister Olive, the author of *The Story of the African Farm*. On the back he wrote, 'I would not lose this letter for a great deal, so when read, please return it. . . . I am glad, for his sake, that he will not be here if trouble comes, but it is bitter hard to feel it is a crime to have fair human sympathy.'[12]

CHAPTER SEVENTEEN

South African Aftermath

THE BRITISH SOLDIERS marched against the Boers under the command of brave and incompetent leaders—Sir George White and Penn Symons and Gatacre and Methuen—who had earned their laurels fighting ill-armed natives in far-off corners of the Empire. They were stopped cold by an all-but invisible mobile enemy armed with high-powered rifles that did not miss. At a dozen points along the frontiers of Natal and the Far North Cape the story was the same—of the triumph of hard-riding straight-shooting farmers over British soldiers led by officers who had profited not at all from the lessons taught by Colley's ill-fated campaign against the Boers nearly twenty years before.

On the veldt humiliation and the smell of death; at home shocked disbelief that quickly gave way to frustration and rage as news of successive defeats and large-scale surrenders trickled in. The British public, denied its heroes, demanded a scapegoat, and the Government was not reluctant to give it one. Butler was the man responsible for England's woes. Butler had betrayed the Empire.

Actually the campaign to denigrate Butler had begun in the summer of 1899, several months before the outbreak of war; there were hints in the London Press of pro-Boer sympathies on his part, and his Grahamstown speech had been generally condemned; but since the War Office naturally divulged no information about its preparations for war in South Africa it was not until the early fighting revealed the weakness of the British forces and the incompetence of British generals that Butler was accused not only of gross neglect of duty but of disloyalty to the Empire. He was, after all, an Irish Catholic, and Irish Catholics were known to be fighting side by side with the Boers.

The men at the War Office did not abandon Butler entirely to the wolves. Before his return from South Africa he had been offered, on Wolseley's recommendation, the home command of the Western District with headquarters at Devonport. He at first declined the post, but later, under pressure from Lord Lansdowne, the Secretary of State for War, accepted, saying that it would be churlish to refuse. A few newspapers expressed surprise and dissatisfaction at the appointment, but the matter would have been shortly forgotten had it not been for the series of disastrous defeats which following immediately the outbreak of war fell on British arms.

So strong was the feeling against Butler—'the best-abused man in England' in the words of a fellow officer—particularly in the West Country following the ignominious surrender of the Gloucester Regiment at Ladysmith, that although General-in-Command of the Western District he was forbidden by the War Office to attend the Queen's visit to Bristol in December 1899, on the grounds that his presence might provoke a riot. The official explanation of Butler's absence, that he was attending a meeting at the War Office, deceived no one.

The public is rarely deceived by official explanations [the *Daily Mail* said editorially], and will accept this one at its true worth. All the world knows that Sir William showed himself in his speeches delivered at Cape Town and in official despatches to be a pro-Boer, and the people of the West of England whence the Gloucester Regiment came, have particular reason for complete lack of sympathy with a general who, to phrase the matter moderately, would have been far better employed preparing for the defence of that part of the Queen's dominions committed to his charge.[1]

Butler himself was stunned by the charges made publicly against him, and hardly less so by the flood of anonymous letters, which, often couched in the foulest language, accused him of monstrous crimes against England and the Empire. So great was his agitation that following the Bristol incident he unwisely wrote to the War Office appealing for a chance to defend himself against the charges of disloyalty and neglect of duty.

Sir: In view of recent circumstances connected with the command of the troops at Bristol . . . I beg to bring to the notice of the Secretary of State for War the fact that for some time past persistent attacks have been made by a section of the London press upon my character as an officer and upon my conduct of military affairs while in command of Her Majesty's troops in South Africa.

In conforming with the rules of the Service, I have taken no notice of these libellous accusations, but I now find that in the immunity which my silence gives my libellers, I am more and more pointed out to the people as being responsible for the existing state of affairs in South Africa, and I have been, in consequence, threatened with insult or violence during the visit of Her Majesty to Bristol. It is said that I am responsible for the surrender of the Gloucester Regiment at Ladysmith, and that it is on that account the feelings of the Bristol mob are incensed against me.

I respectfully submit that the time has come for some action by my military superiors in the matter of these continued attacks—either that I should be given the opportunity of meeting some specific charge in relation to my late command in South Africa, or that they (my military superiors) should do something to vindicate my character.

In suggesting either course I would beg, however, to add that if there should exist any reasons of public expediency or state policy why no steps should be taken at present to put a stop to these libellous attacks, I shall deem it my duty to bear them in silence.[2]

Lansdowne's reply was chilling in its impersonality: 'I am to state that it is not desirable that officers should take note of criticisms in the Press as to the manner in which they have discharged their duties. In the Commander-in-Chief's opinion you have done well to take no notice of the accusations to which you call attention, and he trusts you will continue to leave them unnoticed.'[3]

In November, Sir Redvers Buller went to South Africa to assume command of the British Forces. He went reluctantly (taking with him such bodily comforts as a hip-bath, full-sized bed and enough champagne to float a battleship), for he was long past the time when he enjoyed service in the field, and he knew that in the Boer he was up against a tougher foe than any he had encountered in those earlier wars in which his valour had earned him a Victoria Cross and made him a public idol. Not even Kitchener, not even Roberts, was dearer to the heart of the British public than the stout red-faced West Country squire who in appearance, character and intelligence was the very embodiment of John Bull. With a large, well-equipped army of regular troops Buller failed ignominiously, in the Black Week of mid-December, to force the passage of the Tugela River against an army of farmers and relieve Ladysmith; but even in defeat he remained a popular folk-hero and the unfortunate Butler continued to bear the brunt of public and newspaper criticism for the ineffectiveness of British arms. This in spite of a rumour which eventually gained wide circulation that

Butler had, in fact, warned the War Office repeatedly of the consequences of war in South Africa, and that his silence, following the failure of the War Office to take note of his warnings, had been purchased with the Western Command.

The appointment of Sir William Butler to a high command in England is a complete mystery to many of our correspondents [the *Daily Mail* (the most persistent of Butler's critics) reported], but the more suspicious . . . suggest that this appointment of Sir William Butler is a promotion by way of pacification, that if, indeed, he could speak he could reveal all manner of dreadful secrets. This view is only excusable in that some of the public are not quite themselves at present, and it is obviously inspired by the Dreyfus case.

The plain facts are that a vast number of people believe that General Butler neglected his duty in not preparing Cape Colony against invasion from the Transvaal, whose military strength he, at any rate, must have known; that he left Mafeking, Vryburg, Kimberley and the whole of the Cape Border practically defenceless; and that for some mysterious reasons he had been given a high command in England.[4]

The *Daily Mail* did, however, grumpily admit that 'though a political general, and a little too fond of writing and talking for a soldier, General Butler is at least as distinguished as one or two of the commanders now in South Africa, or ordered there'.

The rumours intensified. Supporters of Butler, and they were many, wrote letters to the newspapers implying that the War Office was concealing vital information which it had received from Butler and ignored in the months preceding the outbreak of the war. Presently the rumours crystallized; became, in the minds of many, an established fact: Butler had indeed sent a confidential report to the War Office in which he stated unequivocally that at least 200,000 men would be needed to subdue the Boers. A surprising number of people had actually seen the report, or been told about it by someone in the War Office. (As late as 1910 the editor of a Tipperary newspaper, in his notice of Butler's death, affirmed that he himself had seen with his own eyes the report calling for 200,000 men, though for the life of him he couldn't remember where.)

In the meantime Butler continued to carry out his duties at Devonport with characteristic thoroughness. Although alleged to be a 'political' general, he gave evidence of great political *naïveté* when, upon the outbreak of war, he at once offered to go to the front in 'any capacity'. Following Buller's crushing defeat at Colenso he was heard to mutter, 'They will have to send for me now.' But for the Government to do so would have been tantamount to political suicide in view of the strength of public feeling against Butler; and there was no suggestion from the War Office that the discredited general be given a chance to redeem himself. So Butler stayed at home and kept quiet while the war dragged on through three weary years, destroying a score of reputations and enhancing none. There were many in England who came to share the *Daily Mail*'s view that Butler was at least as distinguished a general as the blunderers in South Africa who had disgraced British arms; and there was no criticism of Lord Wolseley when, appalled by the slackness he found at Aldershot, he detached Butler temporarily from the Devonport Command to whip the Aldershot garrison into shape. Butler did the job in just four months, then returned to Devonport, where he remained until 1905.

Only once during the war years did he protest what he considered the grossly unfair treatment he had suffered from the War and Colonial Offices. In October 1901, Joseph Chamberlain, speaking in Edinburgh in defence of the Government's bungling of the war, charged that 'there was not one single man who was entitled to the faintest confidence, or even pretended to be an authority on the subject, who anticipated the prolonged resistance we have received'. Someone in the audience shouted Butler's name, whereupon Chamberlain retorted that the suggestion that Butler was an exception to the statement could only be termed a 'fable'.

In anger and bitterness at this revival by the Colonial Secretary of old charges for the sake of political expediency Butler entered into a lengthy and repetitious correspondence with the War Office and the Adjutant-General in an attempt to show that he had, in fact, warned the home Government of the consequences of war with the Boers, and of the probable strength of manpower required to win it. It is further evidence of his political *naïveté* that he seems actually to have hoped to win such an admission from the War Office; but the only admission he could extract was that he had warned the Government of the *political* rather than military consequences of the war and in so doing had committed a grave breach of protocol. Mr. St. John Brodrick, who had replaced Lord Lansdowne at the War Office, wrote to Butler:

Mr. Brodrick has made a careful examination of the documents to which you refer, and fails to find that the language of the Colonial Secretary of which you complain traverses the information conveyed in the documents.

In your despatches you undoubtedly warned the Government that for reasons which you stated the outbreak of hostilities between Great Britain and the Dutch Republics in South Africa might, in the existing state of feeling, produce a racial war, which you pointed out would be 'the greatest calamity that ever occurred in South Africa'.

Your warning to the Government was directed to the political effects likely to occur, whereas the Colonial Secretary spoke of the nature and extent of the military resistance likely to be offered.[5]

The unsatisfactory correspondence terminated when the Adjutant-General, on instructions from Lord Roberts, who had replaced Wolseley as Commander-in-Chief, gave the reason for Butler's recall from South Africa in a letter which must stand as a model of bureaucratic sophistry:

The Commander-in-Chief considers it unnecessary and inexpedient further to discuss this subject. His Lordship has no reason to doubt that you acted to the best of your judgement and ability during the period in question, and he observes that your recall from South Africa was not due to any neglect of military duty on your part but to your resignation on the ground that your presence at Cape Town was likely to be a source of embarrassment to Her Majesty's High Commissioner.[6]

The war dragged to its miserable close; the soldiers and generals came back to a disillusioned disgruntled people; and the Government, shaken by the disastrous prolongation of a conflict which was to have been 'over by Christmas'—Wolseley had predicted November 1899 at the latest—appointed, at the beginning of 1903, a Commission to investigate the conduct of the war in South Africa. The Commission was chaired by the Earl of Elgin, and the members included an old friend of Butler's, Donald Smith (Lord Strathcona and Mount Royal now), the former Hudson's Bay Company Governor who had been responsible for Butler's appointment in 1870 to investigate conditions in the North-West Territories.

The proceedings of the Commission were long and arduous and dull. Numerous witnesses from various government departments were examined; and nearly every general who fought in and survived the war, including Roberts, Kitchener and Buller, appeared and made their depositions—naturally intended to exonerate themselves from responsibility for any of the disasters that had befallen British arms.

Among those who appeared before the Commission—this at his own request—was Butler.

The opportunity was one for which Butler had impatiently waited, when he could cast off the restraints imposed by his profession and defend himself against the charges of incompetence and disloyalty which for four years or more had lain heavily upon him to the destruction of all peace of mind. He had assembled for the Commission an impressive array of documents; he stated his case well, and the members of the Commission treated him with the utmost consideration and respect.

Two points were made clear almost at once—indeed they had been fairly well established in the Commission's examination of earlier witnesses; the utter confusion prevailing in 1899 at the War Office and its inability to give any sort of coherent directives to the Commander-in-Chief in South Africa. To the Commission, Butler quoted from documents he had received from the War Office in the summer of 1899: 'It is difficult to unravel the various directions sent to you from the different branches here, each without the knowledge of the other branches concerned'; and again—'There has been a good deal of confusion at Headquarters from various branches having taken action without reference to the Commander-in-Chief's Department'—and others in a similar vein.

Another point established by the examination was the incomplete control that soldiers responsible for executing plans have in choosing them. Butler quoted for the Commission a passage from a letter he had written to the Adjutant-General, pointing out the absurdity of the communiqué he had received from the War Office shortly after his arrival in South Africa: 'It pressed upon me seizing all the bridges of the Orange River between Cape Colony and the Orange Free State, as well as Van Reenan's Pass and other advance positions in Natal, by the small force under my command. I had, therefore, not only to write a scheme of defence, but I had to argue it against the War Office proposals.'[7]

In addition to establishing before the Commission the significant facts that he was required to base all plans for possible war on the number of troops he had on hand, that he at no time was asked by the War Office to suggest how many troops might be needed to fight the Boers, Butler sought to defend himself against War Office charges that he had been dilatory in preparing his plans for military action. As evidence for the defence he introduced an exchange of letters between himself and Mr. Brodrick, written at the time when Butler was protesting Chamberlain's statement that he had failed to warn the Government of Boer strength. Wrote Mr. Brodrick:

The War Office letter of Dec. 21, 1898, impressed on you the possibility of hostilities with the Transvaal and the Free State, and besides assisting you with a precise recapitulation of the main physical features of the frontier called your attention to secret publications which contained accurate information regarding the military forces of the Republic and the more important strategical points. These publications were in your possession, you had personally the advantage, acquired by previous service in the country, of a general knowledge of the military geography of South Africa and its methods of warfare; and it was open to you to despatch staff officers to examine any particular localities about which you desired further detailed information.

Butler did not miss the opportunity to give a layman, even though a Secretary of State, a lesson in the arts of war. He wrote tartly to Mr. Brodrick:

I respectfully submit there is no analogy whatever between the two cases cited.

The misconception arises from a confusion of ideas between the plan or forecast of war, known as strategy, and the operations which involve immediate action, called tactics.

A glance at the defence scheme of England—which has been many years in preparation, and is not yet complete—will show that a scheme of defence for even a small island is not to be confounded with the operations which a General in the field may be called upon to determine in a few days or hours.

To the suggestions that I might have made use of staff officers for the purpose of visiting various points of the frontier, I reply that I was not disposed to deal at second hand with this important question, even had staff officers been available; but there were none.[8]

As for the secret publications containing accurate information regarding the military forces of the Republic—these were Intelligence reports suggesting that the Boers were not equipped to mount any sort of invasion of the British Colonies. 'Raids, however, of 2,000 to 3,000 men may be expected, and it is against such raids that careful preparation on your part is necessary.'

The examination further established that Butler's difficulties with the home Government stemmed in large part from the Government's inability to decide on any positive policy for South Africa. In a speech to the House of Lords on January 31, 1900, Lord Lansdowne actually indentified the views of the Government with those of Butler and made it clear that had Butler asked for more troops his request would have been refused.

Throughout the summer of last year (1899) [Lord Lansdowne said] the negotiations were proceeding and proceeding hopefully. We received from the South African Republic one proposal after another, each of them apparently more hopeful and encouraging as to a satisfactory issue; and I think we are not to blame if, while these negotiations were going on, we shrank from such measures as, for example, the calling out of the Reserves or the sending of large expeditionary forces which could only be intended for aggressive purposes.[9]

Butler with reason might well ask why he, an officer under orders from the War Office, should be pilloried for failing to insist that the British Government make adequate preparations for a war which, if Lansdowne's words were to be taken at their face value, it did not intend to fight.

In discussing this point with the Commission, Butler scotched once and for all the rumour that he had sent a confidential document to the War Office stating that in the event of war, 200,000 men would be needed to fight the Boers; he had mentioned 40,000 men to Sir Alfred Milner, he had doubled and trebled the figure in conversations with fellow officers; but he had mentioned no number to the War Office. In a somewhat confused statement he attempted to explain why.

It never entered my head to send calculations as to numbers because . . . everything depended on two things, what you were going to fight the Boers on, and how far you were going to push your conquests. If you were going to dictate terms 50,000 or 60,000 or 70,000 men would do it if properly handled. If you were going on the other hand to pursue matters to extreme lengths 'not a shred of independence', 'up to the Limpopo' and the rest of it, then it might take 200,000 men to do it. But to expect a man before you told him you were going to war at all, and when, in effect, you told him you were *not* going to war, when you had already told him . . . he was not to bother his head about it, and was only to make the things that were there efficient, and that the question of reinforcements would not then be considered—to expect him, I say, on such premises to ask you for reinforcements and give you estimates of numbers required for the conquest of the Dutch States is rather a post-diluvial demand.[10]

One man alone, Sir Alfred Milner, knew in the summer of 1899 that war was almost inevitable; and Butler's collision with him was obviously as much due to the indecisive, frequently contradictory orders he received from the War Office as to his personal hostility to the Milner-Chamberlain policy.

In Butler's opinion the real villains of the tragic drama were not, however, Milner and Chamberlain but the South African League and the men behind it—in particular Cecil Rhodes. Of the League and Rhodes, Butler was unable to speak without anger, and he made no attempt to conceal his feelings from the Commission: 'My position was this: Let my Chief at the War Office tell me what to do, and I will do it, but I will not be dragged by Syndicates in South Africa and I will not obey them, they are not my masters.' He himself had incurred the wrath of Rhodes and the League because, as he told the Commission with obvious pleasure in the simple play on words, he had refused 'to confuse Caesar with Cecil'.[11]

In the light of Butler's testimony, that of his successor as Commander-in-Chief in South Africa, General Sir F. W. Forestier-Walker, is of peculiar interest. Forestier-Walker told the Commission that he had taken up his duties on September 6, 1899, only five weeks before the outbreak of war, and that he had received no instructions from the War Office other than to assume command of the forces then in South Africa. 'As to the actual state of affairs and the imminence of war,' he said, 'practically nothing was known beyond the reports which appeared in the daily papers.'

Naturally the new commander had at once gone over the question of defence: 'Sir William Butler had reported shortly before: he had also made proposals for a frontier defense of the Colony with the force that then existed, and practically for the defence of Natal. I wrote home that so far as I could see these views were sound, and that I did not think I could improve upon them.'[12]

It was Butler's contention, and in this he had the tacit support of his successor, that the brave bull-headed officers who assumed command of the British forces in the field on the outbreak of war—White, Penn Symons, Gatacre and the rest—used his plan as the basis for an offensive rather than defensive campaign, with disastrous results.

The subtlest intelligence among the Commissioners was beyond question that remarkable civil servant, Viscount Esher, for many years a shadowy behind-the-scenes figure in the drama of English politics, a 'grey eminence' who was the confidant of prime ministers and the counsellor of monarchs. No more devoted or selfless servant of his country ever lived, and few whose notions were more directly opposed to those that Butler cherished. Esher was a monarchist, a Tory, a hater of democracy and a warm friend and admirer of Sir Alfred Milner. He was without ambition to hold high office—he refused one of the highest, the Viceroyalty of India; the kind of power he enjoyed could be exercised only in secret places out of range of public view. To such an extreme did he carry his passion for anonymity that he left orders (happily ignored) that after his death all personal records and papers should be destroyed.

Esher had agreed to serve on the Commission out of a strong sense of duty, and he did not relish the experience. He found the examination of witnesses tedious, and he was singularly unimpressed by the parade of generals and War Office officials who appeared before himself and his fellow Commissioners. 'Bored to death by the War Commission,' he wrote to his brother. 'It is not an interest which can be revived. It is like an extinct passion—and any attempt to relight the flame is sure to fail. It all . . . seems as flat as possible.'[13]

Although bored he missed little, and his sketches of the witnesses who appeared before the Commission are always fresh and frequently acidulous. Conan Doyle, who had written an on-the-spot history of the war in South Africa, he described as a 'huge elephantine creature with blue eyes. He was jolly, but not very illuminating.'

Esher had never joined in the outcry against Butler. Indeed, he seems to have been one of the few men who realized that Butler's plan for fighting a defensive war had been ignored with evil consequences for British arms. 'But what a national fiasco so far!' he wrote to Sir William Harcourt three months after the outbreak of war. 'The series of horrors culminating with the yielding of the Government to the pressure of those who insisted on the holding and relief of Kimberley.

'And what a justification of the unfortunate Butler!'[14]

(This at a time when every newspaper in England and nearly every citizen were calling for Butler's head.)

The Bulk of the Esher papers was not published until 1934, and it must be a matter of regret that Butler never knew what Esher wrote of him to King Edward VII:

Lord Esher presents his humble duty to your Majesty and begs to say that Sir William Butler was examined today.

In view of the accusation made against Sir Wm. Butler in the winter of 1899, a full opportunity was given to that officer to state his case, of which he availed himself. It is clear that he held strong military and political views of the situation then obtaining, which were not in accord with those of His Majesty's advisers, and Sir Wm. met the usual fate of those who give unpalatable advice. That much of the advice he gave has since proved correct, is not possibly of advantage to him in certain quarters. There is no doubt that he is among the ablest of Your Majesty's servants, and possesses an intellect capable of grasping large problems and of dealing with them in a practical manner. His Irish blood may possibly influence his temper and political judgement, but leaves his military capacity untouched. Upon a highly controversial political question—in which as Acting High Commissioner he became involved—his judgement was possibly faulty, and that is all that can reasonably be urged against him. Intellectually he stands (as he does physically) head and shoulders above the majority of his comrades. His evidence upon the preparation for war, only proved once more that uncertain counsels prevailed throughout the summer of 1899, and that if Sir Wm. was to blame for the strong and clear line of duty he sketched out for himself, this blame may well attach to others for the vacillating course which they, no doubt also actuated by a high sense of duty, found themselves constrained to pursue.[15]

Others besides Lord Esher were impressed by Butler's appearance and testimony before the Commission. The day following the important post of Quartermaster-General. Brodrick himself Esher if he thought Butler should be recommended to the King for the important post of Quartermaster-General. Brodrick himself was not opposed to the appointment, but Lord Roberts and most members of the Cabinet were hostile. In reporting his conversation with Mr. Brodrick to the King, Lord Esher wrote:

Lord Esher ventured to point out that no political question entered into the duties found in Your Majesty's forces; and were Lord Esher in Mr. Brodrick's place, he would prefer a capable administrator, like Sir Wm.

Butler, in the office of Q.M.G., to a less able man whose amiable qualities might be more assured.

Managed with tact, Lord Esher believes that Sir W.B. would not prove the *mauvais coucheur* which he is represented to be.[16]

In spite of Esher's recommendation Butler was not appointed Quartermaster-General—a post he was ideally suited by experience and inclination to fill. Apparently Tory Ministers could not stomach a 'political' general in high place, particularly when his political views were embarrassingly liberal, not to say radical. King Edward VII, who liked Butler personally, seems to have shared the view of his ministers. On one occasion, when inspecting troops under Butler's command at Plymouth, he walked up to Lady Butler and said without preface, 'Your husband is a very fine soldier, Lady Butler, but it is a pity he takes so much part in politics.' He retired a few paces, advanced again on Lady Butler, and repeated in a loud voice, 'Pity! Pity!'

The hearings of the Commission dragged to a close. The generals who had blundered in South Africa were exonerated, Lord Wolseley and the War Office and several Ministers by implication indicted. 'The inevitable conclusion is . . . not favourable to the late Commander-in-Chief, and not wholly favourable to Your Majesty's ministers. In language which will not be found indecorous or discourteous, this conclusion has been made painfully clear.' Thus Esher reported to the King. He did not, however, expect any action to be taken as a result of the Commission's findings, and added to his report to the King what is surely the classic definition of a Royal Commission: 'Your Majesty well knows that Royal Commissions are . . . the expedients employed by politicians to relegate awkward and difficult questions to the official pigeon hole.'[17]

The publication of the Commission report stirred the Press to a brief outburst of indignation and there were demands for the impeachment of Lord Lansdowne. But by 1904 the South African War was an old and unpleasant story best forgotten and the excitement soon died down. No Government fell, no heads rolled. The work of the Commission did, however, have one consequence of the utmost significance—the appointment of a committee chaired by Viscount Esher to reorganize the War Office.

Butler was not appointed Quartermaster-General, but following publication of the Commission report the Government showed some anxiety to make the *amende honorable* by appointing him chairman of a committee to investigate the war stores scandals in South Africa, where, so it was charged by the office of the Auditor-General, contractors selling to and buying from the British Army were growing rich beyond dreams of avarice at the expense of the British taxpayer. From the orthodox commercial point of view the transactions between the contractors and the Army had about them a maniac quality which suggested that the contracts of sale and purchase must have been drafted at a Mad Hatter's tea-party. In summary, the War Office authorized the sale, immediately on the close of the war, of supplies stockpiled at various points; and at the same time authorized the granting by tender of contracts to supply essential goods to the forces still in South Africa. 'The War Office cannot be charged with the base Cobdenite practice of buying in the cheapest market and selling in the dearest,' one observer reported. 'The genius who presided over the Stores Department in South Africa reversed the process. Provisions and forage, having been sold at the price of dirt, were bought back at the price of gold.'[18] What frequently happened was that the same contractor, having bought the so-called surplus stores from the Army for next to nothing—usually with the connivance or through the indifference of the Army Corps officer in charge of stores—immediately resold the goods to the Army at an enormous profit. 'Arrangements were made with due regard for economy, as well as regularity and despatch. The stores were not even removed; they were bought and sold where they stood, the difference between the buying and the selling prices some thousands of pounds a week.'[19]

In many instances there was no evidence of actual dishonesty on the part of the army officers, rather a complete indifference to the price obtained for the goods in their charge, and a lively concern to get rid of the goods as quickly and quietly as possible. In one instance an Army Corps officer sold 70,000 bottles of excellent wine to a contractor at 6d. per bottle and agreed to pay all handling charges on the movement of the huge consignment. It was pointed out that he would have saved his country money had he poured the wine down a gutter.

Neither the War Office nor the Government showed much interest in reports from South Africa of war profiteering; and it was the Auditor-General—responsible neither to the Cabinet nor the Government but to Parliament—who, perceiving from the figures submitted to his office that the contractors were making a killing, reported the matter to the House of Commons. The Public Accounts Committee called for an investigation, and the Butler Committee was accordingly appointed.

In terms of its actual findings the Butler Report inevitably holds little of interest for today. The Committee was severely restricted by its terms of reference (only six cases of alleged misdealings were to be considered), and no witness could be examined under oath. The principals in the inquiry have long since been forgotten, and the findings of the Committee constitute no more than a postscript to one of the unhappiest chapters of South African history. What makes the Butler Report still readable is not its findings of bribery, corruption and nepotism—practices as old, after all, as war itself—but the picturesque phraseology which shocked the orthodox and made Butler once more a whipping-boy for the editorial writers who could not tolerate the 'fanciful levity' of his prose. *The Times*, although in complete agreement with the substance of the Report, severely criticized Butler for 'the extravagant and tasteless rhetoric in which much of the report is clothed. . . . Devices of that order may be calculated to inflame certain kinds of opinion, but they can only excite doubts as to the judicial character of the Report amongst those who are most competent to understand the grave matters with which it deals.'[20]

The fuss about Butler's stylistic extravagances seems out of all proportion to his actual offences. Most of the report is written in clear, vigorous language which strikes a more individual and colloquial note than is common in official documents, and it was only occasionally that Butler allowed his enthusiasm for alliteration—'salaried servant of favoured firms'—and above all fanciful imagery full play:

One is disposed to ask—are the civil offenders who are the object of so much precautionary passion in the Army Form, ever brought to book in the substance? . . . Some clumsy pantaloon in puttees—even some agile harlequin in a helmet—may occasionally be caught, but the oldest member of the Committee has informed his colleagues that in the course of many years' experience he can only call to mind one case where the civil practitioner in a military scandal was brought to justice, and in that solitary instance the offender, when released from 15 months' incarceration, was received by his fellow townsmen with many manifestations of civic triumph.[21]

An eyewitness describes Butler in the throes of composition slapping his thigh and roaring with delight over 'pantaloon in puttees' and 'harlequin in a helmet'—and in almost the same breath expressing regret that he could find no place in the report for a columbine in crinolines.

Following release of the Butler report a Royal Commission was duly appointed to investigate the charges made by the Committee. Expectations were high, especially among Liberal politicians, that the charges would be fully substantiated, their scope perhaps greatly extended. 'The whole history of the South African War . . . has been surrounded with an odious flavour of subterranean finance,' wrote one commentator, obviously hostile to the Government, 'and if Satan's invisible world is at least displayed by the Commission, the picture, however ugly, may be useful. Sir William Butler, whose powers were of course extremely limited, has no doubt that more important personages are in the background than he was able to discover. A full list of the fortunes made by the war is unattainable for the devil cannot be called.'[22]

The findings of the Commission were, however, oddly indecisive, at times contradictory. Of a Colonel Morgan, in the view of the Butler Committee an officer guilty of conspiring most blatantly with the contractors to line his and their pockets, the Commission reported itself unable to find any evidence of fraudulent conspiracy on his part, and having thus in effect dismissed all charges against Colonel Morgan added to the dismissal the extraordinary rider that 'Colonel Morgan can hardly complain if his conduct in these matters has given rise to grave suspicion'. Non-commissioned officers accused by the Butler Committee of accepting bribes were named guilty by the Commission, but commissioned officers accused of similar and even more serious offences were in most instances exonerated on the grounds of invincible stupidity.

In general the tone of the Commission report suggests that the Army Corps officers in charge of buying and selling for the Army, if not actually conspiring with the contractors, were quite unable to cope with them in business dealings. But the Commission dismissed as a 'counsel of perfection' the entirely practicable suggestion of the Butler Committee that immediately following a war 'a specially trained selected officer of high rank, and a small but very capable staff of civil and military officers' be appointed to replace 'the haphazard and wasteful ways of war by regular methods of peace administration'.

The Commission report made few specific recommendations, none of much significance, and together with the Butler report was shortly shelved and forgotten. After all, why worry about a problem which could not possibly arise again until another war broke out?

In October 1905, after nearly fifty years' service, Lieutenant-General Sir William Butler, K.C.B., was placed on the retired list of the British Army.

CHAPTER EIGHTEEN

Celtic Twilight

'UNTIL HIS SIXTIETH YEAR a man belongs to himself; from sixty to seventy to his family; and from seventy onwards to his tribe.' So Butler wrote and professed to believe, and in his own life he adhered to the third part of the pattern. Upon retirement he returned to his native Tipperary, bought Bansha Castle, a substantial country house on the outskirts of Bansha village, and settled down only a few miles from the place of his birth in the heart of the region over which his forebears had once ruled.

Bansha Castle stands almost midway between Tipperary and Cahir on the grounds of a ruined castle which was once a Butler possession. The River Suir runs through the rich meadowlands less than a mile away; and to the south the Galtees, the finest inland mountain range in Ireland, rise in a series of admirably proportioned gradations to a central point more than 3,000 feet above sea-level—the great purple cone of Galtee More. Here Butler lived out the last five years of his life, surrounded by some of Ireland's most picturesque and varied scenery, but unable to suppress entirely the longing, never to be satisfied, to see again the great open prairies of the Canadian West from which the passage of time had removed all imperfections and left only memories of sunlight and distance and the passionate response of life at high noon to the challenge of a new world.

The household was a small one now, for the family were grown up and scattered, and only the youngest of the Butler daughters, Eileen, a lively and intelligent girl in her teens, still lived at home. Eileen did not entirely share her father's pleasure in the Irish countryside. Devonport had been full of the colour and excitement which usually characterize an important military base; by comparison life at Bansha Castle was dull—and occasionally downright difficult, as when her father, convinced for some obscure reason that meat was bad for growing girls, put her on a diet consisting mainly of potatoes and gravy. Fortunately the kitchen staff co-operated in the provision of generous between-meals snacks and she was enabled to bear her father's unorthodox views on diet with comparative equanimity.

Butler's retirement from the Army and his removal to a relatively isolated rural community did not mean a lessening of interest in affairs beyond the bounds of Tipperary. The proposal to build a tunnel under the English Channel, earlier scotched by Wolseley who feared that a tunnel might lend itself to a French invasion, had recently been revived, and Butler gave the proposal his warmest support. He was enthusiastically in favour of closer ties with France, laughed at Wolseley's fears, and in one of his most singular metaphorical utterances appealed against the abandonment of plans 'for the possible conquest by the genius of man over the rude forces of nature . . . because of old-world fears and prejudices—the belated offspring, begotten in the days when the Cocked Hat and Grey Riding Coat of Napoleon were deemed sufficient to frighten all Europe from its propriety'.

In the year following his retirement Butler, having been commissioned by the London *Tribune* to write a series of articles on the state of the Transvaal under British rule, paid a lengthy visit to South Africa. The articles were published in book form under a title, *From Naboth's Vineyard*, the irony of which was not lost on readers of the Old Testament. *From Naboth's Vineyard* is one of the poorest of Butler's books; he found little in the South African scene to excite his imagination—only dismal prophecies fulfilled—and it is obvious that his bitter experiences immediately before and during the South African War had soured his enthusiasm for a country which once excited his warm affection.

He found no reason to modify certain grim predictions he had made about the future of South Africa as early as the 1870s; and no doubt it would afford him a melancholy satisfaction to know that their fulfilment is today being realized. Of local government in the English colonies he wrote: 'Responsible government by a handful of farmers—twelve thousand-acre men more or less—is bound to produce trouble, for legislation for natives will rest chiefly with men who will manage the natives for their own interests.' But the native will not consent to be managed for ever; and it is he and not the white man who must pose the ultimate question in South

Africa: 'The native African has always been the Old World's chiefest puzzle. He has played the same part in the New World; but it is on his own ground—Africa—that he and his question have reached almost insoluble proportions. He is indigenous, strong, active. He can do scores of things which the white man cannot, or will not, do. He possesses qualities of courage, loyalty, power of discipline, honesty and obedience which are not exceeded by any race of men in any part of the world. . . . He watches, waits. He is still a child in many things, but he possesses powers of comparison that are daily growing, and he is expanding that faculty by testing what he is told by what he sees. . . .

'But perhaps the most remarkable thing about him is that while we need him he does not need us; he could do without us, and under the present conditions of life in South Africa nothing is more certain than that we could not do without him.'[1]

Back again in Ireland, Butler settled firmly into the role of man of affairs in his community and country. His activities extended far beyond the range of those normally indulged in by retired military men seeking to maintain some sort of contact with the world from which they are reluctant to withdraw. He was a member of the Senate of the newly founded National University, a Commissioner of the Board of National Education, and a Privy Councillor for Ireland, and in these capacities he worked with enormous energy and an effectiveness which his unorthodox views on the right kind of education for the youth of Ireland in no way diminished. Nor was he content with sitting on boards. Ireland has produced more than her share of orators—not entirely to her gain—and Butler combined a natural talent for oratory with the zeal of the reformer. He looked about him, disliked much of what he saw, and set about the task of making a responsible social being of the Irishman.

Although to the end of his life Butler was in great demand by church and lay societies to provide an evening's entertainment he must have found more frustration than satisfaction in his oratorical efforts. He was not content, as most public speakers are, with the gratification attendant on airing one's opinions to a captive audience—he wanted tangible results to attend his words and the results were not forthcoming. He idealized the countryman of an earlier generation—whom he saw as a cross between Burns's Cotter and Moore's Minstrel Boy—and it was his dream to purge the peasant of his own time of all his vices and follies and restore him to a position he had occupied only in Butler's romantic imagination. Granted the fulfilment of the dream, Butler foresaw an Ireland which, if not free politically, would at least be able to draw comfort from a sense of moral and spiritual superiority to her conqueror.

But moral exhortation is the least rewarding of human activities, and Butler soon discovered powerful affinities between the Tipperary Irishman and the Gold Coast Akim. Like the Akim, the Tipperary man listened attentively to the sound advice Butler gave him and made no effort to follow it, particularly when the advice advocated, as it nearly always did, the twin virtues of temperance and sobriety.

'I know nothing so heart-breaking in Ireland today as the waste which one is compelled to witness on so many sides,' Butler said in a characteristic denunciation of Irish sloth and drunkenness.

Waste of crops and pasture, waste of wood and weed, waste through bog and mountain, waste of farm implements left out to rust in the rains of winter—all over the land.

One thing I do not see wasted—it is drink. I often come upon the butt of a haycock rotting in a field; but I never heard that anyone ever found anything in the bottom of a discarded whisky bottle.

I travel about a good deal, and often get strange sidelights on men and things. I met a man the other day on his way to a fair. 'How is the price of stock?' I asked. 'High,' he answered. 'That ought to bring money into the country,' I said. 'There's no money in the country,' he said. 'It runs out as fast as it comes in.' 'Porter?' I said. . . . 'Yes', he answered. 'And divershun and women's hats. Look here,' he went on, pointing his stick to Galtee More, which was out in his morning majesty, clear of cloud, 'if you were to put a public-house on the top of that mountain tomorrow there would be a road up it the day after.' Ah . . . if we could only get as much public spirit into the land as we have public-house spirit in it, I believe we would be the most prosperous people in the wide world.

No doubt the General's auditors discussed his words with great earnestness over their pots of porter and agreed that a public house on the top of Galtee More would be a fine thing.

Even the ever-loyal Lady Butler acknowledged that as a social reformer Butler was a failure. She reported in her *Autobiography*: 'Sir William spent the remaining days of his life in trying, by addresses to the people in different parts of the country, to quicken their sense of the necessity for industry, sobriety and a more serious view of existence. They did not seem to like it and he was apparently only beating the air.'[2]

He was in distinguished company. 'It is a great fault among you,' Jonathan Swift said to the Irish people in the first of his *Drapier's Letters*, 'that when a person writes with no other intention than to do you good you will not be at pains to read his advices.'

It was unfortunate that Butler's vision of a virtuous peasant living in the kind of bucolic innocence described by Goldsmith in *The Deserted Village* blinded him to the excellent qualities and skills which the peasant of his own day possessed and exercised. Stephen Gwynn tells us that of all his memories of walks and talks with Butler the one that stands out as most vivid and most typical 'pictures him standing at a gate in an old wall near Dublin and while we were waiting for a tram pointing to the excellent rough-casting of the stone wall. "When I was young," he said, "the country was full of men who knew, by inherited tradition, the proper ways of doing that work; now none but a mason could do it, and he would do it badly. The country's life used to turn out peasants who could put their hand knowledgeably to a dozen different jobs; now they do not know even the ordinary work of a labourer." I differed from him, and quoted instances of men I had employed, who, while doing their own work excellently, were always ready to attempt things that lay properly outside it—repairing of machinery and the like—and were generally successful by sheer natural intelligence. "Yes," he said, "that is true; when you get a good Irishman you get the most useful man in the world."'[3]

But the good Irishman was an increasingly rare bird. In his childhood Butler had seen the tragedy of those who were dispossessed of their land and goods through no fault of their own; now, it seemed to him, the tragedy was being re-enacted with the difference that this time the peasant, through self-indulgence and sloth, was himself the agent of the catastrophe.

Not all of Butler's speeches were intended to direct the Irish countryman into sober ways he had no wish to enter. He was a popular orator at literary and historical society meetings, and a number of his best speeches, together with papers on a variety of topics written over a period of many years, were published in 1909, the year before he died, in volume entitled *The Light of the West*. The title derives from a paper on St. Patrick, originally a speech to a Dublin Literary Society, which shows evidence of a diligent reading of secondary sources and a readiness to accept as facts what to the trained scholar are at best uncertainties. Always at his most eloquent and expansive when addressing an audience of fellow Irishmen on an Irish topic, Butler, in estimating St. Patrick's contribution to the civilization and salvation of mankind, allowed his soaring imagination an even looser rein than usual, particularly in his peroration:

The Light came (to America) borne of Ireland's starving children .... Lo! Ere famine's night had passed from Ireland, the Church of Patrick arose o'er all that vast new world of America, from where the great St. Lawrence pours its crystal tide into the daybreak of the Atlantic to where California flings wide her golden gate to the sunset of the Pacific.[4]

Unfortunately, words that sound impressive when given full-bodied utterance before a sympathetic audience have a trick of appearing merely silly in cold print; and although Butler's suggestion that St. Patrick was indirectly responsible for the conversion of the United States to Christianity has the charm of novelty, it is unlikely to find acceptance among Americans of other than Irish blood—particularly the descendants of the Pilgrim Fathers.

The most interesting and original of the papers in *The Light of the West* is one entitled 'Clan and Boat's Crew' in which Butler, drawing on prejudice, intuition and his wide if indiscriminate reading of history, attempts to point up the fundamental difference between the Gael and the Anglo-Saxon. His view of the Gael in Ireland inevitably reflects his idealization of the peasantry, his view of the Anglo-Saxon his hatred of the predator.

The root idea in Ireland has always been the land and what the land produced in corn and cattle. ... The chief and the clan were great and powerful in the exact measure of their ability to maintain or extend the boundaries of their people. ...

The Saxon or English root-idea has been the boat and boat's crew. The Saxon and Norse invaders of the British Isles were sailors first of all. The oar was their spade, the boat's keel their plough, the fishes of the sea were their sheep and cattle. ... Out of this grew a community which has developed the habits, the discipline and the instincts of the inhabitants of a town, changing the rude methods of plunder by force into the modern system of acquisition by trade and commerce. The captain and the boat's crew have given place to the mayor and the corporation.[5]

The fundamental difference established, the lesson to be drawn therefrom inevitably follows. Butler was a staunch Home Ruler, but he was no fanatical patriot; he was candid in his acknowledgement that the intensely individualistic Gael had much to learn from the more communally-minded Anglo-Saxon, hence his advice to the people of Ireland: 'Use your enemies instead of being content to abuse them. Copy the boat's crew—who cut you out of every walk of life because they have learned to pull together.'

Such public admonitions, coming from a man who for nearly fifty years had worn the Queen's uniform, did not entirely commend themselves to a people in whose eyes the Anglo-Saxon was the image of the tyrant and who knew that rowing a boat was hard work. The point of view that saw Butler as an alien among his own people was in no way affected by the knowledge that thousands of brother Irishmen had likewise served in the British Army. They at least had had the grace to keep quiet—they did not take it upon themselves to tell their fellows what to do and how to live.

Although striving to improve the lot of his people and to instil into them a strong sense of social responsibility must have proved, for Butler, unrewarding work, his last years brought him a kind of melancholy content. He was no longer ambitious, no longer dreaming of great achievements, he was satisfied now to be the good citizen, to do something for the love of God. And his writing was more than ever before an agent of consolation and release. His great opus on Napoleon was finished and laid aside; now he had time to work at leisure on his autobiography. And it is by the *Autobiography* that he best deserves to be remembered. Although left incomplete at the time of his death it must rank as his finest book and one of the most readable memoirs written by a soldier of the nineteenth century. The early chapters are the best. Butler was able to recall with almost photographic clarity the experiences of his youth and early manhood, to relive them with undiminished intensity, and to record them in a prose for the most part free of the stylistic excesses which mar some of his earlier work. The most serious artistic flaw in the *Autobiography* is the disproportionate space and emphasis given to his experiences as Commander-in-Chief in South Africa—evidence of bitterness still rankling, old wounds unhealed.

A reading of the *Autobiography* helps to answer a question often asked in Butler's lifetime, and occasionally even today; if he was sincere in his view that war was evil, why did he remain a soldier?

One reason is immediately obvious. All his life Butler was a confirmed romantic who hated the ugly realities of war as they affected the innocent, but who responded with adolescent enthusiasm to exposure to danger, the matching of wits against an enemy in a game in which the stakes were life itself, and to exploring, on campaigns and leaves, strange places of the earth. These were the attractions which held him faithful to a profession in which the material rewards were few. Early in his military career, at a time when he was embittered by lack of promotion and seriously considering resigning his commission he had written:

Here was the rub—when every fibre of one's existence beat in unison with the true spirit of military adventure, when the old feeling, which in boyhood had made the study of history a delightful pastime, in late years had grown into a fixed unalterable longing for active service, when the whole current of thought ran in the direction of adventure, no matter in what climate, or under what circumstances—it was hard, beyond the measure of words, to sever in an instant the link that bound one to a life where such aspirations were still possible of fulfilment; to separate one's destiny for ever from the noble profession of arms, to become an outsider . . . to admit that the twelve best years of life had been a useless dream, and to bury oneself far away in some western wilderness out of reach or sight of the red coat or sound of bugle.[6]

Butler's campaign and combat experiences in Egypt and the Sudan did a good deal to modify the glamour of the bugle call, but to the end of his life he idealized the professional soldier just as he did the Irish peasant and the North American Indian. Properly employed, the professional soldier was an agent of justice, and enemy of evil, his virtues and obligations admirably summarized in a passage from Massinger's *A New Way to Pay Old Debts* which Butler loved to quote:

If e'er my son
Follow the war, tell him it is a school,
Where all the principles tending to honour
Are taught, if truly followed: but for such
As repair thither, as a place in which
They do presume they may with license practise
Their lusts and riots, they shall never merit
The noble name of soldiers. To dare boldly
In a fair cause, and for their country's safety
To run upon the canon's mouth undaunted;
To obey their leaders and shun mutinies;
To bear with patience the winter's cold,
And summer's scorching heat, and not to faint
When plenty of provision fails, with hunger,
Are the essential parts make up a soldier . . .

That the soldier's purpose was sometimes perverted to evil ends by his employers did not render the soldier or the profession of arms the less noble. Butler firmly believed that given the present state of man the soldier had a vital role to play in society, and above all the *thinking* soldier who acted as an essential check on the manipulations of financiers and the stupidities of politicians. He would have approved whole-heartedly the United Nations and looked on an international armed force dedicated to preserving peace in all corners of the earth as fulfilling the loftiest conception of the soldier's role in an imperfect world.

The *Autobiography* was not published until the year following Butler's death. His daughter Eileen, who acted as his literary executor, in her innocence submitted copies of the MS. simultaneously to three publishers and to her acute embarrassment received almost immediate acceptances from all three. It was the most enthusiastically received by the Press of all Butler's books and gave the reviewers an admirable opportunity to sum up the virtues and defects of the author himself, each according to the political inclinations of the publication for which he wrote. The reviewer for the *Spectator*, recalling the War Stores Scandals report and the extraordinary stir that it created, reminded his readers that

the language of it was sometimes so inappropriate that one was astonished that an officer of Butler's experience should have employed words which were unquestionably sincere, but which must have appeared to anyone who did not know him to be the epitome of levity. Thus the luxuriant but unschooled mind of Butler stultified his great abilities, and made him in relation to the modern state a public servant *manque*. There was room, and plenty, for his liberalizing tendencies. It is necessary that such voices as his should be heard. But at the most critical moments of his life he intervened in the wrong way.[7]

The radical *Nation* would have no truck with such chiding, however gentle:

All the soldierly qualities were his, and his mind was cultivated to take full advantage of them. In two things alone he failed. Through some strange kink of temperament, his sympathy was always given to the weak, the injured, the oppressed. And through some unfortunate perversion of mind he was able to foresee with unerring intuition the natural consequences of military and political errors . . .

He looked too far ahead (in South Africa). But let us remember what we threw away to please a few purblind politicians and astute financiers.

We threw away the one supremely able man that South Africa held on our side—the one man whose strategical power and knowledge of the country might have averted disaster. 'It was lucky for us, General, that you were not in the field,' said one of the Boer generals to him after the war. Yes, it was lucky for them.[8]

It remained, however, for the less violently partisan *Spectator* reviewer to write the words which might well stand as Butler's epitaph: *He had an inexhaustible fund of pity, and indignation quick as a flame.*

The last years of Butler's life were busy, crowded years. He was as active mentally as he had ever been, and the writing of his memoirs and the work that he did as a public service must have satisfied to some extent two of the deepest urges within him—to express his own individuality and to do something for his fellow men. But in spite of his capacity to retain old interests and assume new, his last years were shadowed by a melancholy at odds with his usual robust optimism. In part it was no more than the natural accompaniment of old age—the shadow that gathers about life's close; in part the consequence of disillusionment resulting from intimate association with his own people—the real-life Tipperary Irishman had little in common with Butler's idealization of him; most of all from a weakening of faith in the value of life itself. The men he had known in youth, and particularly the splendid brotherhood of the Ring who long ago had had the world at their feet, who were born, they believed, to achieve greatness and knew they would never die, epitomized for Butler in his darker hours the futility of human endeavour and the insignificance of all things mortal. For men of the Ring were nearly all gone long since; they lay dead and forgotten in graves scattered all round the world—'one at Prahsu, another under Majuba, another in the middle of the desert of Bayuda, another at Spion Kop, another under the sea near St. Helena, another in the sands at Tel-el-Kebir, another in the veldt at Magersfontein'.[9] And some who survived the perils of battle had better died in action. Buller lived out his last years in bitterness and humiliation, and Wolseley, long since overshadowed by new gods—notably Kitchener—and a victim of premature senility, faded out of life long before the actual time of dying. When in 1908 Butler visited Wolseley for the last time his old chief did not know him. Did Butler then recall the lines from Johnson's *Vanity of Human Wishes*, with which he was familiar?

From Marlborough's eyes the streams of dotage flow,
And Swift expires a driveller and a show.

And yet, looking back over the course of his own life, he could hardly feel that whether he had lived or died made no difference in the sum of things. He had hurt a few men and helped many; he had fought all his life against the things he believed were evil and defended those he thought were good—the distinctions he made between them were not merely traditional and unthinking—and one would like to believe that at the end he held firmly to the truth of what he had written years before in words which constitute a moving affirmation of faith in the significance of each man's efforts, however humble, to create a society founded on truth and justice:

In human effort there can be no finality. Liberty must grow with knowledge, must progress with progress, and yet both knowledge and progress are ever raising up fresh dangers to liberty even as they open fresh possibilities to it also. That is the difficulty. The combat must be everlasting. The road has no final halting-place; and it is right and proper that it should have none. As fitly might the husbandman of last year's harvest expect to reap a crop from his old labour, as the political reformer look for a spot on the roadway of human liberty where he can cry 'Stop!' and lie down in peace.

And it is this necessity of attempting the unattainable—this law of perpetual conflict with wrong—this ever recurring fight of day with darkness—that gives to man's life on earth its nerving necessity, its ceaseless ideal, its sole nobility. For, as no man can finish the task, so no man may despair of helping it forward, be his labour ever so humble, or his effort ever so hidden. If he can only loosen the smallest fragment of foundation in the great fortress of human oppression—if he can but rough-hew a single stone or mix the mortar with which some future master-mason will build and shape a fairer edifice—his task is worth all the thought and labour of a lifetime.[10]

For Butler himself the long day's task was nearly done. In the spring of 1910 he was visibly failing; but an attack of influenza which confined him to his room was not considered serious by the doctor who attended him. He was greatly cheered by a message from Theodore Roosevelt, ex-President of the United States, then on a lecture tour of Great Britain, expressing his warm admiration of *The Great Lone Land* and the hope that he might shortly meet its author. Butler replied by telegram through the friend who had conveyed Roosevelt's message to him: 'Regret extremely unable to leave room owing to chill. Please express to Mr. Roosevelt honour I feel at his kind message, and reference, which I shall always prize, to my little book of nearly forty years ago.'

It is a pity the two men did not meet, for they were temperamentally closely akin and held many things in common—above all an abiding love of the vast lonely spaces of the far West. But shortly after the exchange of courtesies with Roosevelt Butler's condition suddenly worsened; a hitherto unsuspected heart condition revealed itself; and on June 7, 1910, he died.

There is infinite pathos in the fact that on the day of Butler's death Field-Marshal Lord Wolseley, in a moment of lucidity, wrote a letter to his old companion-in-arms in which—all differences forgotten—he paid moving tribute to a friendship of more than forty years and bade unwitting farewell to a fellow soldier and comrade who had already passed beyond reach of his voice:

My Dear Butler:

Today's newspapers state that you are very unwell. I earnestly pray that this note may reach you in the enjoyment of rapid recovery and that I may soon hear of you being the strong merry comrade you always were to me. I always looked upon you as a host in yourself, ready to undertake any difficult job, and the more dangerous it was the more you enjoyed it. May God in his mercy soon restore you to your family and all your friends, of whom none have ever valued your friendship more than your very attached friend and old comrade,

Wolseley

Of the many tributes paid him following his death Butler himself would surely have relished most of all those from prominent men of his own community who, while sincere in their recognition of his worth, ingeniously contrived to turn praise of the dead man into praise of themselves. Typical of such tributes is the eulogy delivered by the Ven. Archdeacon Ryan, P.P., to the members of the Tipperary Executive Council:

Most of them (members of the Council) had probably seen and known General Butler, and certainly he was one of those magnificent figures who once seen was always remembered; for if ever there was a typical Tipperary man in the openness and manliness of his face as well as the magnificence of his stature it was General Butler (Hear, hear). And what he exhibited in his face and in his physique he acted in real life; for though he was a member of an alien army, and so, in a sense, an alien to the governed people of Ireland, he never lost the instincts of nationality that he drank in with his mother's milk. (*Subdued applause.*)[11]

In a little poem found among his papers after his death Butler had expressed the wish to be buried in Irish soil—

> Give me but six-foot three (one inch to spare)
> Of Irish earth, and dig it anywhere;
> And for my poor soul say an Irish prayer
> Above the spot . . . .

His wish was granted. He was buried in the little country churchyard of Killardrigh—at his own request outside the family vault, in the good earth itself. The cortège—gun-carriage, military detachments of the Connaught Rangers, the Royal Field Artillery and the 18th Royal Irish, followed by a straggling line of peasants who had come to honour the dead man and marvel at the greatest spectacle the countryside had ever seen—wound its way along honeysuckle-scented lanes under a serene sky. The band of the Royal Irish played the Dead March, the Royal Field Artillery fired a salute of six guns over the grave. Their duty done, the men in uniform marched back to where they had come from, the peasants hurried away to the nearest public house to drink to the General's memory and afterwards say a prayer for his soul—and there remained only the quiet fields under a quiet sky and near by the River Suir sliding past on its way to the sea and farther off the grand upthrust of the Galtees and all around him the silence and the solitude in which he had always been at home.

Notes

CHAPTER 1: THE BUTLERS OF BALLYCARRON

1 Butler, Sir W. F., *An Autobiography*, Constable, London, 1911, p. 4.
2 Butler, *The Light of the West*, Preface, M. H. Gill, Dublin, 1909.
3 Butler, *Red Cloud*, Sampson Low, London, 1882, pp. 7–10.
4 Butler, 'Cromwell in Ireland', from *Studies in Irish History*, (ed. Barry O'Brien), Macmillan, London, 1903.
5 Butler, *Autobiography*, p. 12.
6 Ibid., p. 11.
7 Butler, *The Life of Sir George Pomeroy-Colley*, J. Murray, London, 1899, p. 9.

CHAPTER 2: STATIONS OF THE EAST

1 Lunt, J. D., *Scarlet Lancer*, Harcourt, Brace and World, New York, 1964, p. 171.
2 Butler, *Autobiography*, p. 70.
3 Ibid., pp. 70–71.
4 Ibid., pp. 15–16.
5 Butler, *Far Out: Rovings Re-Told*, Isbister, London, 1881, p. 258.
6 Ibid., p. 261.
7 *The War in South Africa.* Report of His Majesty's Commissioners, 1904, Cd. 1789–1790–1791.
8 Ibid.
9 Butler, *Autobiography*, p. 19.
10 Ibid., p. 28.
11 Ibid., pp. 36–37.
12 Ibid., p. 39.

CHAPTER 3: THE BURNING PLAINS

1 Butler, *Autobiography*, pp. 39–40.
2 Ibid., pp. 40–41.
3 Butler, *The Light of the West*, p. 39.
4 Ibid., pp. 50–51.

CHAPTER 4: YEARS OF THE LOCUST

1 Butler, *Autobiography*, p. 77.
2 Ibid., p. 82.

[3] Ibid., p. 89.
[4] Ibid., pp. 95–96.
[5] Butler, *The Great Lone Land*, Sampson Low, London, 1872, p. 63.

CHAPTER 5: A ROVING COMMISSION

[1] Butler, *The Great Lone Land*, p. 42.
[2] Wolseley, Field-Marshal Viscount, *The Story of a Soldier's Life*, Constable, London, 1903, Vol. 1, pp. 20–21.
[3] Butler, *The Great Lone Land*, pp. 101–3.
[4] Ibid., p. 133.
[5] Ibid., p. 134.
[6] Ibid., pp. 140–1.
[7] Ibid., p. 190.
[8] Steele, Colonel S. B., *Forty Years in Canada*, McClelland, Goodchild & Stewart, Toronto, 1915, p. 24.

CHAPTER 6: THE GREAT LONE LAND

[1] Butler, *The Great Lone Land*, Appendix, pp. 352–5.
[2] Ibid., pp. 199–200.
[3] Ibid., pp. 205–6.
[4] Ibid., pp. 217–18.
[5] Larmour, Major Robert, *Canada's Opportunity*, William Briggs, Toronto, 1907, p. 12.
[6] Butler, *The Great Lone Land*, pp. 240–1.
[7] Ibid., pp. 242–3.
[8] Hamilton, Mrs. A., *These Are the Prairies*, Regina, 1948, pp. 87–89.
[9] Butler, *The Great Lone Land*, p. 262.
[10] Ibid., pp. 274–5.
[11] Butler, *Far Out: Rovings Re-Told*, p. x.
[12] Butler, *The Great Lone Land*, pp. 286–7.
[13] Ibid., p. 331.
[14] Ibid., pp. 338–9.
[15] Ibid., pp. 385–6.

CHAPTER 7: THE WILD NORTH LAND

[1] Butler, *Autobiography*, pp. 128–9.
[2] Butler, *The Wild North Land*, Sampson Low, London, 1873, pp. 105–6.
[3] Ibid., pp. 90–91.
[4] Ibid., pp. 216–17.
[5] Ibid., pp. 161–2.
[6] Butler, *Far Out: Rovings Re-Told*, p. 45.
[7] Butler, *The Wild North Land*, pp. v–vi.

CHAPTER 8: THE STORY OF A FAILURE

[1] Butler, *Akim-Foo: The Story of a Failure*, Sampson Low, London, 1875, p. 28.

[2] Lloyd, Alan, *The Drums of Kumasi*, Longman's, London, 1964, p. 62.
[3] Butler, *Akim-Foo*, pp. 136–7.
[4] Butler, *Autobiography*, p. 154.
[5] Butler, *Akim-foo*, pp. 193–4.
[6] Butler, Ibid., pp. 118–19.
[7] Wood, Field-Marshal Sir Evelyn, *Winnowed Memories*, Cassell, London, 1917, pp. 275–6.
[8] Reade, Winwood, *The Story of the Ashanti Campaign*, Smith, Elder, London, 1874, pp. 366–7.
[9] Wolseley, *The Story of a Soldier's Life*, II, p. 342.
[10] Reade, *The Story of the Ashanti Campaign*, p. 367.
[11] *Illustrated London News*, April 4, 1874.
[12] Butler, *Autobiography*, pp. 164–65.

CHAPTER 9: SOUTH AFRICAN INTERLUDE

[1] Butler, *Autobiography*, pp. 176–7.
[2] Ibid., p. 181.
[3] Butler, *Far Out: Rovings Re-Told*, pp. 206–7.
[4] Haggard, Sir Rider, *The Days of My Life*, Longmans, London, 1926, pp. 50–51.
[5] Butler, *Autobiography*, p. 188.
[6] Ibid., p. 191.
[7] Ibid., p. 191.

CHAPTER 10: PAINTER OF HEROES

[1] Dickens to his wife, 10–28–53.
[2] Meynell, Alice, *Prose and Poetry*, Jonathan Cape, London, 1947, p. 227.
[3] Butler, Elizabeth, *An Autobiography*, Constable, London, 1922, p. 3.
[4] Meynell, Wilfred, ed., *The Art Annual*, London, 1898. p. 3.
[5] Butler, Elizabeth, *Autobiography*, p. 156.
[6] Meynell, Wilfred, *The Art Annual*, p. 31.
[7] Butler, Elizabeth, *From Sketch-Book and Diary*, London, 1909, p. 5.
[8] Ibid., pp. 5–6.
[9] Ibid., pp. 9–10.

CHAPTER 11: BATTLES AND BOOKS

[1] Butler, *Autobiography*, p. 196.
[2] Ibid., pp. 201–2.
[3] Ibid., pp. 208–9.
[4] Ibid, p. 214.
[5] Butler, *A Narrative of the Historical Events Connected With the Sixty-Ninth Regiment*, W. Mitchell, London, 1870, p. 92.
[6] Ruskin, John, *The Bible of Amiens*, George Allen, London, 1908, pp. 22–23.

[7] Butler, *Far Out: Rovings Re-Told*, pp. 309–11.
[8] Butler, *The Invasion of England*, Sampson Low, London, 1882, p. 26.
[9] Ibid., pp. 65–66.

CHAPTER 12: TEL-EL-KEBIR

[1] Butler, *Autobiography*, p. 219.
[2] Ibid., p. 231.
[3] Ibid., p. 245.
[4] Ibid., pp. 243–4.
[5] Wood, *Winnowed Memories*, pp. 275–6.
[6] Butler, *Autobiography*, pp. 247–8.
[7] Ibid., p. 237.

CHAPTER 13: THE CAMPAIGN OF THE CATARACTS

[1] Churchill, Winston, *The River War*, Eyre & Spottiswoode, London, 1899, p. 12.
[2] Ibid., p. 46.
[3] Butler, *The Campaign of the Cataracts*, Sampson Low, London, 1887, pp. 141–2.
[4] Hamilton, General Sir Ian, *Listening for the Drums*, Faber & Faber, London, 1944, p. 175.
[5] Ibid., p. 176.
[6] Butler, *Autobiography*, p. 284.
[7] Ibid., pp. 285–6.
[8] Lady Wolseley to Lord Wolseley, Dec. 25, 1884.
[9] Wolseley to Lady Wolseley, Dec. 23, 1884.
[10] Ibid., Dec. 31, 1884.
[11] Churchill, *The River War*, p. 67.
[12] Ibid., pp. 66–67.
[13] Butler, *Autobiography*, pp. 292–3.
[14] Butler, *Charles George Gordon*, Macmillan, London, 1887, pp. 254–5.
[15] Butler, *The Campaign of the Cataracts*, pp. 367–8.
[16] Butler, *Autobiography*, p. 311.
[17] Ibid., p. 338.
[18] Ibid., p. 343.

CHAPTER 14: MAN OF HONOUR

[1] *Vanity Fair*, Dec. 25, 1886, p. 375.
[2] Ibid., p. 375.
[3] Ibid., p. 375.
[4] *The Times*, Dec. 21, 1886, p. 9.
[5] *Vanity Fair*, Dec. 25, 1886, p. 373.
[6] Ibid., p. 374.

[7] *The Standard*, London, Dec. 27. 1886.

The account of the trial is based on the exhaustive contemporary newspaper accounts, in particular that of *The Times*.

CHAPTER 15: THE YEARS OF PEACE

[1] Butler, *Sir Charles Napier*, Macmillan, London, 1890, p. 76.
[2] Butler, *Charles George Gordon*, pp. 78–80.
[3] Ibid., p. 213.
[4] Butler, *Napoleon on St. Helena* (unpublished MS.).
[5] Butler, Eileen (Lady Gormanston), *A Little Kept*, Sheed & Ward, London, 1953, p. 33.
[6] Butler, *Autobiography*, p. 361.
[7] Ibid., p. 374.
[8] Butler, Elizabeth, *An Autobiography*, pp. 218–19.
[9] Wood, Field-Marshal Sir Evelyn, *Winnowed Memories*, p. 116.
[10] Ibid., p. 21.
[11] Butler, Elizabeth, *An Autobiography*, p. 236.
[12] Butler, Eileen, *A Little Kept*, p. 33.
[13] Ibid., pp. 34–35.
[14] Butler, *Sir Charles Napier*, p. 212.
[15] Wolseley to Lady Wolseley, Oct. 2, 1890.
[16] Butler, *Charles George Gordon*, p. 51.

CHAPTER 16: ACCORDING TO HIS LIGHTS

[1] Gollin, AM. M., *Proconsul in Politics*, Blond, London, 1964, p. 30.
[2] Kerr, Phillip, *The Nation & the Athenaeum*, 23 May, 1925.
[3] Garvin, J. L., *The Life of Joseph Chamberlain*, Macmillan, London, 1934, Vol. III, p. 452.
[4] Butler, *Autobiography*, pp. 400–1.
[5] Ibid., p. 403.
[6] Gollin, *Proconsul in Politics*, p. 607.
[7] Headlam (ed.), *The Milner Papers*, 1897–9, Cassell, London, 1931, pp. 402–3.
[8] Butler, *Autobiography*, p. 418.
[9] Ibid., p. 441.
[10] *Milner Papers*, pp. 425–6.
[11] Telegram, Milner to Chamberlain, 24,6,99.
[12] Walker, Eric, *W. P. Schreiner*, O.U.P., London, 1937, p. 177.

CHAPTER 17: SOUTH AFRICAN AFTERMATH

[1] *Daily Mail*, London, Nov. 6, 1899.
[2] *Minutes of Evidence*, Royal Commission on the War in South Africa, 1903 (59537).

[3] Ibid., (59537).
[4] *Daily Mail*, Dec. 20, 1899.
[5] *Minutes of Evidence* (59537).
[6] Ibid. (59537).
[7] Ibid. (13416).
[8] Ibid. (59537).
[9] Lord Lansdowne to the House of Lords, Jan. 31, 1900.
[10] *Minutes of Evidence* (13520).
[11] Ibid. (13621).
[12] Ibid, (13657 seq.)
[13] *The Journals and Letters of Reginald, Viscount Esher* (ed. M. V. Brett), Ivor Nicholson and Watson, London, 1934, p. 373.
[14] Ibid., p. 251.
[15] Ibid., p. 374.
[16] Ibid., p. 376.
[17] Ibid., p. 419.
[18] Paul, Herbert, 'The Butler Report', *The Nineteenth Century and After*, July 1905, p. 167.
[19] Ibid., pp. 170–1.
[20] *The Times*, London, June 15, 1905, p. 9.
[21] *Report of Sir W. Butler's Committee*, Blue Book (Cmd. 2435).
[22] Paul, *The Butler Report*, p. 171.

CHAPTER 18: CELTIC TWILIGHT

[1] Butler, *From Naboth's Vineyard*, Chapman and Hall, London, 1906, p. 80.
[2] Butler, Elizabeth, *An Autobiography*, p. 309.
[3] Gwynn, Stephen, 'The Writings and Opinions of General Sir William Butler', *The Nineteenth Century and After*, Feb. 1911, pp. 314–29.
[4] Butler, *The Light of the West*, M. H. Gill, Dublin, 1909, pp. 26–27.
[5] Ibid., pp. 156–7.
[6] Butler, *The Great Lone Land*, p. 7.
[7] *The Spectator*, March 11, 1911.
[8] *The Nation*, March 11, 1911.
[9] Butler, *Autobiography*, p. 148.
[10] Butler, *Napoleon on St. Helena*.
[11] *Clonmel Nationalist*, June 15, 1910.

Bibliography

Works consulted include the following:

AMERY, L. S., *The Times History of the War*, 1900–9.

BLUNT, W. S., *My Diaries*, Martin Secker, London, 1921.

—*Secret History of the English Occupation of Egypt*, Fisher Unwin, London, 1907.

BRACKENBURY, SIR H., *The River Column*, Blackwood, Edinburgh, 1885.

—*Narrative of the Ashanti War*, Blackwood, Edinburgh, 1874.

—*Some Memories of My Spare Time*, Blackwood, Edinburgh, 1909.

BUTLER, EILEEN (LADY GORMANSTON), *A Little Kept*, Sheed and Ward, London, 1952.

BUTLER, ELIZABETH, *An Autobiography*, Constable, London, 1922.

—*From Sketch-Book and Diary*, Constable, London, 1909.

BUTLER, SIR WM., *A Narrative of the Historical Events Connected With the Sixty-Ninth Regiment*, Mitchell, London, 1870.

—*The Great Lone Land*, Sampson Low, London, 1872.

—*The Wild North Land*, Sampson Low, London, 1873.

—*Akim-foo: The Story of a Failure*, Sampson Low, London, 1875.

—*Far Out: Rovings Re-Told*, Sampson Low, London, 1881.

—*Red Cloud*, Sampson Low, London, 1882.

—*The Invasion of England*, Sampson Low, London, 1882.

—*The Campaign of the Cataracts*, Sampson Low, London, 1887.

—*Charles George Gordon*, Macmillan, London, 1887.

—*Sir Charles Napier*, Macmillan, London, 1890.

—*The Life of George Pomeroy-Colley*, John Murray, London, 1899.

—*From Naboth's Vineyard*, Chapman and Hall, London, 1906.

—*The Light of the West*, Gill, Dublin, 1909.

—*An Autobiography*, Constable, London, 1911.

—*Napoleon at St. Helena* (unpublished MS.).

CHURCHILL, WINSTON, *The River War*, Eyre & Spottiswoode, London, 1899.

CRANKSHAW, EDWARD, *The Forsaken Idea*, Longmans, London, 1952.

CURTIS, EDMUND, *A History of Ireland*, Methuen, London, 1936.

D'ARCY, W., *The Fenian Movement in the United States*, Catholic University of America Press, Washington, 1947.

DUNBOYNE, LORD, *Butler Family History* (privately printed), Kilkenny, 1966.

ESHER, VISCOUNT, *The Journals and Letters of Reginald, Viscount Esher* (ed. M. V. Brett), Ivor Nicholson & Watson, London, 1934.
EVANS-GORDON, MAJOR, *The Cabinet and War*, Constable, London, 1904.
FLYNN, PAUL, *The Book of the Galtees*, Hodges, Figgis, Dublin, 1926.
FURNEAUX, RUPERT, *The Zulu War*, Lippincott, N.Y., 1963.
GARVIN, J. L., *The Life of Joseph Chamberlain*, Macmillan, London, 1934.
GLEICHEN, LORD EDWARD, *With the Camel Corps Up the Nile*, Chapman & Hall, London, 1888.
GOLLIN, A. M., *Proconsul in Politics*, Blond, London, 1964.
GWYNN, STEPHEN, *The Charm of Ireland*, Harrap, London, 1934.
HAGGARD, RIDER, *The Days of My Life*, Longmans, London, 1926.
HAMILTON, IAN, *Listening for the Drums*, Faber & Faber, London, 1944.
HAMILTON, ALBINA, *These Are the Prairies*, School Aids, Regina, 1948.
HATTERSLEY, ALAN, *Portrait of a Colony: The Story of Natal*, O.U.P., London, 1938.
HUYSHE, GEORGE, *The Red River Expedition*, Macmillan, London, 1871.
KRUGER, RAYNE, *Goodbye, Dolly Gray*, Lippincott, N.Y., 1960.
LARMOUR, ROBT., *Canada's Opportunity*. A Review of Butler's 'Great Lone Land', Briggs, Toronto, 1907.
LEHMANN, JOSEPH, *All Sir Garnet*, Cape, London, 1964.
LESLIE, SHANE, *Salutation to Five*, Hollis and Carter, 1951.
LLOYD, ALAN, *The Drums of Kumasi*, Longmans, London, 1964.
LUNT, BRIGADIER J. D., *Scarlet Lancer*, Harcourt Brace, N.Y., 1964.
MACDONALD, CAPTAIN JOHN, *Troublous Times in Canada*, W. S. Johnston, Toronto, 1910.
MAGNUS, PHILIP, *Kitchener*, Dutton, N.Y., 1959.
MARAIS, J. S., *The Fall of Kruger's Republic*, O.U.P., London, 1961.
MEYNELL, ALICE, *Prose and Poetry*, Cape, London, 1947.
MEYNELL, VIOLA, *Alice Meynell*, Cape, London, 1929.
MEYNELL, WILFRED, *The Art Annual: The Life and Work of Lady Butler*, London, Xmas, 1898.
MILLIN, SARAH GERTRUDE, *General Smuts*, Faber & Faber, London, 1936.
MILNER, SIR A. (ed. HEADLAM), *The Milner Papers*, Cassell, London, 1931.
MOOREHEAD, ALAN, *The White Nile*, Hamish Hamilton, London, 1960.
O'BRIEN, BARRY (ed.), *Studies in Irish History*, Macmillan, London, 1903.
O'CONNOR, FRANK, *Munster, Leinster and Connaught*, Hale, London, 1950.
READE, WINWOOD, *The Story of the Ashanti Campaign*, Smith, Elder, London, 1874.
ROBINSON, SIR JOHN, *A Lifetime in South Africa*, Smith, Elder, London, 1900.
RUSKIN, JOHN, *The Bible of Amiens* (ed. Cook and Wedderburn), George Allen, London, 1908.

STACEY, COLONEL, *The Nile Voyageurs*, The Champlain Society, Toronto, 1959.
STANLEY, H. M., *Coomassie and Magdala*, Harper, N.Y., 1874.
STEELE, COLONEL S., *Forty Years in Canada*, McClelland, Goodchild & Stewart, Toronto, 1915.
STRACHEY, LYTTON, *Eminent Victorians*, Garden City, N.Y., 1918.
SYMONS, JULIAN, *Buller's Campaign*, The Cresset Press, London, 1963.
TURNER, J. P., *The North-West Mounted Police*, King's Printer, Ottawa, 1948.
VULLIAMY, C. E., *Outlanders*, Cape, London, 1938.
WALKER, ERIC., *A History of South Africa*, Longmans, London, 1941.
W. P. Schreiner, O.U.P., London, 1937.
WARD, W. E. F., *A History of Ghana*, Allen & Unwin, London, 1948.
WILSON, BECKLES, *Lord Strathcona: The Story of His Life*, Methuen, London, 1902.
WOLSELEY, SIR G., *The Story of a Soldier's Life*, Constable, London, 1903.
WOOD, SIR E., *Winnowed Memories*, Cassell, London, 1917.
WOODHAM-SMITH, CECIL, *The Great Hunger*, Hamish Hamilton, London, 1964.
WORSFORD, BASIL, *Lord Milner's Work in South Africa*, Kegan Paul, London, 1913.

Index

624205
HI
REF
CIR
SR
REF
CIR
SEP 1968